# A History of
# Literacy and
# Libraries
# in Ireland

To my son

PATRICK

# A History of Literacy and Libraries in Ireland

## The long traced pedigree

Mary Casteleyn

Gower          A Grafton Book

Published by
Gower Publishing Company Limited,
Gower House Croft Road
Aldershot Hants GU11 3HR
and
Old Post Road
Brookfield
Vermont 05036
USA


Printed in Great Britain by
Redwood Burn Limited, Trowbridge, Wilts.

Library of Congress Cataloging in Publication Data

Casteleyn, Mary
    A history of literacy and libraries in Ireland – (A Grafton book)
    Includes index.
    1. Libraries – Ireland – History
    2. Books and reading – Ireland – History
    3. Education – Ireland – History
    4. Literacy – Ireland – History
    I. Title
    Z792.5.A1C37 1983      027.0415      83-15412


British Library Cataloguing in Publication Data

Casteleyn, Mary
    A history of literacy and libraries in Ireland – (A Grafton book)
    1. Libraries – Ireland – History
    I. Title
    027.0415   ZZ792.5


ISBN 0-566-03478-6

# Contents

Acknowledgments     vii

1    Bardic and monastic literature     1

2    Education in Ireland up to 1831     15

3    Early publishing and printing     42

4    Great private collectors and their libraries     63

5    The subscription and society libraries     89

6    University libraries and the National Library     120

7    Repeal reading rooms and *The Nation*     140

8    Adult education and the Mechanics' Institute libraries     151

9    The public library movement up to 1922     170

10   Public libraries in Northern Ireland since 1922     198

11   Public libraries in the Republic since 1922     211

References     236

Bibliography     237

Index     243

# Acknowledgments

I am most grateful to many individuals and organisations for invaluable help given to me during the preparation of this book, and I wish to express my appreciation to them. Particular thanks must go to Dermot Foley, former Director of An Chomhairle Leabharlanna, for his patient assistance and encouragement, also to Seamus O'Conchubhair, County Librarian of Kildare, and to Mairín O'Byrne, Librarian of the City and County of Dublin, and her deputy, Deirdre Ellis-King.

Grateful acknowledgment is also made to Tom Armitage, the present Director of An Chomhairle Leabharlanna, for his generous help and encouragement. I am also indebted to James Fogarty, County Librarian of Kilkenny, to Mrs B. Foster of the Limerick County Library, and to J.P. McCarthy of the Library of the University College, Cork, for their assistance, freely given. Many other librarians throughout Ireland have also given generously of their time and knowledge and I would like to express my sincere thanks to all of them.

For permission to reproduce illustrative material I am grateful to Thomas Armitage, to J. Hayes, County Librarian of Wicklow, to W.R.H. Carson, Chief Librarian of the Southern Education and Library Board, to Cork City Library, and to the Carnegie United Kingdom Trust. Special thanks are due to the National Gallery of Ireland for permitting the reproduction of a photograph of *Reading The Nation* by Henry McManus.

Acknowledgment is also made to Macmillans for allowing me to quote the list of publications of the Kildare Place Society from Kingsmill Moore's *An Unwritten chapter in the history of education* (Macmillan, 1904); and to Gill and Son for permission to reproduce the list of parish libraries in Kildare and Leighlin, 1820 – 1829, from the Revd Martin Brenan's *Schools of Kildare and Leighlin, 1775 – 1835* (Gill and Son, 1935).

Thanks are also extended to the staff of Westminster City Libraries Bibliographical Services for their help in obtaining materials through the inter-library loan system, and also to the staffs of the British Library (Newspaper Library) and the British Library (LA Library). I also acknowledge the kind assistance given by Michael Leader and Nigel de la Poer, who allowed me access to their private libraries.

Last but not least I thank the Oxford University Press for permission to use the quote 'The long-traced pedigree', which is taken from a poem

'This night sees Ireland desolate' by Andrais MacMarcuis, included in *The Irish tradition*, by Robin Flower, published by OUP in 1947.

Mary Casteleyn

# 1    Bardic and Monastic literature

Libraries in Ireland have a long but distinctly chequered history over a period of 1,500 years. There are many references in the oldest extant Irish literature, both religious and secular, proving that the Irish people had books well before the arrival of Christianity in the fifth century and indeed had developed many useful arts, being skilled and artistic craftsmen. The pagan Irish had a knowledge of letters, and whilst a great deal of their learning was memorised, some of it was written in books or cut into ogham inscriptions on stone or wood. Acthicus of Istria, a Christian philosopher of the fourth century, recorded in his book *Cosmography of the World* that after leaving Spain he hastened to Ireland where he spent some time 'examining the books'. This would seem to indicate that on visiting Ireland he found collections of books and that he spent some time examining them.

None of the pagan books have survived. Indeed no Irish document has been preserved that is earlier than the seventh century but there is evidence that these manuscripts had been copied from others that went back at least one century, if not two. Irish scholars of the fifth century recorded in writing not only the laws, bardic and historical poems of their own time but also those preserved from earlier times. Amongst all Gallic people there were three kinds of men held in high regard. These were the Druids, the bards and the poets, and the Vates-deviners and natural philosophers.

The Druids of pagan Ireland were concerned with divine worship, performance of sacrifice, interpretations of ritual questions, and with resolving disputes. Younger men gathered round them for instruction and held them in high esteem. These young men spent twenty years under training, learning by heart a great many verses so as not to neglect the cultivation of the memory and prevent the rule becoming common property.

The Druids, as pagan theologians, with a traditional theory of life directly opposed to the teachings of the Christian missionaries were naturally the chief enemies of the early missionaries and were represented as such in their teachings. With the coming of Christianity the Druids gradually lost their influence and ended up as mere soothsayers, discredited because of their superstitious practices. Their influence in pre-Christian Ireland was nevertheless considerable.

The Brehon laws give us a valuable insight into social conditions and the state of the culture achieved by the pagan Irish. According to tradition it was St. Patrick who persuaded King Laoghaire to codify the laws in AD 438. The development of such a detailed code evolved over many generations suggests a fairly high degree of culture. As further evidence in the Tripartite Life of St. Patrick, it states that when St. Patrick arrived at the king's court the Druids already possessed books, and when at a later date St. Patrick decided upon revising the Brehon laws, the books in which they were written down were laid before him. That there exists no written record, except in stone, earlier than the seventh century can be credited to the enormous destruction of books by the Danes. But all the Irish bardic tales and the existing lives of St. Patrick agree than when he arrived in Ireland he found the country full of literary and professional men.

Ireland is in the unique position of being the only part of the Celtic world that was never brought under the influence of the Roman army and is consequently one of the few countries of Western Europe whose civilisation developed along native lines. Roman learning was only introduced into Ireland in a peaceful manner as early as the fifth century, and the introduction of classical learning is again popularly ascribed to St. Patrick. However, the seeds of classical learning had found their way to Ireland as early as the first and second decades of the fifth century by scholars fleeing their own countries as they were invaded by the Goths and other barbarians.

As well as the Druids there existed bards and a superior class of poets called Filid. Whilst the bards were considered as minstrels without much learning, the Filid not only composed verses but preserved the old epic literature of the nation. They were also skilled in genealogy and topography. There was a strong tradition of oral teaching in pre-Christian Ireland and even after the introduction of a general written literature, oral teaching and memorising remained a feature of the secular schools. Indeed the qualifying tests for the order of poets was the number of stories known by heart. The following is a table indicating the number of stories each grade of Fili had to know:

the *Oblaire* or lowest grade of Fili knew seven stories
the *Taman*, ten
the *Drisac*, twenty
the *Fochlocon*, forty
the *Macfuirmid*, forty
the *Doss*, fifty
the *Cana*, sixty
the *Clú*, eighty

the *Ánruth*, one hundred and seventy five

the *Ollam* or poet of the highest grade knew three hundred and fifty stories

It took between nine and twelve years training to learn 250 prime stories and 100 secondary stories.

The poets in Ireland were rich and of high social standing. The Ollam was allowed to have 24 attendants, the same number as a provincial king, and had the privilege of sitting in the banqueting house with the king when he visited the palace. The exalted place held by these poets in early Irish society marks the love of the more traditional type of literature in sagas, poems and songs which was nearly universal in Ireland at this time.

The ancient Irish invented and practised a unique form of writing called ogham. Druids and heroes of the ancient epics are shown to have made constant use of ogham writing usually on wooden staves. The ogham alphabet devised by the Filid is based on the Latin alphabet and the Irish probably became familiar with the use of the letters and the Roman alphabet through trade with the Continent or from Romanised Britain during the first and second centuries onwards. The alphabet itself was called *Faiodh* or *Faodh* which means voice. This ogham script was quite unsuitable for the recording of literature which was only retained as an oral tradition at this time. The ogham script consists of a number of short lines, straight or slanting, and drawn either below, above or through one long stem line, (see Figure 1.1). However basic, this writing is quite ingenious and skilfully devised. Vowels which are most frequently used are the simplest to inscribe.

The Irish attribute the invention of ogham to the god Ogma, one of the leading Tuatha De Danann, who was also supposed to be skilled in dialects and poetry. Whilst Irish literacy can be identified in many of the modern Irish words for books (*leabhra*), reading (*léigheadh*), writing (*sgríobhadh*), letters (*litreacha*), pens (*pinn*) and vellum (*meamram*), there are other words used to identify early Irish writing materials. These are *taibhli fileadh* or tablets of the sages, and *tamhlorg fileadh*, which translates as the 'sages headless staves'. The Brehon laws prescribe that a poet may carry a *tabhall-lorg* or tablet staff. It has been suggested that these tablet staves were in the form of a fan which could be closed up in the shape of a square stick, upon the lines of which the poets wrote in ogham, probably the outlines of narratives and genealogy. According to one of the most ancient epics, inscribed tablets were in use in the reign of King Art, son of Conn, in the second century, and according to the *Four Masters*[1] these tablets had been preserved in the treasury at Tara until it was burnt by Dunlang, son of Enna, in AD 241.

## FIGURE 1.1  OGHAM ALPHABET

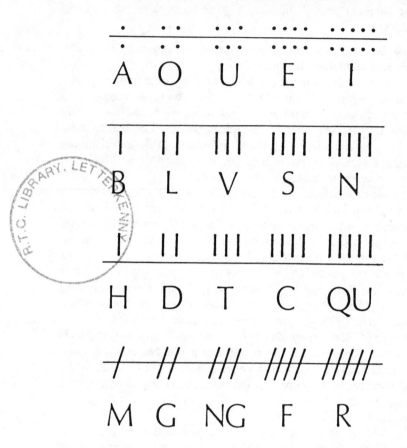

Schools had been in existence under the sway of the Druids in pagan Ireland. Cormac MacAirt, king of Ireland from AD 254 to AD 277 founded three schools. They were of three distinct types, one for the study of military science, one for the study of law, and one for studying literature. In these schools the tradition of oral teaching was universal, and even after the introduction of written literature this oral tradition was retained by the secular schools.

Certainly the tradition of the Bardic school dates from at least pre-Christian times when the aspiring poet spent one year studying magical incantations. Although many ancient books, sagas, annals and poetry have survived, there are frequent allusions in them to earlier and lost manuscripts and books, particularly a great skin book in which pagan tales were written. Other books are recorded as being ascribed to Cormac MacAirt (the Saltair of Tara). Another lost

4

book is called the *Cin of Drom Snechta* and is often referred to both in the *Book of the Dun Cow* (*c* AD 1100) and in the *Book of Ballymote*. The book is attributed to the fourth century and certainly before the coming of St. Patrick.

The most famous Irish literature of this period is the *úrsgeul* or romance told in the form of narrative prose or verse. The bards from all over Ireland had to know the same standard stories but they probably did not learn them word for word, rather the highlights of each story which they then embellished and filled in. This accounts for the discrepancies in the stories that have been handed down to us. Their authorship is unknown, but they are mythological, heroic and Fenian, the great source of Irish history and legend.

St. Patrick had not managed to convert the whole of Ireland by the time of his death in AD 461. To continue his work he established a school at Armagh in AD 450 to train the native Irish for the Ministry and to spread the Gospel. Students there learnt Latin and sometimes a little Greek. To supply the various churches with books a special house was established in which students were employed as scribes. Other schools were gradually set up and these laid the foundation of the seats of learning which made Ireland the land of saints and scholars in the sixth to the ninth centuries. There were in fact over 160 monasteries in the sixth century, and at least another 120 others were founded by Irish monks in Scotland, England and on the Continent, with missionaries penetrating to France, Belgium, Germany and Italy. This Irish Mission, as it is known, is one of the most important cultural phenomena of the early Middle Ages. These monks and scholars were famous for their learning and also for their wrangling spirit which often involved them in controversy.

The monks left Ireland for a variety of causes. One was the act of sacrifice at leaving their own country to be an exile for Christ. Another reason was the Irish desire to travel inherent in the national character. One has only to think of the voyages of St. Brendan in the sixth century to realise the truth of this. But a further reason was the attraction of famous centres of learning on the Continent where their own scholarship and poetry would be welcome. Later when the raids of the Danes made life difficult for cultural pursuits the attraction and call of the foreign cultural centres was considerable and the Irish impact on Carolingian culture is great, as well as their contribution to the role of education under Charlemagne.

One other reason could also have encouraged the Irish monks to cast their lot overseas and that was the quarrelling at home in Ireland. St. Columba left the country under very strange circumstances in what can only be recorded as the first known case of Irish copyright. Columba was visiting Finnian of Druim Finn and his host lent him a book which he had brought back from a visit to Rome. It was supposedly the famous O'Donnell Cathach which later became the O'Donnell battle talisman. The Cathach or Battle Book was preserved in the O'Donnell family for hundreds of years and was said to bring them victory when carried three time clockwise around the field of battle.

St. Columba, who was a great lover of books, secretly copied out the Cathach during several nights in Finnian's church. Finnian, however, discovered what Columba had done and strongly objected to the copying having been done without his permission, therefore he claimed the copy as his own. Columba refused to give it up and the dispute was taken to King Diamuid at Tara, the seat of the High Kings of Ireland. There were no known Brehon laws dealing with books and the nearest the High King could find was the sentence 'le gach boin a boinín', which translates as 'with every cow her calf'. The King therefore decided in favour of Finnian saying 'With every book its son-book, as with every cow her calf'. This decision so infuriated St. Columba that he cursed the High King and walked out.

The judgment, as well as the slaying of the son of the King of Connaught who was under the protection of St. Columba, enraged the saint so much that he appealed to his cousins, the northern princes Fergus and Donall, to avenge him. They raised a great army against the High King and a fierce battle was fought between the mountain of Ben Bulben and the sea in which King Diamuid was defeated with the loss of three thousand men. Soon after this St. Columba as a penance decided to leave Ireland. He set sail from Derry in AD 593 with an entourage of twelve monks, determined to convert as many souls to Christianity as had fallen at the battle of Cooldrevna. St. Columba was, of course, a member of the learned order of poets and his zeal for copying books is well-known apart from this particular story, as is St. Finnian's jealousy in regard to his own books.

St. Patrick and other early Irish Christians spent much of their time converting the pagans and building churches. The saints of the sixth century however were able to consolidate this work and spent much time founding monastic institutions and teaching in schools and colleges, (see Figure 1.2). Books were copied and multiplied to an amazing extent. At the same time the professional bards were also flourishing in Ireland and it was said that nearly one-third of the men of Ireland belonged to the poetic order. The most famous schools were those set up by the three patron saints of Ireland, St. Patrick's at Armagh in AD 450, St. Brigid's at Kildare in about AD 487, and St. Columba's at Iona in AD 563. But there were at least sixteen

## FIGURE 1.2 MAP SHOWING MAJOR MONASTIC SITES

Christian schools in Ireland in the fifth century, and another thirty established between the sixth and the eighth centuries. These include the more famous monastic schools of Bangor, founded in AD 559, Clonard in AD 520, Clonmacnois where Alcuin was educated in AD 544 to 548, Lismore founded in AD 635, Monasterboice founded about AD 500, and Mungret dating from about the year 551 AD.

The clergy and the monks took the place of the Druids as the theologians and philosophers of the nation, and it followed naturally that they should also devote themselves to the furtherance of study and learning. In the sixth century the monks usually came from the well-to-do classes who could afford to have their children fostered, which was a very old Irish custom. Latin learning predominated in the monasteries, the Holy Scriptures being widely studied. But whatever language the monks wrote in they usually spoke Irish and preached in Irish to the people. Profane literature was read to increase mastery of Latin and for its general usefulness in understanding the sacred texts. This Latin learning was propagated by books, while the traditional Celtic culture had been spread by mouth only.

The monks were responsible for devising a scheme of writing Irish based on the Latin model and they developed a scheme of orthography which made it as easy to write in Irish as in Latin. With this development it became possible to record the old Irish literature more fully than had been possible using the ogham script. The monasteries began to record, assimilate and foster the national culture which placed them in positions of extreme influence and strength.

The monastery was usually a group of buildings surrounded by a rampart made of earth or stone walls. Within the monastery would be the church, oratories, refectory, kitchen, school and the armarium which was a special chamber for the preservation of books and literary apparatus. In all the monasteries there were usually generous supplies of books available for study.

The library or *teach screptra* was an important feature of every monastic school, and was stocked with textbooks and general reading. Books were stored in satchels containing one or more volumes and hung on racks or pegs around the room. These satchels were of embossed leather and decorated with ornamentation usual in Irish art, and were used to carry books from place to place.

A charming legend that no doubt has an element of truth in it refers to this practice of hanging the book satchels on the walls. St. Lon of Garad in Ossory hid his books from Columba who was his guest. Columba was so infuriated that he left a curse upon Lon Garad's books. 'May that as to which thou hast shown niggardliness be of no profit after thee!' In the ninth century a chronicler noted that this was fulfilled for the books still remained and no man read them. It was also reported that when Lon died all the book satchels of Ireland fell down! Alternatively it is reputed that the book satchels in the cell of Columba fell down and that all in the house wondered and were silent at the noisy shaking of the books.

In the schools the monks produced their own books, carrying out this work in a special room called the *scriptorium*. Very often the educational work of the scriptorium and the library was hardly less important than the work done in the classroom or school, but schools are mentioned in connection with most monasteries, and their fame extended throughout Europe.

Dagobert II, King of France in the seventh century, was educated at Slane in Ireland. Aldfrith, King of Northumbria, was also taught in Ireland during the same century, as was Aigilbert, first bishop of the Western Saxons. Both Alcuin and Bede refer to crowds of Anglo-Saxons who went to Ireland and who were provided with food, books to read, and gratuitous instruction. At that period the Irish language was held in considerable repute, even by the British monarchs, for when Aidan preached to the Northumbrians in Irish, King Oswiu was able to interpret his discourse to the people.

The books produced in the scriptorium supplied the texts for the school, service books for the church, and more general works for the library. The younger members of the community and students sat there writing out and reproducing books before the introduction of the printing press. To alleviate boredom many manuscripts carry fragmentary notes in the margins. The monks of course would be under a strict rule of silence in the scriptorium.

Beeswax tablets were used to teach reading and writing, as were slates and pencils. Parchment was prepared from the skins of goats, sheep and calves which were finely polished. Parchments were re-used by deleting the original script and writing either between the lines or across them to form palimpsests, as they were known. The ink was made of carbon and lampblack, and pens came from the quills of geese, swans and crows. The scribe sometimes wrote with a book resting on his knees with a flat board for support, but as writing became more elaborate and decorative a desk would have been used with a maulstick to support the wrist.

The scribe was usually selected because of his scholarship on the one hand and his skill with the pen on the other. To copy a book was considered very meritorious work, especially if the book were of the Holy Scriptures. The Brehon laws describe the same penalty for the murder of a scribe as for the murder of an abbot or a bishop. The abbot sometimes combined the office of scribe with his other duties, this office being held in such esteem that it was frequently recorded that certain saints were excellent scribes, and the office of abbot or bishop is mentioned as if it were of secondary importance. The scribe was an artist and transcription was practised as an ascetic occupation by some monks, the skill having been acquired after years of training and practice. The *Four Masters* records the obituaries of 61 eminent scribes who lived before AD 900, forty of whom lived between the years AD 700 and 800.

The monks were not only scribes but also artists. They illuminated their books with such skill that the colours after one thousand years are still bright and beautifully preserved. They lavished all their artistic ability on these illustrations, and their work was done at a time when the fine arts had practically disappeared from the Continent. The most famous of these books still existing is without doubt the *Book of Kells*, probably written at Iona and brought to Kells for safety in the ninth century, and it now remains pre-eminent among the illuminated manuscripts of the world. Others which have survived are the *Psalter of St. Columcille* (St Columba), the *Book of Dimma*, containing the four Gospels, rituals and prayers from the fourth century, and the *Book of Armagh*, as well as the *Book of Durrow*, the *Book of Molling*, and the *Book of the Dun Cow*, so called because the original from which it had been copied had been written in the sixth century on the favourite cow of St. Ciaran of Clonmacnois.

Since the Scriptures were the chief books studied they were also the most frequently transcribed. Other ecclesiastical writers were not neglected and the profane authors were also known and copied, thus preserving them for posterity. Profane authors included Persius, Virgil, Horace, Sallust, Ovid and Juvenal, and the Christian poets transcribed included Juvencus, Prudentius and Ausonius, as well as the writings of St. Jerome, St. Augustine, St. Cyprian and St. Gregory the Great. Pastoral cycles of Anatolius, Theophilus, Dionysius, Cyrillus, Morinus and Victoius are cited as well as Origen and Philo. It is not unreasonable to assume that these works must have been widely taught and read.

Lay schools continued to exist alongside the monastic schools but the teaching was done by the Christian Ollamhna or doctors who took the place of the Druids. The system of lay schools had come near to extinction but at the Convention of Drum-Ceata in AD 573 St. Columba, who had received part of his education in the Bardic schools, pleaded their cause so well that the whole system was reformed and a new scheme was devised by Dallan Forgaill, the chief poet of Ireland. There was to be a main school or college for each of the five provinces, and under these there were to be smaller schools, one in each tuath or district. The heads of these schools were the lay Ollamhna, doctors of literature and poetry. The lay schools were limited to secular learning and there was more learning by rote than in the monastic schools where pupils were encouraged to question and explain.

Despite all this the vast majority of the people could neither read nor write, but they were not uneducated. The carvings and sculptures on the High Crosses erected at the time were used to instruct the common people, but they also had education of another kind. Every hamlet had its amateur reciters. People listened to recitations of poetry, historical tales and legends, and this practice was as common as is reading the newspaper today. Douglas Hyde underlines the perseverance of this oral tradition in recording that he heard from illiterate peasants of the early twentieth century stanzas composed in the thirteenth century that had been handed down by word of mouth.

The extent of the libraries and the educational work of the Irish monasteries can be seen by the number of manuscripts produced by the Irish monks which are now preserved all over Europe. It is known that books were plentiful in Ireland up to the time of the Danish invasions at the end of the eighth century. But the Danes seemed to be particularly vengeful in their destruction of the monasteries. All the books they could find were either burnt or were thrown into the nearest lake or river. One of the aims of the Norsemen had been to destroy learning and 'it was not allowed to give instruction, no scholars, no clerics, no books, no holy relics were left in church or manstery through dread of them. Neither bard nor philosopher nor musician pursued his wonted profession in the land'.

Clonmacnois was plundered or burnt on ten separate occasions by the Danes; Bangor suffered terribly at the hands of the Norse invaders who slew as many as 900 monks according to St. Bernard. It is amazing that any single book survived. This pillage went on for two centuries until the defeat of the Danes at the battle of Clontarf in the year AD 1014. During this period of domestic upheaval the monks fled overseas taking many manuscripts with them. Because of this great destruction by the Danish insurgents there are no firm statistics about the value or the contents of the great Irish monastic libraries, but the European establishments at St. Gall and Bobbio provide examples of what were once the holdings of these libraries.

The library at Bobbio contained about 700 volumes at the end of the tenth century. Of these 479 had been acquired from unstated sources, 220 were presented by named scholars, and 43 were given by the Irish monk Dungal of Pavia. The catalogue lists both Greek and Latin classics, including Terence, Ovid, Lucretius, Virgil, Lucian, Martial, Juvenal, Claudian, Cicero, Seneca, the elder Pliny, Persius, Horace, Demosthenes and Aristotle. Bobbio, founded by St. Columbanus, was undoubtedly one of the most important collections of books rivalled only by the library of St. Gall in Switzerland. In the ninth century the St. Gall library contained 533 volumes and was famous even in the Middle Ages. Unfortunately many of the books were borrowed by ecclesiastics attending the Council of Constance in the years AD 1414 to 1418, and they failed to return them. It is known, however, that the library contained works by Cicero, Livy and other classical writers, including Vitruvius, Priscian, Quintilian and Lucretius.

But all over Europe there are manuscripts copied by Irish monks in the seventh, eighth and ninth centuries. These are bound together into codices which are named either after the principal work included or after the monastery in which they were written. The Irish script was carried overseas and taught in the schools Irish monks founded in Europe. Irish writing flourished at Luxeuil in France, Würzburg in Germany, St. Gall in Switzerland and Bobbio in Italy.

The libraries of the monasteries at Würzburg and Reichenau seem to have been important and, whilst there is no existing catalogue of the library at Würzburg, there is a catalogue of the contents of Reichenau made between the years AD 822 and AD 838 which lists 415 manuscripts. It is known that the monastery at Resbacus (Rébais) had manuscripts copied there of the works of Terence, Virgil, Horace, Cicero, Donatus, Priscian and Boethius.

Full of missionary zeal, the Irish founded monasteries in a number of western European countries. Among these were:

*France:* Remirmont, Besançon, Poitiers, Bezières, Brezille, Romain-Moutier, Cusance, St. Ursanne, Fleury, St. Riquier, Jouarre, Reuil, Rébais, Faremoutier, St. Maur-les-Fosse, Lagny, Mourtier-la-Celle, Caubabec, Hautvilliers, Moutier-en-der, St. Salagerga, Meaux, St. Saens, Fontenelles, Jumièges, Stavelot, Corbie, Anegry, Luxeuil, Fontaines, Ferrières, Péronne, Toul, Amboise, Beaulieu, Starsbourg.

*Italy:* Bobbio, Taranto, Lucca, Faenza, Fiesole.

*Netherlands:* Namur, Liège, Gueldres, Fosse, Haumont, Soignes.

*Germany* and *Switzerland:* Hohenaug, Würzburg, Memmingen, Erfurt, Freyburg, Schüttern, Ettenheimünster, Mentz, Cologne, Nuremburg, Altomünster, Ratisbon, Constance, St. Gall, Mont. St. Victor, Bregens, Reichenau, Seckingen.

The most important Irish foundations in England and Scotland were at Durham, Iona, Jarrow, Lindisfarne, Melrose, Ripon, Wearmouth, Whitby and York.

The Irish monks were not only the guardians of the earlier cultures and responsible for transmitting these to Europe, they were also scholars and researchers. One of the best-known was Virgilius, bishop of Salzburg who lived in the eighth century. His Irish name was Fearghal. He cultivated the profane sciences and maintained that the sun and the moon passed under the earth and that there must be people living on the other side of the earth. He was Bishop of Aghadoe in Ireland, and had no doubt been educated in an Irish monastic school and had gained a reputation as a scholar before he left Ireland.

Another scholar was Dicuil who died in AD 825. He was also interested in the secular sciences, notably geography, and had probably been a pupil at the monastery of Clonmacnois. He is the first writer to refer to Iceland and to give authentic information about the Faroe Islands. From his writings it is obvious that he had read Pliny, Solinus, Isidore, Virgil, Crosius, Servius, Homer and Herodotus. Dungal, who lived in the ninth century, was not only a poet and theologian, but studied astronomy and was head of the school at Pavia. Dungal also wrote poetry, and in a poem he sent to Charlemagne he describes himself as an Irishman. Dungal gave many books to the library at Bobbio, notable among these was the *Antiphonary of Bangor* which was a book of hymns used by the community at Bangor and is possibly the actual book he himself used when he was a pupil there.

John Scottus was of Irish birth and education and was by far the most distinguished scholar and philosopher in Western Europe in the ninth century. He was familiar with the works of Aristotle and Plato as well as with those of St. Augustine and St. Basil. He was also a professor of mathematics and dialectics, and could write verses in Greek. He was an inmate of the palace of Charles the Bald, grandson of Charlemagne, who was a zealous patron of literature. In AD 851 Scottus published his *Liber de Praedestinatione* or book of pre-destination which gave rise to much controversy. He was also the only man at the French court able to translate the writings of Dionysius the Areopagite, whose works had been given to Louis the Debonair in the year AD 828.

The Irish influence on the scholarship of the age has already been noted but it is not unsignificant that these missionaries loved literature and the classics and delighted in poetry and music. Their learning and their schools were in all probability the greatest educational factor in early medieval times.

In the year AD 1002 Brian Boru came to power as undisputed High King of Ireland when he defeated the Danes at the battle of Clonray. From then until after his death in AD 1014 there was a period of re-growth. Brian Boru found the monasteries so destroyed and depleted of learning that he sent men overseas to buy books in an effort to restore something of what had been lost. He not only funded these purchases himself, he rebuilt churches and monasteries, and re-founded the schools. His efforts were extremely effective and he thought in terms of institutions for the entire island, restoring communications and spreading learning. It was a time of recovery from the Danish raids, and an era of reform.

This eleventh century revival of the arts and learning ended abruptly with the arrival of the Normans in the twelfth century. The building of fortified castles replaced the building of churches, and the arts of the illustrator and scribe were halted by the new Norman regime. All Irish art and literature now ceased.

Most of the old Irish literature was kept alive by the bards who over a period of four centuries passed down the old stories from one generation to another. Few new epics or poems were written, and those that were tended to be in the old style. Bards attached themselves to ancient families and by the fifteenth and sixteenth centuries there were large collections of poetry preserved in the houses of the old Irish families. When these houses were destroyed their archives and libraries of books were lost or carried overseas with the exiles. The function of the bards in the sixteenth century was to record genealogies, wars and the histories of the tribes and their chiefs. These traditions gradually faded away until few would commission or buy a poem from the bards. The poet John O'Higgin records that men were too frightened of the foreigners to buy a poem. In fact it was probably the poverty of the time, brought on by constant warring, that prevented the Irish from continuing the custom. The bards of the sixteenth century were usually men of wit and learning, full of national feeling, who travelled the length and breadth of the island. After the Cromwellian wars in the seventeenth century the idea of the bard was merged into that of a musician and harpist in the minds of common men, but in fact these had originally been two distinct professions.

# 2    Education in Ireland up to 1831

Before looking at the use of books and libraries after the sixteenth century it is important to consider the state of education in the country and the state of literacy of people in Ireland. The bardic schools had been the ancient professional schools of the Irish and these had survived until the 1640s after which they had been forced to close down when their patrons had become landless, homeless or had fled the country altogether. The bardic schools had represented the nearest thing to university education in the country while they existed, and they had supplied the people with a long line of poets, historians and brehons right down to the middle of the seventeenth century. They had been purely secular schools, teaching through the medium of the Irish language with a lengthy and arduous course of study lasting at least six to seven years before a degree was conferred. These schools had been well-supported by many Irish chiefs and by the Anglo-Norman lords.

Edmund Campion, who visited Ireland in 1570, described one of these schools at work.

> They speak Latine like a vulgar language, learned in their common schooles of leach craft and law wherein they begin children ... I have seen them where they kept school, ten in some one chamber, groveling upon couches of straw, their books at their noses, themselves lying flatte prostrate, and so to chante out their lessons.

The problem with the schools was that they kept alive the spirit of nationality and were a direct threat to the English authorities. As a result of this nationalistic outlook they were persecuted from the reign of Henry VIII to that of Charles I. Eventually only poetry was studied at these schools which became known as 'Courts of poetry' where poetry was learned, recited and discussed down to the nineteenth century. The much earlier tradition of people sitting down at the end of the day to listen to stories and poems continued to be practised. In both the eighteenth and the nineteenth centuries visitors to Ireland recorded the existence of the bards or *Seanachies* and how it was common practice even among the poorest people for the bards to recite ancient poems about heroes, battles, love and hospitality.

The bards also met together to recite traditional stories. During these sessions if any one of them repeated a passage that appeared to be irrelevant he was stopped by the others and then each would give their versions of the way it should be recited. Any dispute was put to the vote and the final decision became the version to be used in future. In this way the authenticity of the ancient stories was preserved down the years to modern times.

The national traditional literature eventually became the possession of the landless Irish peasants and the tillers of the soil. Thus, the great literary achievements of previous generations were not lost but were preserved by the peasantry into whose ranks the hereditary poets, teachers and genealogists had become absorbed after their patrons and lords had fled the country.

So much literature was confined to memory because the Irish as such had little access to the printing press, and while Irish remained the general language of the people these verses were preserved. The people themselves were too poor to have the verses put into print: they kept copying and re-copying their old stories in manuscript form, sometimes producing new poetry. The great watershed was the famine in the mid-nineteenth century. In the horror and desolation that followed in its wake many of the old manuscripts were lost and the ancient literary tradition of Ireland became submerged, hardly surviving the famine, the fever, and massive emigration.

Up to this time Irish had usually remained the native tongue of the Gaelic Irish and indeed of many of the old Norman Irish families. Many attempts had been made down the years to enforce the use of English but usually to no avail. Nearly all the peers in the Dublin Parliament in 1541 were of Norman or Anglo-Irish descent, yet only the Earl of Ormonde could understand English. A letter to the English Privy Council confirms that in 1569 even the scions of the best houses could neither speak nor understand English.

Whenever they could the Irish tried not to neglect their learning and literature, but there are accounts of old families with their learning in disrepute. Foreigners in their midst have related how some members of these old families allowed their tailors to cut up the leaves of old manuscript books to be sewn into long pieces to make up their measures or patterns.

With the suppression of the monasteries in 1539 the monastic schools disappeared where the English rule held sway, but some monks continued to educate the sons of the old houses. In Donegal, for example, monastic education continued until the late sixteenth century. The Franciscans, sponsored by the local chieftains, diffused learning among the poorer classes who were addicted to booklore. At this stage many peasant lads were familiar with Virgil, Horace, Homer and genealogies of the Milesian princes. Even under the Commonwealth period this kind of education continued, although the schoolmaster often taught with his life at risk if he were caught. The least that could happen was to be transported in Connaught. If they were found to be corrupting the youth of the nation with Popish principles such schoolmasters were to be secured and put on board a ship bound for Barbados.

The Jesuits also entered the country after having finished their education abroad and they too attempted to instruct the children of the native Irish. In the days of the Commonwealth these schools were conducted furtively usually in wretched hovels beside ditches. By 1682 education was on a sounder footing with the people still retaining an ardent desire for their children to be educated, instruction being given to Catholic children by private professors as they were not allowed to have public schools of their own.

After the victory of William of Orange at the Battle of the Boyne in 1690 the situation for Catholics took a turn for the worse and under the penal laws introduced from 1695 – 1727, education for Catholics was forbidden under the severest penalties, whether at home or overseas. Catholic bishops and priests who had previously educated the Catholic children were compelled to leave the country and were not allowed to re-enter.

## FIGURE 2.1   A HEDGE SCHOOL

From *Sketches of Irish Character* by Mrs S. C. Hall, London, 1855.

On the whole the education of most Catholics was left to the lay schoolmasters who dared to risk their liberty. Schools were set up in remote mountain regions where the danger of discovery was slight. These unlicensed and illegal schools, known as Hedge schools, flourished all over Ireland until the beginning of the nineteenth century and were the source of most surreptitious education during this time. The Hedge schools were basically peasant institutions, maintained by the people who were always keen for their children to learn to read and write, (see Figure 2.1). The normal instruction was in reading, writing, arithmetic, Latin, Greek and mathematics, and very often the language of instruction was Irish, not English. These schools were the most vital force in education in the eighteenth century. By the nineteenth century they outnumbered all other kinds of schools and their very national character was responsible for the introduction of the state system of education in 1831.

The teaching of the Hedge school masters had a profound effect on the continuing national identity of the Irish people and many famous Irishmen received their education in these very primitive conditions. Daniel O'Connell, born 6 August 1775, was taught by the very respected David Mahony, and right down to the present century their influence continued to be exerted through their pupils. Michael Collins was born in 1890 to a father 75 years of age who had received his instruction from the Hedge school master Diarmuid O'Suilliobhain in the wild, inaccessible regions of West Cork in the 1820s. His teaching was a direct influence on the development of the national leader. Collins' father, who was no mean scholar and although only a farmer was a widely read man familiar with the classics, formed the child's mind and encouraged him to read and to seek learning and education. These men were curious products of the penal code whose advocation it was, seated behind some dyke or hedge out of the way of informers to teach pupils 'feloniously to learn'.

The Halls[1] however record the following and paint a very different and official image.

> The Irish schoolmaster has been pictured by nearly every writer of fiction who has dealt with the Irish character and although commonly presented as odious and dangerous the portrait has been seldom overdrawn. The high estimate in which the people generally hold 'learning', a fact on which we cannot lay too much stress, induced them not only to tolerate his evil habits, but tacitly to allow him a very perilous influence over their principles and conduct. Upon this topic it is needless to enlarge: there is abundant evidence by which the origin of

nearly every illegal association may be traced to the cabin of the village schoolmaster.

In the year the book was published the Halls say that the 'Cottage classics of Ireland' were the only books in circulation in the cabins of the humbler classes. These titles include Ovid's *Art of love, Moll Flanders* and *Irish Rogues and Rapparees.*

An Act of Parliament had established parish schools in 1537 which required every clergyman to make arrangements for the keeping of a school 'for to learne English'. These and other English schools existed with the intention of weaning the people away from their own customs and traditions and existed in conflict with the national ideas of education. The parish schools were intended for the lower classes of the Irish people but in 1570 another Act was passed to establish free schools in every diocese with the schoolmaster to be of English birth. These were aimed at the middle classes. The foundation in 1591 of Trinity College completed the Tudor system of education in Ireland. Under the reign of Charles I some free schools of Royal foundation were set up and later in the seventeenth and eighteenth centuries a few classical schools were established out of private funds. One example of this type was Kilkenny College, founded in 1684 by the Duke of Ormonde. This is where Dean Swift received his early education.

Charter schools were another attempt to instil an English education upon the native Irish. Both the Acts passed during the reigns of Henry VIII and Elizabeth I had failed, and William of Orange in 1695 directed that these Acts be put into force more strictly. The Act further imposed fines and prison sentences upon any person of the Popish religion who instructed any youth within the realm. Irish people had been looking towards Catholic Europe and sending their children to be educated there, but this too became illegal in that any parent sending their child to France or to Spain for education ... 'Being lawfully convicted shall lose and forfeit all ... goods and chattels.'

The constant undermining of the government system of education was felt acutely as a severe problem by the ruling authorities and in 1709 yet another Act was passed lamenting the failure of the previous laws and stipulating that if any Protestant schoolmaster employed a Popish assistant to teach, that Protestant would be prosecuted as if he were a Catholic and would 'incur such pains, penalties and forfeitures as any regular Popish convict is liable unto by the laws and statutes of this realm'. The carefully thought out laws to Protestantise and Anglicise education were definitely not working. Despite the penal laws Catholic children were still sent

19

overseas to be educated and illegal education abounded.

The idea of charity schools was introduced to Ireland in the first decade of the eighteenth century with the intention that they should be established in every parish to instruct Irish children gratis in the English tongue together with the catechism and religion of the Church of Ireland. The idea was to clothe and decently educate the children of working class people, and to wean them away from the influence of the Church of Rome and thus stabilise the Protestant hold over Ireland. By 1719 there were 130 charity schools in Ireland and there were plans to open more. The big problem was that being day schools the children returned home each evening to their Catholic environment. Catholic parents only sent their children to these schools for the meals they received, and for the suit of clothes and the industrial training they obtained. Catholic private education continued underground and it was reported that nearly every parish had a Popish school with Catholic masters teaching surreptitiously in defiance of the laws. Many Papists kept schoolmasters in their houses under the guise of servants, and even Protestant families kept Catholic schoolmasters in their homes as they were usually cheaper to hire than the Protestants.

A House of Lords Committee set up in 1729 reported that there were at least 549 Popish schools in existence. This figure is probably very inaccurate as it would not have been possible for any official committee to obtain a precise figure since the very existence of the Popish schools was kept quiet from the authorities. The eventual result of the Committee's investigation was the establishment of residential charity schools under Royal Charter, where the children of Papists could be educated well away from parental influence, be brought up as good Protestants, and thus secure the kingdom of Ireland from the potential danger from the great number of Papists in the country. The Charter was issued by George II on 24 October 1733. The aim of these schools was to teach the Protestant religion, reading, writing and simple crafts such as spinning and farming skills. The children from the schools were to go eventually as apprentices to good Protestant families, armed with their own copies of the Bible, the Book of Common Prayer, and *The Whole Duty of Man.*

In 1743 James Blow, a Belfast bookseller, presented 100 Protestant catechisms and 50 Psalm books to the Ballynahinch Charter School probably as part of the proselytising efforts of the school, rather than for the establishment of a library.

By 1750 there were 33 residential Charter schools in the country, but however worthy their aims they were destined to failure. The schools were not popular with the Catholics who tended to avoid sending their children to them. Under an Act of Parliament children found begging in the streets or wandering as vagrants were taken compulsorily to the schools and parents were denied access to them. Children were supposed to be fed, clothed and instructed up to the age of 14 years. But the system led to enormous abuses with children overworked, badly fed, ill-clothed and instruction badly neglected. The Charter schools became a conspicuous and monstrous failure.

As the masters of the schools were allowed the profits from any labour the children might undertake, very often the children were kept long after they should have been apprenticed and were usually overworked. Worse still, the female pupils were often debauched either by the masters or by the inspectors send round by the Incorporated Society for the Promotion of Protestant Schools in Ireland. Despite these well-recognised evils, the schools continued to receive support from the Government.

Enlightened Protestants tried to establish other methods of education for the masses in Ireland and the Hibernian Society was just such a body. It was founded by the well-intentioned Thomas Sheridan in 1757. His aim was to improve education solely by the study of the English language and the art of speaking. 'In all their pursuits of this kind, the pleasure arising from their skill in the true art of reading would smooth the way before them and render their whole progress not only easy but delightful'. It was not really surprising that this scheme and others like it were doomed to failure before they had hardly started. In fact many Protestants realised that the illegal schools would not be suppressed. Over the next decades they began to look at ways of making the illegal schools less of a threat and accepting their existence provided that they conformed and were not subversive or disloyal to the existing political situation. Henry Grattan reflected this new thought. He wrote:

> I should recommend that in those parish schools the Christian religion should be taught but that no particular description of it should form part of their education ... and I would submit as a proper matter of education in those schools not only the study of the English tongue, reading, writing and arithmetic: but also the study of certain books of horticulture and agriculture, together with treatises on the care of trees.

Under Grattan's Parliament an Act was passed to allow persons professing the Popish religion to teach school in this kingdom, and for the regulating of the education of the Papists. This was in 1782 and under this Act a Catholic schoolmaster was permitted to teach providing he first took an oath of allegiance to the Crown and also that he obtained a licence to teach from the Protestant bishop of the diocese. Although the issue of these licences varied throughout the country Catholics now began to teach openly with or without the licence. At the same time the infamous Charter schools began to come in for more criticism from the leading Protestant members of the community. John Wesley on his visits to Ireland reported the squalor of these schools in 1785 where no master or mistress was to be found and the children were dirty and in rags. Wesley also visited Ireland in 1773 and had reported on the bad condition of the Charter School at Castlebar – 'the whole a picture of slothfulness, nastiness and desolation'. He could find no evidence that the children were being taught anything at all.

The philanthropist John Howard visited some Charter schools near Dublin and found them to be a disgrace to Protestantism, at variance with their aims and bound to encourage Popery in Ireland. When in 1787 he was asked to make a further inspection of the schools he found the children were neither well-fed nor well-clothed, and the backwardness of the children in book learning was due to the fact that there was no time for it since the children were being employed to work for the masters. Howard reported that he found the children of the Hedge schools much more advanced than those of the same age in the Charter Schools, as well as being cleaner and more wholesome.

A committee of inquiry set up by the Dublin Parliament also asked the Inspector General of Prisons, Sir Jeremiah Fitzpatrick, to report on the schools. He visited 28 schools and found the conditions appalling with the children being forced to work for the masters who made a profit from their labours, also the masters were not concerned about the propagation of the Protestant religion nor concerned about education. Despite these reports and a very genuine concern felt by the Commissioners, the schools were not condemned outright and Parliament continued to vote money for the Society, as much as £12,000 being voted in 1789 and the annual subsidy was increased after that.

In 1792 an Act was passed by the Dublin Parliament stating that 'it was not expedient any longer to make such a licence necessary and that ... it shall not ... be necessary that the licence of the ordinary be obtained'.

Another Act was passed in 1793 'for the relief of His Majesty's Roman Catholic subjects in Ireland' which provided that the Papists were no longer liable to any special penalties if they chose to educate their children as Catholics, nor was it an offence for Catholics to teach. It became lawful for Papists to hold or to take a degree or be masters or fellows of 'any college to be hereafter founded in this kingdom, providing that such a college shall be a member of the

University of Dublin and shall not be founded exclusively for the education of the Papists ... and to be a member of any lay body corporate, except the Holy and Undivided Trinity of Queen Elizabeth, near Dublin, without taking the oath of allegiance'.

Life was not all that easy even when the penal laws were relaxed. The Jesuit College at Clongowes which opened in 1814 had considerable difficulty in claiming a cargo of books from Italy, destined to be the nucleus of the college library and which had been driven ashore by a storm in Carlingford Lough. The Lord Lieutenant refused to release the shipwrecked books without detailed justification for the titles being supplied by the head of the college. The prospectus of the college had been supplied but to no avail and a petition went forth in order to claim their books.

> May I venture to recall my humble memorial to Your Excellency's gracious consideration. The books are destined to form a small library for my establishment. I have now drawn a much larger view of the school than the prospectus affords. I hope Your Excellency will not deem it tedious as it was written in compliance with the request which Your Excellency was pleased to express.

Ultimately the shipwrecked books were allowed to be removed to the college.

The government lent great support and granted monies to many Protestant educational societies which sprang up at the beginning of the nineteenth century. These were very often Bible Societies, so called because the Bible was used as a school book in all their schools.

In 1801 a grant of £300 was given to the Association incorporated for Discountenancing Vice and promoting the knowledge and practice of the Christian Religion. A grant of £9,000 was made in 1823 indicating the rise in its importance as far as the government was concerned.

The London Hibernian Society, founded in 1806, was supposed to be undenominational but clearly was not, for by 1824 this Society had 950 schools in existence. The Baptist Society, established in 1814, set up the majority of its schools in Connaught and used Irish as the language of instruction. But although its activities were supposed to be educational they were obviously of missionary intent. The bent towards proselytism was evident everywhere.

There were occasional exceptions. Lady Castlereagh's school at Newtownards opened in 1812 and had a juvenile library attached to it which was opened with the aid of a grant from the parish. With the help of private donations the school was able to spend £16 on books in 1814. The books were non-sectarian, selected by the different clergymen of the parish, and the school was also supported by a donation from the Quakers. One of the most important gifts to the school was the grant of a collection from the Kildare Place Society in 1823.

The Irish Society for Promoting the Education of the Native Language was founded in 1818. Its objectives were to instruct the native Irish in their own vernacular language, to learn how to employ it as a means of obtaining an accurate knowledge of English, and also for their moral amelioration to distribute amongst them the Irish version of the Scriptures, the Irish prayer book and such other works as may be necessary for the school books, disclaiming at the same time all intention of making the Irish language a vehicle for the communication of general knowledge.

There was also a Sunday School Society which by 1824 had as many as 1,699 schools and the Irish Society which had 83 schools. In 1821 it was ascertained from the population census that schools for the instruction of the lower orders had since 1811 increased from 4,600 to upwards of 8,000.

In fact there were two mass movements which effectively spread libraries for children throughout Ireland. One was the Kildare Place Society and the other was the Sunday School Society (SSS). Sunday schools had existed earlier, in Ulster particularly as early as 1770, but until the SSS was formed these were badly organised and established only spasmodically. The SSS realised the importance of libraries and urged Sunday schools to purchase the publications of the Kildare Place Society and the Religious Tract Society. Sunday schools sprang up all over Down, one of the earliest and strongest being at Rathfriland where the Sunday School Union Committee had established a library of religious books for the teachers and pupils. In 1822 the same committee had started a lending library of tracts to lend to children, as well as the Rathfriland Sunday School Union Circulating Library to which teachers in Sunday schools within the Union had access. Those who taught in the Sunday schools received books weekly as the children received the tracts. This circulating library went from strength to strength and by 1835 it possessed 888 volumes. As the schools were generally small, it was usually through forming unions of several schools that adequate libraries could be formed. The libraries in Sunday schools obtained their income from two sources, donations and church collections.

The largest and most influential of these educational societies was the Society for Promoting the Education of the Poor in Ireland, usually referred to as the Kildare Place Society after its Dublin address. It was founded in December 1811 and was to confer lasting benefits on the Irish educational scene. The founders of the Society had been carrying out their ideals from temporary premises and they needed a site for the building of a model school, with offices and residences for the staff. The government granted them £6,980 to purchase a site in Kildare Place. The Society had made it clear that the principles forming the charter in regard to education were for 'all classes of professing Christians, without interfering with the peculiar religious opinions of any ... the Scripture without note or comment to be used, excluding all catechisms and books of religious controversy'.

The aim was to open schools divested of all sectarian distinctions. The committee consisted of members of the Irish Church, Roman Catholics, Nonconformists, and also the Society of Friends who were keenly concerned with education in Ireland. The Society established schools wherein the poor might be instructed to read, write and learn arithmetic, and where the Scriptures without note or comment should be used, thus avoiding the potential accusation of proselytising. The Society set about building and furnishing schools and training teachers. Many school books were inaccessible to the poor because of their price. Organisations like the London Hibernian Society made good this deficiency by insisting on the use of the Bible for all purposes. Hedge schools used anything that came to hand. The Society determined to alter all this by the production of its own books which were to sell at reasonable rates. Libraries were to be established and attached to each school so that what was learnt in the schoolroom could be developed by futher reading. To this end a Book Committee was set up to consider the publication of educational works and suitable literature for the home, and later a Library Committee was formed when grants of 'Libraries' (sets of the Society's cheap books) began.

The second Parliamentary grant of £6,000 was to go towards this publishing work and the Society became the first educational publishers of their time. From 1817 annual Parliamentary grants were voted in aid of the general educational work of the Society until they reached the annual sum of £30,000.

One of the special features of the Society's work was the granting of its publications to form libraries of instructive and interesting books in connection with each school. As their publications increased in number, the school library system was extended and libraries or complete sets of books were given freely wherever responsible institutions of any kind signified a willingness to undertake their safe custody. By 1831, upwards of 11,000 of these libraries had been formed. In 1815 only three educational books had been published by the Society but by 1824 all the books required by the demands of the time had been published, and in some subjects such as geography and needlework, the Society had out-distanced all competitors. Many of these educational books were being sold in editions of 5,000 and 10,000. In another line the establishment of libraries of healthy books to a large extent purified the market of immoral literature.

Previously a Cheap Book Society had been formed in 1814 with the purpose of providing healthy literature but it did not have the resources to cope with such a large undertaking. Some of the members of this Society also sat on the committee of the Kildare Place Society, and very soon the latter took over the books, property, organisation and goodwill of the Cheap Book Society. They published first a book called *Hints and Directions for Building, Fitting up and arranging School Rooms*. A Dublin spelling book was published next, not a book as such but a series of tablets mounted on cards to be used for class purposes. Following the Dublin spelling book came the Dublin reading book. Other school works were speedily published, including the *General Geography* which sold not only in Ireland but wherever the English language was spoken. In addition, the Society published maps at the low price of 3d. each. Other publications included a book on needlework by Miss Lancaster, Joseph Lancaster's sister, and the *Schoolmaster's Manual*, a guide to the teaching of spelling, reading, writing and arithmetic.

The book committee of the Society aimed to produce a series of cheap, well-printed books, priced so as to undercut their rivals and tempt customers to buy them. A literary assistant had orders to pass nothing to which any exception could be taken, and at least two members of the committee had to testify from personal perusal as to the fitness of the book for publication. Some books were read by all members of the committee before being accepted. After this sifting process the books were sent up to obtain the approval of the general committee, but approval could not be obtained until the works had lain for at least a month on the table for personal inspection.

Sales of these books actually began in November 1817, by which time seven titles had been produced. The most remarkable feature of the books was their price. They were sold either in sheets or bound. Neat, strongly bound volumes sold for 8d. each (5 sheets or 450 pages) or 3d. (2 sheets or 180 pages). Other publishers were offering books at 1s.4d. each, so the undercutting made the Kildare Place Society books attractive.

Books were not advertised through the newspapers in the usual way, but they were so much in demand that they sold immediately and within six months new editions were needed. Private patrons lodged orders in advance for the books as they appeared, while booksellers and hawkers found it to their advantage to become regular buyers. By 1831 the sales for that year had reached 1,464,817. Their first desire had been to get the books read, so the first titles aimed to amuse, instruct and to compete successfully with the dissolute publications of the day. In the end the library had books of lasting value and contained a large proportion of religious, moral and educational works. (See Figure 2.2 for the list of books).

The books of the Kildare Place Library were also sold in England and Scotland. The British and Foreign School Society made a feature of the library in their lists. Books found their way into regimental libraries. They were exported in large numbers to India, and when a project was started for supplying the coastguards of the United Kingdom, an application was made to the Kildare Place Society which resulted in a first order for nearly 13,000 volumes. By 1823 the book committee was able to report that except in Belfast their cheap books were everywhere supplanting pernicious literature. This provision of good cheap literature was envied by the English public: a member of the British and Foreign Society said: 'I do greatly admire those little publications, and almost envy the Irish poor the privilege of such valuable reading whilst our own population remain unsupplied'.

The Revd. Charles Bardin was appointed as literary assistant in 1818 and remained in the post until 1827. It fell to him to do the writing, re-writing and editing of the library of Cheap Books, although the committee was ever watchful much of the credit for the excellence of these books must go to him. Many of the travel books were the product of his pen. In 1827 he was appointed to the curacy of Dundalk and even though he resigned his post as literary assistant he continued to write for the Society and devoted much of his time to supporting and promoting the Society's interests in the diocese of Armagh.

The Society was also responsible for publishing in Irish. The first to recognise this need had been the Irish Society and the London Hibernian Society. These societies founded schools where Irish was taught, yet the only book available for instruction in Irish was the Bible. The Educational Society extended a helping hand by providing them with suitable publications in the way of readers and spelling books. Their intention was the advancement of the peasantry which in their estimation depended upon their learning English and to this end they produced educational books in the Irish language and the Irish characters but they always took care to print the English in parallel columns with the Irish as they felt this was the best way of encouraging the intelligent study of English. At this time the proportion of the population understanding English amounted to

# FIGURE 2.2 PUBLICATIONS OF THE KILDARE PLACE SOCIETY

SOCIETY FOR PROMOTING THE EDUCATION OF
THE POOR OF IRELAND.

The following works, forming a lending library, have been
published by the Society, and are now on sale at
their Depository, Kildare Place, and at Messrs. J.
Nisbet & Co., Berner-street, London.

RELIGIOUS, MORAL, OR ILLUSTRATIVE OF SCRIPTURE.

Scripture Zoology,
Manners and Customs of the Israelites,
Selections from the Psalms, Proverbs, &c.
Sturm's Reflections,
Views of the Creation,
The Bee, a Collection of Poems,
Scripture Geography,
Destruction of Jerusalem,
History of Joseph and the Creation,
Nature Displayed,
Moral Essays,
The Wreath, a Collection of Poems.

INSTRUCTIVE IN ARTS OR ECONOMY.

Treatise on Practical Mechanics,
The Cabinet of Arts,
The Cottage Fireside,
Richard M'Ready, the Farmer Lad,
James Talbot, and—'The Widow Reilly,
Hints to Farmers,
Useful Arts and Manufactures,
The School Mistress,
Tim Higgins, the Cottage Visiter (sic),
The Pedlars.

NATURAL HISTORY.

Natural History of Remarkable Beasts,
  „        „        Domestic Animals,
  „        „        Animals,
  „        „        Trees,
Animal Sagacity, Exemplified by Facts,
Natural History of Fishes,
  „        „        Birds,
  „        „        Insects,
  „        „        Reptiles,
Picture of the Seasons.

VOYAGES, TRAVELS, &c.

Voyage of Commodore Anson,
  „,    in the Arctic Regions, 1818-19, & 20.
Byron's Narrative,
Discovery of America by Columbus

History of Prince Lee Boo,
Voyages and Travels in the Islands of the Pacific Ocean,
Voyages in the Northern Pacific Ocean,
   ,,    the Arctic Regions, 1821 to 1825,
Dangerous Voyage of Captain Bligh,
Life of Captain Cook,
Shipwreck of the Alceste and Medusa,
History of Mungo Park,
Travels in the Arctic Regions,
   ,,    North America,
   ,,    South America,
   ,,    England and Wales,
   ,,    Sweden, Denmark, and Norway,
   ,,    Spain and Portugal,
   ,,    Northern Italy,
   ,,    Southern Italy,
   ,,    European Turkey,
   ,,    Switzerland,
   ,,    Africa,
   ,,    South Eastern Asia,
   ,,    South Western Asia,
   ,,    Northern Asia,
   ,,    European Russia,
   ,,    Germany,
   ,,    Northern France,
   ,,    Southern France,
   ,,    Greece.

MISCELLANEOUS.

Elizabeth, or the Exiles of Siberia,
Entertaining Medley,
Robinson Crusoe,
History of the Robins,
Wonders of the World,
Keeper's Travels, and Select Story Teller,
Amusing Stories, and Mungo the Traveller,
Gleanings, and—William, an Orphan,
Fables of Æsop,
Miscellany,
New Robinson Crusoe,
Scrap Book,
Isaac Jenkins, and a Friendly Gift for Servants,
Little Jack, and—The Brothers,
Selection of Poems.

about one in four.

School libraries were formed to encourage deserving pupils. If the system had no need of books during school hours, it placed no difficulty in the way of the circulation of books in the hours of leisure. All the pupils were made aware of the existence of the school library, but only the meritorious were allowed the privilege of borrowing. To obtain a place upon the library register became a legitimate ambition. The proper handling of books and their punctual return were safeguarded by the required use of a form prepared for the purpose. A lending library was attached to every Kildare Place school.

The work of the Kildare Place Society stimulated the foundation of schools in every part of Ireland because they supplied the necessary plans to build schools, contributed to their construction and to purchasing the equipment. Important from the point of view of this study is that they were publishers on a large scale, publishing on their own initiative all the necessary school books and editing them into a cheap and convenient library which became highly valued not only in Ireland but throughout the rest of the United Kingdom. This was perhaps the Kildare Place Society's greatest achievement. Unfortunately by 1825 the Board of Education was reporting that the Society was failing to produce universal satisfaction.

Members of the Church of Ireland objected to the Society because the Bible was read to children without note or comment. Catholics opposed it for the same reason, but also because the schools were being used for proselytising, although for some years after the foundation of the Society Catholics had supported it. But by 1824 less than twelve per cent of Catholic children were receiving education in the Society's schools.

The Kildare Place schools fell further into disrepute with the Roman Catholic population after 1826 when the Catholic bishops published a series of resolutions laying down educational requirements particularly in the use of books. They demanded that no book should be used for the instruction of pupils of which the Roman Catholic bishop of the diocese had not approved, and by requiring that no teacher should be appointed without reference to his religion. The Roman Catholic Education Society denounced the Kildare Place Society as anti-Catholic and un-Christian. Politicians like O'Connell made the destruction of the Society part of the emancipation programme. By 1831 the last government grant had been made to the Kildare Place Society, the main stumbling-block being the reading of Scriptures without comment and the absence of denominational teaching.

But before its decline, the Kildare Place Society had published in 1824 a little leaflet entitled *Hints on the formation of lending libraries in Ireland*, and this contained much useful advice to those who might wish to set up libraries without limiting its application to the formation of libraries in schools. It was felt that if the people were learning to read as fast as the schools appeared to be developing then good literature needed to be provided for them. The Society for Promoting the Education of the Poor of Ireland decided to donate to anyone desirous of forming a lending library two or more copies of their publications.

Libraries could acquire as many as 100 to 150 books in this way and at no expense, thus providing a good foundation to any proposed collection. Ever practical the leaflet goes on to say that the restraint imposed on the Society in the formation of schools would not apply to others who wished to establish libraries and recommended that means of religious improvement be sought. It advised that if a library was exclusively religious its success would not answer expectations, and that it would be prudent to admit works on other subjects! Libraries should provide a variety of reading matter on the most interesting subjects – religion, history, poetry, biography, travel, arts and sciences. The variety of choice of books on sale led to difficulties of selection, and one object of the leaflet was to give guidance in book selection, also advice as to where the books selected could be purchased. Lists of books to the value of ten guineas is given, plus those titles which were available free of charge from the Society. All the recommended books were obtainable from Mr Tims at 85 Grafton Street, Dublin, except those issued by the Society. Most of them could also be obtained at the repository of the Religious Tract and Book Society in Sackville Street. A deduction of ten per cent was allowed by both bookshops if the purchases were to go towards the formation of a lending library, and where the books were paid for in ready money. It was stated that ten guineas should be enough to provide for the establishment of a lending library.

The leaflet went on to list a further 45 titles suitable for addition to the lending library which would be:

> unsuited for the mere peasantry but extremely desirable for persons somewhat superior to them in condition. Even in the upper ranks it will sometimes occur that a few families may wish to join in establishing a library of this kind exclusively for the use of their respective households, separate from any similar libraries for public use.

No book is listed that can point to any matter of controversy between Protestants and Roman Catholics.

The Society was extremely comprehensive in its dealings and even refers to the necessity of properly bound books and that Mr Tims 'has accordingly made arrangements for the books supplied by him to be properly bound in a durable and uniform manner at the additional rate of 5d. for the large volumes and 4d. for the smaller volumes'. It goes on to say that the Kildare Place Society books will not need this extra reinforcement but that it will still be necessary for all the other books.

Mr Tims further undertook to provide the books packed in boxes so constructed as to form a bookcase when hung up. Vacant space was allowed for the Society's own titles. Ever resourceful, Mr Tims also ensured the carriage of the books purchased from the Society gratuitously with additional volumes purchased at his shop. When the books bought did not exceed ten guineas in cost the bookcase was three feet high and three feet broad, and was supplied for 13s.6d. At a cost of 7s.7d. Mr Tims undertook to provide a book ruled for the purpose of recording the issue and return of books to the subscribers.

The leaflet includes details of preparing a basic catalogue.

> There should be an alphabetical catalogue of the library with a number prefixed to each volume in the catalogue, the numbers beginning from unity under each letter in the alphabet and that corresponding numbers and letters should be marked strongly on the covers of the respective volumes. The account book should also have a separate page for each book, in which are to be entered the periods of its being lent to each of the subscribers and also of its being returned, thus ascertaining where each volume is, through whose hands it has passed, and how long it has been detained.

It was recommended that a subscription of a small sum should be charged to the tune of about 10d. during the quarter of the year to use one volume at a time, with the liberty to change it as often as desired, with the loan of two volumes being charged at 1s.8d. per quarter and three volumes being charged at 2s.6d. for the quarter. Alternatively the Society recommended that each person who subscribed £1 should be allowed ten transferable tickets for one year, each entitling the bearer the use of the library at the rate of one volume at a time.

The value of the Society's work in establishing libraries becomes very apparent on reading this leaflet.

The setting-up of the Board for National Education in 1831 meant that the Parliamentary grants were transferred from the Kildare

Place Society to the new national system. From the above it will be seen that the education of the great mass of Irish people had been left to chance or to what they could arrange for themselves. In 1824 the number of schools in the country was reported as 11,823, although this figure must be regarded as suspect. Only 1,727 of these were Society schools. The number of pay schools receiving no assistance from the state was 9,352, with the Hedge schools forming the majority.

The Hedge schools in Ireland date back to the seventeenth century when the Popish schoolmasters are referred to in the Cromwellian records as people 'who taught the Irish youth, bringing them up in idolatry, superstition and evil customs'. However, it was not until the beginning of the eighteenth century that the term Hedge school really began to mean anything. As the law forbade the Popish schoolmaster to teach, he was compelled to teach secretly, and because householders could be penalised for harbouring a Popish schoolmaster very often the master taught outside in a quiet place, on the sunny side of the hedge hidden away from chance passers-by, with one of the pupils placed as lookout to give warning of the approach of any stranger. In winter he moved from place to place dependant upon the hospitality of the people. As the laws against Catholic education were relaxed he usually set up a small school in a cabin or in a barn, but the term Hedge school was still retained.

Latocnaye, a Frenchman who walked through Ireland in 1797 carrying an umbrella and a pair of dancing pumps, wrote an interesting description of one of these schools, describing it as a wretched windowless building, only five feet high, stinking and extremely uncomfortable for both master and pupil.

Pat Frayne's school at Skelgy, Co. Tyrone was a sod house, scooped out of the bank on the roadside, with upwards of one hundred scholars, male and female. Lord Palmerston wrote of his Irish speaking tenants in Co. Sligo attending the Hedge schools in miserable mud huts where boys learned reading, writing, arithmetic, Latin and Greek.

As the schoolmasters were often on the run the education of Irish children flourished in the remoter regions where they were less likely to be caught. The schools in the Munster area, particularly in Kerry, provide ample evidence of this. Even Sir Robert Peel, as chief Secretary for Ireland, stated:

> I do not wish to see children educated like that part of the country ... where the young peasants of Kerry run about in

rags, with a Cicero or a Virgil under their arm. In my opinion this is not the best education which will fit them for the usual purposes of life.

As Chief Secretary for Ireland Peel had placed entire control of the new grants for education in the hands of the Kildare Place Society from 1816.

There was a strong desire amongst the poorer classes to be educated and the reputation of the Munster schools, especially those of Kerry, was very long standing. Classical learning was fairly common among the poor and the lower orders included many good Greek and Latin scholars not able to speak the English tongue. There was actually a need among the poorer classes for this kind of classical education. They usually had stong ties with France and Spain. Sir James Caldwell stated in 1764 that there was not a family which did not have a relation in either the church, the army or in trade in those countries, and that in order to qualify their children for foreign service the children are all taught Latin in schools housed in poor huts in the southern part of the kingdom. From all over Ireland scholars travelled to be taught the classics by these masters in the south. 'Amongst the most uncultivated part of the country many may be found who whilst not speaking a word of English are good Latin scholars'. In 1830 Sir Thomas Wyse wrote to Dr James Doyle Bishop of Kildare and Leighlin, stating that the lower classes in Ireland proportionately to their position were better educated than the middle and upper classes.

The passion for knowledge was occasionally flamed by the kidnapping of a schoolmaster. In a mountainous and backward area of Kerry the local people, unable to persuade the schoolmaster to come to such a poor area, took him by force. He was given accommodation and made comfortable but was not allowed to wander more than a mile. Here he was kept until he had educated at least one of the pupils to the level where that pupil would be able to teach the other children. The Halls state that such occurrences were not uncommon.

The founder of the Royal Dublin Society, Samuel Madden placed the sense of education very clearly when he stated that 'As the Irish are not naturally fond of labour crowds of them waste their time and substance as poor scholars to qualify them for the laziest kind of life and hardly ever return to the plough and the spade.'

Books were expensive items in Ireland and were rarely bought by the lower classes as their cost could represent, even for the cheapest book, more than two or three days' wages. Schoolbooks were available, sometimes written by a schoolmaster, whose friends would subscribe to it in order to get it printed. Some schoolmasters could not always afford printed books and kept manuscript copies, sometimes selling these to other masters. There were certain standard arithmetic books available, namely Voster's *Arithmetic*, and similar titles by Gough, Thompson, Darling and Deighan were also very popular. Other books that the masters taught from were Bonnycastle's *Geometry and Algebra*, and Keith's *Trigonometry*. Deighan, being Irish, was popular and he also wrote other books on such subjects as geography, bookkeeping and algebra. It must be borne in mind that the children attending the Hedge schools were usually Irish speaking and there was very little that had been printed in the Irish language in the eighteenth century. A grammar of the Irish language had been published, an English/Irish dictionary, a catechism in the Irish language with corresponding pages in English had been printed on the Continent during the eighteenth century, but normally printed books in Irish were rare.

It was mainly the books for learning to read in English that came under a great deal of criticism. Books being expensive were prized and valuable items. Many peasants had to purchase books from the hawkers and pedlars who distributed the products of the usually Catholic (and illegal) press. It is sometimes difficult to obtain a fair impression of the kind of books that were available, and the surveys done by the authorities are sometimes tinged with the wish to condemn rather than to evaluate. The returns provided by the Catholic clergy sometimes paint a different picture about the books that were available.

Protestants reporting on the reading matter available to school children in the Hedge schools were usually concerned with whether the literature could be regarded as inflammatory as regards the political situation. The Hedge schools are described as miserable, which they undoubtedly were, and the books in them were described as worthless. Hely Dutton in 'A Statistical Survey of the County of Clare' gives a list of books that he found in use in County Clare. As well as a few spelling books the other cottage classics were reported to be:

> *History of the Seven Champions of Christendom*
> *Montelion, Knight of the Oracle*
> *Irish Rogues and Rapparees*
> *Freney, a notorious robber* (teaching them the most dangerous mode of robbing)
> *Jack the Batchelor*, a noted smuggler
> *Fäir Rosamund and Jane Shore*, two prostitutes
> *Donna Rosina*, a Spanish courtesan

Ovid's *Art of love*
*History of Witches and Apparition*
*The Devil and Dr. Faustus*
*Moll Flanders* (highly edifying no doubt!)
*New System of Boxing*, by Mendoza

Later writers were to complain that the books in the Hedge schools were 'political and religious ballads of the vilest doggerel'. Also available were books which had political and historical significance for Catholics, such as:

*The Battle of Aughrim*
*The Siege of Londonderry*
*History of the Young Ascanius* (a name by which the Pretender was known)
Ward's *Cantos* (A poem written by Thomas Ward called England's Reformation)

Other books frequently found in the homes of the poor Catholics were:

*History of Reynard the Fox*
Aesop's *Fables*
*The Arabian Nights' Entertainments*
*The Forty thieves*
*The History of St. Patrick*

Sometimes political pamphlets found their way into the schools and were used to teach children to read. Most of these books would have been very cheaply produced in Dublin, Limerick and Cork, where pirating was quite usual. In Dublin there were at least four booksellers distributing these sixpenny books, but they were probably the only printed books to which the vast majority of the people had access.

Some semi-religious societies tried to suppress these licentious books and nearly all the Societies, such as the London Hibernian Society and the Hibernian Bible Society all found these books nonsensical and foolish. The Association for Discountenancing Vice and Promoting the Knowledge and the Practice of the Christian Religion actually brought the law into play to prevent hawkers selling the books. The Dublin Parliament imposed a tax on the hawkers, pedlars and petty chapmen who went around the country selling books. The tax was 20s. a year and could be shared between the informer and the Incorporated Society for the Promoting of Protestant Schools in Ireland.

The teaching of history was not approved either, as particularly in the Hedge schools it laid the foundation for discontent and disaffection and the general intent was to suppress all reading matter that did not specifically encourage piety, morality and industry. Greek and Roman histories were frowned upon because they were felt to encourage ideas of democracy. Richard Lovell Edgeworth spoke of them as 'to inculcate democracy and a foolish hankering after undefined liberty is not necessary in Ireland'.

In fact most of the books read by children were used as just that – readers. Although these were usually cheap editions very few of the books were actually bad – merely romantic which suited the Irish character very well. Each child brought to school a book bought by the hard-pressed parents and read his or her lessons from it. These books were not used as class books for teaching. Many books were of sound literary value such as *The Vicar of Wakefield*, Drake's *Voyages*, *The Life of Buonaparte* and *Don Quixote*.

A very different picture is drawn by the Parochial School Returns compiled in the dioceses of Kildare and Leighlin in 1824. This is a record compiled by the parish priest in each of the parishes in these dioceses, and is a history of what was achieved by the people and the priests in these areas from 1752 to 1824.

The Confraternity of the Christian Doctrine existed to teach the Roman Catholic religion and catechism to the children and although not formally in existence in the penal times its aims were being carried out secretly in the mass houses, cabins and huts of the people. In the 1820s it was reported that both sexes were taught in separate houses by pious persons who generally belonged to the Confraternity of the Christian Doctrine. In Abbeyleix as well as instruction in the chapel on Sundays there were also Sunday evening schools established in the remote parts of the county where 600 children received moral and religious education. Other parishes also had school houses or chapels used for instruction. In the parish of Clane, Co. Kildare, there were seven different schools teaching a total of 320 children. The instruction in these schools was usually very thorough, covering a good grounding in the faith as well as an acquaintance with the recognised authorities on the ascetic and spiritual life. In connection with every chapel there was usually a parochial library, situated in the vestry, and this was available for the people of the parish as well as for the confraternity of teachers.

> There is a circulating library at Tullow where about 100 religious books are contained and to which teachers and parishioners have access.
> In the chapel of Carlow besides catechisms there is a parochial library to which teachers have access consisting of 280 volumes of religious books.
> In Goresbridge and Paulstown there is a library kept in the

vestry for the use of the Sunday School and in the chapel for the use of the parishioners.

In Clonbullogue Chapel the books in these schools are 106 volumes of religious works which are sometimes read out in the chapel on Sundays and Holydays but generally read by the people at their respective houses.

These are details taken from the returns issued by the Royal Commissioners to all parish priests and ministers in Ireland during the summer of 1824 and are taken from the abstract of parochial returns furnished in the second report of the Commissioners of Irish Education Inquiry 1826. The holdings of these parish libraries were mainly religious books, for example, the Bible (Douai version), *Sinners' Guide, Life of Christ, Charity and Truth, Moral Extracts, Elevation of the Soul to God*, Butler's *Feasts and Fasts, Imitation of Christ*, by Thomas a'Kempis, *Think Well On't*, Challoner's *Meditations, Parsons Christian Directory*, and *Lessons for Lent*. Other books would include catechisms and prayer books (See illustration taken from Schools of Kildare and Leighlin on the number of books in these parish libraries – Figure 2.3).

Many of the schools referred to in these returns are in fact Hedge schools and whilst it is obvious that many of them were for little children and dealt with basic reading, writing and arithmetic, at least sixteen of them are referred to as teaching the classics. They also list the books available in the schools where Latin, Greek and French were taught. The books were Homer, Virgil, Cucero, Horace and the Greek Testaments. The Hedge schoolmasters were frequently the scribes of the parish and the people to whom all applied if they wanted to have letters or petitions written. These teachers were nearly all men, although there were dames' schools for younger children.

Another fact about these schools is that the masters were very often sanctioned by the parish priests. They taught the catechisms every day so that the term Hedge school became synonymous with Catholic school. Many Protestants attended these Catholic pay schools, and this was especially noticeable in Northern Ireland. Despite their learning the masters were poor men, who were badly paid or not paid at all. The fees were low. For example, William Connell of Boly, parish of Rathaspic, had an annual income of £5. 5s. paid by the pupils at 1s.3d. per quarter and 7s.6d. per quarter for two classical scholars. Denis O'Neil of Rahanna had a total income of £15 annually. Some of this was received from wealthy patrons but most of the income came from quarterly rates charged to the pupils – 2s.6d. for readers and writers, 1s.8d. for spellers, 5s.0d.

# FIGURE 2.3  LIST OF PARISH LIBRARIES IN KILDARE AND LEIGHLIN, 1820 – 29

## KILDARE AND LEIGHLIN
### PROGRESS, 1820–1829

| Parochial Area | Members in Confraternities | Parish Library Volumes | Schoolhouses | Scholars |
|---|---|---|---|---|
| Leighlin | 109 | 78 | Old Chapel | 932 |
| Tullow | Many | 200 | Built 1826 | 1000 |
| Baltinglass | 154 | 246 | 2 built 1818-29 | 909 |
| Ballinakill | 435 | 221 | 2 built lately | 670 |
| Borris | 313 | 466 | 1 built lately / 1 to be built immediately | 920 |
| Mountmellick | 150 | 480 | 3 built lately | 700 |
| Clonaslee | 87 | 28 | Building | 280 |
| Rathvilly | 196 | 488 | 1 built lately / 1 to be built | 1000 |
| St. Mullins | 130 | 60 | 1 built lately / 1 to be built | 500 |
| Paulstown | Many | 113 | Built lately | 342 |
| Mountrath | 200 | 200 | Built lately | 350 |
| Raheen | 200 | 75 | Building | 500 |
| Abbeyleix | 310 | 160 | Built lately | 640 |
| Killeshin | 181 | 180 | Built | 600 |
| Ballon | 88 | 229 | 2 Schools | 263 |
| Kill | 148 | 62 | School | 300 |
| Arles | 430 | 294 | 3 built | — |
| Tinryland | 200 | 60 | Built | 400 |
| Ballyadams | 400 | 303 | 2 built / 1 to be built | 930 |
| Rosenallis | 55 | 90 | To be built | 250 |
| Portarlington and Emo | 789 | 281 | 5 built | 350 |
| Clonbullogue | 107 | 271 | 2 built | 350 |
| Stradbally | — | 50 | No School | 450 |
| Monasterevan | — | 666 | 3 built | 800 |
| Philipstown | 370 | 200 | 2 Schools | 700 |
| Carbery | Few | 37 | Building | 240 |
| Newbridge | 30 | — | 1 built | 300 |
| Hacketstown | 16 | 98 | 2 built | 610 |
| Naas | — | 350 | Built | 473 |
| Dunane | 67 | — | No School-house | 342 |
| Clonegal | 48 | 98 | 2 building | 500 |
| Allen | 100 | 66 | 2 built lately | 272 |
| Rhode and Edenderry | 250 | 140 | Schools, but not attached to Chapels | 500 |
| Myshall | 305 | 108 | No School-house | 690 |
| Clonmore | 225 | 203 | 2 built lately | 500 |
| Kildare | 297 | 567 | 4 built lately | 400 |
| Suncroft | 10 | 100 | School-house | 200 |
| Ballyfin | 30 | 25 | Built lately | 200 |
| Bagenalstown | 261 | 390 | 3 Schools | 900 |
| Killeigh | 195 | 275 | 3 built lately | 500 |
| Graig | 150 | 137 | 4 built lately | 600 |
| Balyna | — | 83 | 2 built / 1 building | 360 |
| Carlow | — | 360 | Built many years | 916 |

*From* Revd Martin Brenen *Schools of Kildare and Leighlin*, 1775-1835, Gille, 1935

39

for teaching the English grammar, and 11s.4½d. per quarter for teaching bookkeeping.

William White at Raheen at the foot of Mount Leinster had an annual income of £2 raised in fees from the scholars. Many masters complained of not actually getting paid, and frequently the children did not attend in the winter months. Despite this many of them possessed their own libraries and one might well wonder where they managed to get the money to acquire these books. The poem called the *Song of the Books* is a lament composed by Tomás Ruadh O'Sullivan, who had been sponsored by Daniel O'Connell, when he lost his books in a crossing at Derrynane Harbour, the boat being wrecked and all his books going to the bottom of the sea. He states that most of his boooks were written with the pen and therefore copied by him, not printed books. His list of books is most impressive.

In the early nineteenth century nearly every Irish village possessed manuscripts written in the Irish script, the products of the schoolmaster. Usually there were sagas of heroes, tales of Fingal, Oscar Ossian or stories about St. Patrick. Sometimes the classics were translated into the Irish, sometimes they were prayers, recipes or charms. These manuscripts would be brought out to be read aloud when large numbers of people would gather round the fire in a cabin for that purpose, (see Figure 2.4). The authorities in complaining of the pernicious literature in English being sold by hawkers to the peasantry seemed to be unaware of the totality of the Irish culture and learning which was being perpetuated.

### FIGURE 2.4   SCHOOLMASTER READING ANCIENT STORIES TO THE PEOPLE

# SONG OF THE BOOKS
### by Tomás Ruadh O'Sullivan

There were Deehan and Dowling and Voster in it
And De Catone and Bonicastle
And Duggan's laws relating
To the moon's age;
And Moran, the adventurous one,
Who wrote about the sea
And gave us a true account
Of the ebb of the tide.
There was Euclid too
By Owen May

There were Comerford and O'Halloran
And Keating's book of history
And the sweet Psalter of Cashel
Of which he treats;
There was an account of the Battle of Clontarf
Where Brian rid us of the Danes,
And how Malachy defeated
The enemy in combat

There was Paul O'Brien, the grammarian,
Who put Irish into shape for us
And gave us the rules of song and story
So that all could read them.

If I walked through Ireland and Scotland
And France, and Spain and England,
And yet again if I travelled
In every direction under the moon,
I would not get as many books
That were so full of knowledge and wisdom
Or of such benefit to me
Although now they are gone.

# 3    Early publishing and printing

Records of the book trade exist from as early as 1545 when James Dartas of Dublin purchased a consignment of school service books for which he paid 76s.11d. in London. However, the earliest printer to arrive in Ireland was Humfrey Powell who came to the country in 1550 with his printing press, intent on being an instrument for the promotion of Protestantism. He presided in the vicinity of the old Crane in Dublin. His edition of the Book of Common Prayer is believed to be the first book printed in Dublin, together with: '*A Briefe Declaration of certain principall articles of religion*' Imprynted at Dublin by Humfrey Powell the 20 of January 1566.

He was obviously appointed an official printer as the book states: 'Imprynted at Dublin in Saint Nycolas Street by Humfrey Powell Prynter appoynted for the Realme of Ireland'. He had practised in London as a printer before his arrival in Ireland and his name appears in the Charter of the Stationers' Company in 1566 at which period he was resident in St. Nicholas Street, Dublin.

The first book to be published in the Irish language was issued in 1571 and was an Irish alphabet and catechism:

> Precept or instruction of a Christian, together with certain articles of the Christian rule which are proper for every one to adopt who would be submissive to the ordinance of God and of the Queen in this kingdom: translated from Latin and English into Irish by John O'Kearney: printed in Irish in the town of the ford of the Hurdles (Dublin) at the cost of Master John Ussher, Alderman, at the head of the Bridge, the 20th day of June 1571. With the privilege of the great Queen, 1571.

Gilbert White in his *History of the City of Dublin* refers to Nicholas Walsh, minister of St. Werburgh's from 1571 to 1577 and subsequently Bishop of Ossory, who was the first to introduce Irish types into Ireland: Queen Elizabeth, at her own expense, having provided a printing press and a fount of Irish letters.

Alderman John Ussher took an active part in the affairs of the city and had the idea of establishing a university twenty years prior to the foundation of Trinity College in a letter addressed to Lord Burghley. Addressing Lord Burghley was probably in vain. When Queen Elizabeth I suggested that in giving education to the people which she intended when she founded Trinity her purpose would be aided through the medium of the spoken language, and she suggested the appointment of an Irish professorship. This idea found no favour with her Premier. 'What!' said Burghley, 'encourage a language more nearly allied to canine barking than to the articulation human?' – and he illustrated his most calumnious assertions by pronouncing the cacophonous alliteration:

> D'ibh, dubh, damh, obh, amb, which pronounced as
> div, duv, dav, ov, av (a black steer drank a raw egg)

Ussher was a well-respected character and when he died in 1629 he was succeeded by his son Sir William Ussher in whose house the first extant Irish version of the New Testament was printed:

> The New Testament of Our Lord and Savious Jesus Christ, faithfully translated from the Greek into Irish by William O'Donnell. Printed at the town of the Ford of Hurdles, in the house of Master William Ussher, at the foot of the Bridge, by John Francke, 1602.

The dedication of the work includes an address to James I which refers to Queen Elizabeth.

> and even in the beginning of her most happie raigne, out of her motherly care and princely bountie, provided the Irish characters and other instruments for the presse, in hope that God in mercy would raise up some to translate the Newe Testament into their mother tongue.

These first Irish books appeared from the presses to state in simple terms the Protestant religion for the native Irish. The Irish Franciscans in Louvain and the Low Countries were responsible for publishing some works of the Catholic Doctrine in Irish. These books were written in simple intelligible prose by such men as Archbishop Florence Conry, Hugh McCagwell and Bonaventure Ó Heoghusa. These writers and others like them very often came from the old Bardic schools and by tradition deferred to the ancient learned classes of Ireland, prefacing their books with apologies for the basic language that had been used. The hereditary scholars still retained the respect of their exiled brethren and even though they had lost their wealthy patrons they still held the key to all the ancient heritage of Irish scholarship – history, chronicles, genealogies, Brehon law and poetry. But their arrogance did the Irish language more harm than good because they despised the simple colloquial language of the people. Because of them Irish remained remote from the printing presses while English became the usual language of the printer.

During the seventeenth century many exiled Irish scholars

established colleges and houses in Louvain, Paris, Lisbon, Prague, Salamanca and Rome. From these centres priests were educated to return to Ireland as missionaries. Here in these continental houses they laboured to preserve Ireland's past, setting up printing presses and having books printed in Irish. Books of piety and devotion written for the people at home were smuggled into Ireland sometimes by the barrel-load.

It was almost as if the printing presses had never been invented as the professional Irish scribes continued to copy out in beautiful script the prayer books and devotional manuals many of which had been reprinted even a century before in Louvain and elsewhere on the continent. These members of the hereditary scribal families survived to the beginning of the nineteenth century, and being deferred to by the people they hindered rather than helped the efforts of those who sought to provide a printed literature for the Irish speaking readers. With their old-fashioned rules and linguistic conventions they kept the language in an historical strait-jacket that bore little resemblance to the ordinary everyday language spoken by the people. These scribes could raise as much as £5 for a volume of manuscript from eager patrons who saw them as the guardians of the ancient ways. Thus almost by default and through the vicissitides of the penal times English won the day as the output of the printing presses was made available to the people.

During the Commonwealth period an order was sent to Ireland conceived in the full spirit of arbitrary power:

> That the printer (for there was but one) in Dublin should not suffer his press to be made use of, without first bringing the copy to be printed to the clerk of the Council who, upon receiving it, if he found anything tending to the prejudice of the Commonwealth or the public peace and welfare, should acquaint the Council with the same, for their pleasure to be known therein.

After the Restoration at a meeting of the first Parliament to be held in Ireland in July 1661 the House of Lords ordered that:

> All the Bibles that had been printed by the late Usurper's Printer, calling himself Printer to His Highness the Lord Protector, should have the title-page where those words are printed torn from them; and that no sale be made within this Kingdom or any Bible with the said title-page; but that new title-pages be printed by Mr. John Crooke, His Majesty's Bookseller, whereof all booksellers are to take notice.

Later there was a thriving book business in Dublin, most of the trade being confined to Castle Street, Dame Street and Skinner's Row. Towards the end of the reign of Charles II, Richard Pue, a printer, founded Dick's Coffee House in Skinner's Row. This became a fashionable establishment and two Dublin booksellers started book auctions at Dick's. A room at the back was hired for the same purpose by John Dunton, the eccentric London publisher who brought a large collection of books and manuscripts to Dublin for sale in 1698. Dunton's auctions were patronised by the chief noblemen, clergymen and scholars.

After the second auction another bookseller contracted with Pue to hire the sale room occupied by Dunton. This was Patrick Campbell, a Scotsman. Like most of the coffee houses in Dublin Dick's was on the drawing room floor and one of the shops underneath was occupied by Thomas Cotter, bookseller and publisher, while at the rear was the establishment of Aaron Rhames, publisher of a Saturday periodical called the *Diverting Post*. Nearly all the principal auctions of books, land and property were held at Dick's which was in existence for nearly a century. *Pue's Occurrences*, published at Dick's Coffee House, was a Tory paper first issued around 1700 in quarto size, from which it gradually grew into large folio. Richard Pue died in 1758 and was succeeded by his nephew James Pue who in turn died in 1762. Sarah Pue then published the paper but it eventually became the property of John Hillary the bookseller of 54 Castle Street. It ceased publication about 1792.

Robert Thornton had his shop in Skinner's Row at the sign of the Leather Bottle from 1685 to 1718. He was a bookseller and was appointed as the King's Stationer in 1692, being the first to hold that office. He issued the first Dublin newspaper called *The Dublin News Letter* in 1685, prior to *Pue's Occurrences*. Alderman James Malone was appointed with Richard Malone as King's Printer in 1689 by James II. He issued various publications of the Jacobite Government which were later industriously sought out and destroyed by the Williamites. Some of his pamphlets were rigidly suppressed. In 1707, along with Luke Dowling, another Roman Catholic bookseller, he was tried at the Queen's Bench for publishing and selling a book called *A Manual of Devout Prayers*. They were convicted and sentenced to pay fines of 300 marks each. On appealing they stated that the said book had been on sale in Dublin for the past twenty years. It had been sold by both Protestant and Popish booksellers: it contained prayers for the Pretender and had been distributed originally at the time of the proposed invasion by the French king in order to make the population rise. Malone and Dowling who had no such intention had their fine reduced to 5 marks and were released from confinement.

Being a publisher in Ireland was not always easy. John Harding, publisher of the *Dublin News Letter*, issued Swift's *Drapier's Letters* in 1724. He was publicly prosecuted by the government for publishing this, and was thrown into prison where he died. His widow Sarah was ordered to be taken into custody in October 1725 for having printed a poem called 'Wisdom's Defeat' which commented adversely on circumstances connected with the passing of an address to the King from the House of Lords. It was declared by them to be 'Base, scandalous and malicious, highly reflecting upon the honour of their House and the peerage of this Kingdom'. The sheriffs of the city of Dublin were ordered to direct the said scandalous pamphlet to be burnt by the hands of the common hangman before the gate of the Parliament House and also before the Thosel of the City. The persecuted distributor of this political satire survived her imprisonment, unlike her unfortunate husband, and in 1728 published *The Intelligencer*, a journal conducted by Swift and Dr Sheridan.

The first King's printer in Ireland whose patent is enrolled was John Frankton who was appointed to the office by James I in 1604. He continued to be the principal publisher until 1617 when the patent was granted to Felix Kingston, Matthew Lownes and Bartholomew Downes, stationers and citizens of London who in 1618 erected a 'factory for books and a press' in Dublin and commenced by publishing the Irish Statutes. The Company of Stationers continued to publish in Dublin up to the time of the Civil War in 1641. Many booksellers suffered during this time and John Crooke and Richard Sergier who kept their stationers' shop well-furnished with merchandise and English books stated that 'the loss they have sustained by this present rebellion, besides the utter decay of their trade to their undoing and the further loss they must needs suffer in the stock of books now lying dead on their hands'. At this time they were owed upwards of £600 by both Protestants and Papists who had lost all through the rebellion. It was, after all, difficult for the book trade and culture to blossom during an uprising. John Crooke afterwards recovered his fortunes as he was appointed King's Printer in 1660.

In the reign of James II, Eliphal Dobson, the most wealthy Dublin bookseller and publisher of his day, had a shop at the Stationers' Arms. He was attainted in the Parliament of 1689 and returned to his former habitation after the evacuation of Dublin by the Jacobites. Mr Dobson was a great dissenter, but his pretence to religion 'does not make him a jot precise. He values no man for his starched looks or supercilious gravity, or for being a churchman,

Presbyterian, Independent etc. provided he is sound in the main points wherein all good men agreed'. Dobson was succeeded by his son and namesake and later in 1737 another bookseller Stearne Brock was at the same site.

According to Gilbert White, after the Restoration the number of printers in Dublin rapidly increased and in the middle of the eighteenth century the city could boast of many respectable publishers but after the union with England the amount of works published in the metropolis of Ireland decreased by eighty per cent.

A Committee for Conducting the Free Press was set up in 1764 and published a second volume of the *Freemans Journal*. The first volume had been produced by the publishers Alexander MacCulloh, bookseller in Henry Street and William Williamson, bookseller at Maecena's Head in Bride Street and had been printed in September 1763 by order of the Committee for Conducting the Free Press. Afterwards the Committee set up their own press at St. Audoen's Arch and started to print it for themselves in September 1764. Those concerned with its production were Dr Lucas, Henry Brooke, the first editor, Bernard Clarke of Mary's Abbey, John Grant, a merchant and the woollen drapers Tandy and Braddell. In the 1770s the paper became the mouthpiece of Flood, Grattan and other opponents of the administration of Lord Townshend. Although constantly denounced by the authorities the *Freemans Journal* was in literary ability and arrangement superior to other papers of the day and had the merit of publishing independent and original political essays. *The Censor* has been the first paper to do this, and the *Freemans Journal* was the second.

At the sign of 'Mercury' in Parliament Street was the shop of James Hoey, a young Catholic bookseller and publisher, son of James Hoey of Skinner's Row. He published a newspaper called the *Mercury* which was the organ of the Irish Government during the Viceroyalty of Lord Townshend from 1767 to 1772. The *Mercury* was full of satires and epigrams against Dr Charles Lucas and the Committee for Conducting the Free Press, as the editors of the *Freemans Journal* called themselves. The latter tired of being lampooned as a Puritan committee declared that the writers of the *Mercury* were a knot of Jesuits employed by Hoey to subvert the state.

Hoey's brother was an associate of George Faulkner, known as the prince of Dublin printers. A character of great importance in his own day, he owned a bookshop and printing establishment in Skinner's Row where he started to publish the newspaper, the *Dublin Journal*. He also worked in connection with Swift. A zealous and active advocate for the relaxation of the penal code, he is recorded by Matthew O'Conor as the first Protestant who stretched his hand to the prostrate Catholic.

A vignette of these early booksellers is provided by Dunton who described Nat Gun, publisher and bookseller.

> This son of a Gun gave me a hearty welcome; and to do him justice he's as honest a man as the world affords; and is so, esteemed by all who know him. He understands stenography as well as bookbinding; and he himself is a sort of shorthand character; for he is a little fellow, but one that contains a great deal; and as he is a most incomparable writer of shorthand, so he speaks it as well as he writes it; to complete his character he is a constant shopkeeper.
>
> This Gun was a constant and generous bidder at my auctions, where he bought a quantity of books, which he as honestly paid for.

James Carson, the publisher of the *Dublin Intelligence* which contained a full and important account of the foreign and domestic news, also published a Saturday newspaper called *The Dublin Weekly Journal*. We find him complaining in 1729 that people instead of buying his paper for three halfpence, usually borrowed it from hawkers at 'a halfpenny a read'.

Jacques Fabrij, *marchand libraire Français*, sold books in Dame Street in 1704 and the Revd. Jean Pierre Droz, a clergyman of the Reformed Church of France, published in 1744 the first original and critical periodical to be printed in Ireland. This was called *A Literary Journal*. His objectives were in his statement of design:

> As foreign books are only known from the French journals, published abroad, understood by few and read by fewer, my intention is to give English abstracts of the most important foreign books, German, Dutch, French or Latin ... I shall chuse the best extracts to be found in the great variety of foreign journals; give them either whole or in part, according to the importance of the subject; enlarge upon what shall be judged to be of the greatest moment; and suppress what appears to be of small use. I shall also give abstracts which are not to be met with in any journals; in short I shall use my best endeavours that nothing be omitted that may render this work agreeable or useful to the public ... All books of note published abroad, of which no abstract is given, shall be exactly mentioned at the end of each volume, with whatever happens remarkable in the Universities of Muscovy, Sweden, Denmark, Germany, Holland, Switzerland and France.

This periodical came out every quarter at the rate of one shilling and sixpence, English money, each part.

Droz' accounts of contemporary continental literature given under the title of 'Literary News' at the end of each number were exceedingly ample. The essays were usually on theological and scientific subjects and almost excluded any literature in Ireland. In the whole work there are only three papers treating Irish subjects. However, Droz was probably quite a shrewd character as he imported considerable quantities of foreign books, published a series of French comedies and also several works written by the French refugees in Ireland. The journal continued to appear until June 1749 and on his death in December 1751 his countryman Des Voeux made an unsuccessful attempt to revive the periodical.

John Magee at 41 College Green was an extensive lottery broker and published *Magee's Weekly Packet* or *Hopes Lottery, Journal of News, Politicks and Literature*, first issued in June 1777 and with each of the early numbers was given a lottery ticket with the chance of a prize of £50. Competition among the many publishers of newspapers must by that time have been particularly fierce and illustrates that the present-day idea of bingo or roulette through the newspapers is not a new one!

A circulating library was kept at 5 College Green in 1798 by Vincent Dowling, but he was a restless person and he tried a variety of occupations including running a coffee house, a registry office for procuring situations, and a company for insuring persons against being drawn for the militia. He was an able and witty writer, and produced many ballads and *jeux d'esprits* against the union with Great Britain.

Nearly all the booksellers had signs displayed outside their premises to attract customers, and the fronts of their shops were a jumble of books, leaflets, pamphlets, lottery tickets and patent medicines. The booksellers chose heads of famous writers such as Milton and Swift to display on their signs, but they used others signs as well. In the seventeenth century books could be found at the sign of the horseshoe at Samuel Dancer's, and at Robert Thornton's at the sign of the Leather Bottle. William Williamson in the late eighteenth century sold books at Maecena's Head, and John Watson at the Bible and Crown in the early eighteenth century. George Grierson was at the sign of the Two Bibles in Essex Street from which press emerged the first Irish edition of *Paradise Lost* in 1753, and who held the office of Official Printer. Richard James was at Newton's Head in 1756 and Robert Main sold books at the Erasmus Head in 1747. Thomas Whitehouse, another bookseller, kept his shop under the Cocoa Tree Coffee House in the vicinity of the

Custom House and the Anne and Grecian, a suite of rooms in a house at the foot of the bridge where books were often sold by auction in the evenings.

In the 1770s most of the Catholic printers and booksellers were around the region of Cook Street, the same area which had been associated with printers from the time of the establishment of the first press in 1551. The printers in order to ply their trade had to belong to the Guild of St. Luke, the activities of which were largely confined to Dublin. Like all the other guilds at this time it was exclusively Protestant. The guild levied a quarterly fee from Catholic printers but no Catholic was entitled to become a freeman or a full member of the guild. Moreover, officers of the guild were required to take the oath of supremacy which at that time no Catholic could take. Restrictions only allowed Catholic printers to take two apprentices.

It was mainly due to the Catholic committee that Catholic printers were eventually admitted as full members of the Guild of St. Luke in 1793, the first Catholic printers to be admitted being Pat Wogan, Richard Cross and Matthew Cary. This committee was comprised of a group of laymen representing the Catholic merchant class, but led by a few Catholic noblemen, and their job was to manage Catholic affairs. Experienced men, their policy was one of passive loyalty, taking what they got and using every influence and peaceful means to achieve more.

Most Catholics operated in a small way, producing prayers and devotions for the Catholic chapels in the area of the back lanes around Cook Street. For larger works, the Catholic printers sometimes joined together, pooling their resources to print large and expensive volumes. For these major works Catholic printers canvassed for subscribers, and out-of-print works were produced with the support of the clergy, Catholic merchants and tradesmen, Catholic gentry and other booksellers who sometimes ordered up to fifty copies. During the late eighteenth century Catholics were just beginning to emerge from the effects of the worst aspects of the penal code, and the numerous but poor Catholic printers in Dublin were valuable auxiliaries in making the Catholic voice heard.

Patrick Lord, at the sign of the Angel and the Bible in Cook Street, was a poor Catholic printer who published in 1755 *Case of the Roman Catholics* which became a best-seller in its day. It was advertised in Pue's, Faulkener's and Williamson's papers. Lord was so worried about printing this book that he often stopped his press on account of being told that he would find no sale for the book. Secrecy was often the order of the day. When he published in 1759 *Historical Memoirs of the Irish Rebellion of 1641* the proof sheets were sent to his friend Reily, who carried them at dead of night to the house of Dr John Curry, the author.

The printers and booksellers during the eighteenth century had to cater for popular taste and produce books that would sell widely. Hence they turned their attention to the production of spelling books, primers, collections of fairy tales, folk tales, and accounts of highwaymen, rapparees and rogues whose stories were avidly sought by the majority of the submerged masses. Almanacs were one of the period's best-sellers. They contained calendars and lists of fairs to be held, and were packed with conundrums, puzzles, riddles, mathematical problems and astrological lore. These were published by John Whaley, a compiler of prophetic almanacs and compounder of medicines to cure all diseases! Others who published almanacs at this time were Andrew Cumpsty, John Knapp at the sign of the Dyal in Meath Street, and John Coats of Cork.

Until the Act of Union in 1801, when the Copyright Act of 1711 was extended to Ireland, Irish publishers had maintained the right to reproduce British publications for the Irish market, but the new law deprived them of this. Up to this time many Irish publishers had literary agents in London whose business it was to procure works in sheets before publication, enabling the Irish to bring out contemporaneous editions or sometimes to outstrip their English counterparts. This extension of the Act had the effect of practically destroying the flourishing book business in Ireland, particularly the Dublin trade where in the eighteenth century there were in the region of nearly two hundred different printers, publishers and booksellers. Irish printers had been free to produce anything which was outside the monopoly of the King's printer but from 1739 they were prevented from importing publications into England but at that time still had the home market and the colonial markets.

The chapmen helped to distribute the early publications of the printers and booksellers, which were the cheap books or chapbooks of all kinds – folk tales, tales of rapparees and highwaymen, little devotional works, and so on.

Luke White was a most successful chapman who started his career as a wandering hawker of books which he carried to various parts of the country. It was reported that old men used to remember seeing him with his cargo of portable literature on his back, practically bent double with the load, toiling upon a blustery day along the road and driving a hard bargain for Corderey or Cornelius Nepos at the door of a village school. When he had amassed enough money he set himself up at a stall in a small alley called Crampton Court, and soon afterwards purchased a bookshop. Book piracy was not illegal in Ireland and he consequently became a publisher and as a buccaneer of literature made a profitable trade. Luke White died in 1824 an amazingly rich man but sad to relate his fortune came not from books, although these undoubtedly put him on the first few rungs of the ladder toward success. Instead some of his money came from lottery speculations, but his main wealth accrued from his loan negotiations with the government.

The Dublin publishers relied on the chapmen to sell their works outside Dublin in the country generally. The publishers gave great encouragement to the country merchants and others who bought to sell again. Such merchants qualified for special terms and in the country areas books and pamphlets were sold with stationery, seeds, patent medicines and many other goods. Books were sold by Hely and Dillon of Cork, Carpenter of Newry, Finn of Kilkenny, Callwell and Maguire of Waterford, Gorman and Hackett of Clonmel, and Nowlan of Carlow. The last-named may well have acted as an agent for the parochial libraries in the diocese of Kildare and Leighlin already mentioned in Chapter 2. Various solidarities, confraternities and Catholic book societies all helped to disseminate Catholic literature, and some spent their time reading books of piety to the sick, invalids and those who were unable to read for themselves. Throughout this period most Catholic homes had access to these kind of books which were read and discussed within the home circle. A Catholic Book Society of Dublin was founded in 1827 with the support of the Bishop of Kildare and Leighlin, Dr James Doyle. It was promoted from the bookshop of William J. Battersby who published, *inter alia*, the *Irish Catholic Directory*.

Many Catholic printers irked by the restrictions in Ireland fled to America. One such was Matthew Cary, himself a voracious reader, clandestinely subscribing to a circulating library to read novels and romances. He was apprenticed to Thomas McDonnel, a printer and bookseller, but had a tremendous chip on his shoulder because of the wrongs done to the Catholics of his day. Unknown to anyone he wrote and published an inflammatory pamphlet urging the immediate repeal of the penal code. His father bundled him off to Paris in 1781 where Cary was engaged to work at the printing office run by Benjamin Franklin at Passy. He was consulted by Lafayette at the time of the proposed French invasion of Ireland. After a year he returned to Dublin and became editor of a paper called the *Volunteer Journal*. One issue which was especially vitriolic against the government led to Cary's arrest, but he escaped and fled to Philadelphia, the then acknowledged literary centre of America. Patrick Byrne, one of the principal political publishers of his day, was another Dublin printer who, after being arrested in 1798 for his nationalistic convictions, made his way·to Philadelphia.

The distinction of calling oneself printer and bookseller was then much sought after, and the Catholic booksellers began to emerge from the back streets of Dublin. In a way this was unfortunate, because the language of Dublin and of the printing presses was now English, and the submerged Irish language of the countryside did not come to the surface. This dissemination of English language printing by the Dublin Catholic printers contributed towards the Anglicisation of Ireland.

During the eighteenth century the terms printer, publisher and bookseller were frequently interchangeable. Many produced newspapers and pamphlets of political satire, but some of these newspapers did not survive for very long. Many were just casual or jobbing printers concerned with the production of ephemera. Dublin apart, printing in the seventeenth century was known only at Belfast, Cork, Kilkenny and Waterford, but the output from these places was not enormous, and printing there was introduced mainly for administrative reasons in the 1640s. The period of the greatest printing activity lasted from 1766 to about 1790. The first printers in Belfast came from Glasgow. Limerick also became an important printing centre.

The printers of Dublin established an institution called the Asylum for Aged Printers in 1832 for the care of aged and infirm members of the trade who were no longer able to support themselves. This was supposedly the first attempt of any of the operative classes to provide for their superannuated members. According to the Trustees, among whom was George A. Grierson, there was no other employment where the maturity of life was so short or the decline so helpless since the sedentary and peculiar nature of the work tended to an early waste of human strength.

Taxes in Ireland on newspapers were introduced more as a means of controlling the press rather than raising revenue, and on the whole the newspaper tax and tax on pamphlets was lower than in England. The arrival of the newspapers in the 1760s marked a big increase in the printing output of the country, although the circulation of some of the newspapers was extremely low.

The potential reading public in the country areas would have been small and at first the printing presses catered for the middle classes and for the non-Catholic community. Printers were often stationers and booksellers as well as dealers in medicine and hardware, some were also wine merchants or auctioneers. Robert Greer of Newry ran a subscription library whilst being a jobbing printer and binder, as well as having a stationery business. Chapmen who sold their wares at school houses, convents and cabin doors were known as 'Flying Stationers' and had material specially produced for them by some provincial printers. William Young of Armagh advertised in 1805 that from his shop chapmen and dealers could be well supplied with pictures, pamphlets, school books and stationery.

James Blow of Belfast contracted to print 8,000 Bibles over seven years for George Grierson, the King's printer of the day, but Grierson was his father-in-law and that amount of printing at that time outside Dublin was unusual. There was generally not much printing done outside Dublin, and with improved communications in the nineteenth century provincial printing declined even more as books could be more easily supplied from Dublin, although provincial newspapers continued to do well. The average circulation for a newspaper in Ireland in the 1830s was 547 copies. Only the well-to-do and the middle classes could afford newspapers as the taxes kept the prices high and as a result the circulations were low. The bulk of the 41 stamped newspapers in 1821 had a circulation of less than 400, although at the close of the eighteenth century the *Belfast Newsletter* was claiming a circulation of 3,000 and the *Northern Star* claimed 4,000. These may well have been exaggerations.

In the history of book production in Ireland one of the most remarkable features were the brilliant and magnificent bindings produced in the late seventeenth and eighteenth centuries, the style and technique of which are unmistakeable. The Parliamentary Records of the Irish Commons and Lords were bond annually between 1697 and 1798, and represented the most splendid achievement rivalled only by French bindings. These books perished during the Civil War that raged in Ireland in the 1920s, but photographs and rubbings taken by Sir Edward Sullivan in 1904 have survived. There were few Catholic books with expensive bindings. They were quite rare before 1775 as on the whole the Catholic population did not have the means to pay for luxury work, besides which devotional works tended too be used until they fell to bits.

There appears to be scant information available on circulating libraries and a perusal through town and county directories of the eighteenth and nineteenth centuries throws a tantalising but very faint light on the situation. Gilbert White's *History of the City of Dublin* lists vast numbers of booksellers, printers and publishers, but in the whole of his comprehensive work he mentions only two circulating libraries. One was run by Alexander Stewart who kept a circulating library in Dame Street in 1774. He is mentioned in an article by Paul Kaufman 'Community lending libraries in eighteenth century Ireland and Wales' (*Library Quarterly*, October 1963, vol. XXXIII no. 4) as A. Stuart, 'at the circulating library in Dane (sic)

Street, 1774 – 1789.' Another circulating library mentioned by White is that of Vincent Dowling, a publisher and proprietor of the Apollo Circulating Library at College Green in 1798. White makes no mention at all of the engaging Mrs Lord of Dublin, quoted by Kaufman, and who when an irate father made violent protests about the lending of unsuitable novels to innocent young girls, explained that she carefully underlined the passages of dubious reading in order to warn the readers what to skip!

On 4 April, 1810 Mrs M. Trench was to write from England to Mrs Mary Leadbeater at Ballitore, the Quaker village in Kildare:

> I am now relieved from my long fast as to reading. You know the difficulty of getting books in Dublin, even to buy; and I, who have already so many, and so little space wherein to put them, wish only to have the majority of those I read, which is out of the question in Dublin, as it does not afford as good a circulating library as is found down to the sixth rate provincial town here. In London a guinea a quarter gives one everything one could wish.

By 1824 Pigot and Co's *City of Dublin and Hibernian Provincial Directory* lists seven circulating libraries for Dublin alone. There are:

Richard Fitzgibbon 18 King Street
Sarah Flanaghan, Kingstown
Jane Ganly, 174 North King St. (also listed as a stationer)
T. Henscholl, 36 Naussau Street (also listed as bookseller)
John Kempston, 31 Lower Sackville Street (marked as "extensive")
Rebecca Ledford, 53 Golden Lane
Margaret Milton, 52 Lower Kevin Street

In addition for the capital there are 25 bookbinders listed and 92 persons listed as booksellers and stationers. The Directory is too early to list the circulating library run by D. Jacotin referred to in Kaufman's article of which a catalogue from 1803 has survived listing English, French and Italian scores.

The *Dublin Evening Mail* for 12 January, 1827 carries an advertisement for the Circulating Library at 43 Lower Sackville Street which reads as follows:

> Thomas Webb in directing the public attention to his new catalogue just published takes opportunity of observing that the very flattering encouragement he has hitherto obtained from his unwearied exertions to anticipate the wishes of his

subscribers, has been his constant inducement to make such great addition to the collection that a perusal of the catalogue will prove that his library cannot be surpassed by any in the City, for the taste, variety and selection of its volumes. He can assure his friends and subscribers that he relies on his own assiduous exertions and the excellence of his Books to retain the public patronage and confidence that without parade or puff he is proud and grateful to acknowledge he now so largely possesses.

| TERMS | For a set or part of a set of books | | | For 8 vols in town or 12 in the country | | | For 12 vols in town or 18 in country | | |
|---|---|---|---|---|---|---|---|---|---|
| | £ | s | d | £ | s | d | £ | s | d |
| Yearly | 1. | 1. | 0. | 2. | 2. | 0. | 3. | 3. | 0.* |
| Half yearly | | 12. | 0. | 1. | 4. | 0. | 2. | 0. | 0. |
| Quarterly | | 7. | 0. | | 14. | 0. | 1. | 1. | 0. |
| Monthly | | 3. | 0. | | 6. | 0. | | 9. | 0. |
| Weekly | | 1. | 0. | | 2. | 0. | | 3. | 0. |

*Subscribers of this class are entitled to get introduced into the library any work not already in the collection. Books sent to subscribers in all parts of the Kingdom in any quantity. Boxes with locks and keys always ready.

A very similar advertisement appears in the issue for 14 February, 1827 for the circulating library operated by Westley and Tyrrell, proprietors of the Circulating Library and Reading Room, 11 Lower Sackville Street. Conditions seem slightly better however, and subscribers of two guineas or upwards have the liberty of access to a commodious reading room in which London and Dublin newspapers and the various magazines, reviews and reports of societies are always kept. Books are also sent to subscribers in all parts of the Kingdom and in any quantities on payment of a proportional subscription. Catalogues and boxes with locks and keys are always ready. Here they add that libraries are purchased and that country libraries and book societies are supplied at the shortest notice and on moderate terms. (See Figure 3.1).

Interestingly there was a Music Circulating Library in existence which advertised in the *Dublin Evening Mail* in 1824. This was the Royal Harmonic Saloon and Musical Circulating Library run by I. Willis of 7 Westmoreland Street, Dublin and of 22 Southampton Street, London. This library stocked airs, songs, ballads, serenades

# FIGURE 3.1 WESTLEY AND TYRELL'S CIRCULATING LIBRARY ADVERTISEMENT

CIRCULATING LIBRARY and READING-ROOM, 11, Lower Sackville-street, corner House of Lower Abbey-street—WESTLEY and TYRRELL, Proprietors.

It is with much pleasure that the Proprietors are able to announce, that their Second Supplementary Catalogue is ready for the Press; and they are proud to be able to assert, with confidence, that the present additions will present to the Public, a Library containing double the number of Books of any other to which they have access in this Country. A large number of every New Work is placed in the Library the moment it appears.

The Proprietors beg to return their thanks for the extraordinary degree of public favour with which they have been honored, and to express their determination of meriting its continuance, by the liberality of their arrangements, and the most assiduous attention to the wishes of their Subscribers.

| TERMS. | For a set or part of a set of Books. | | | For eight Vols. in Town, or twelve in the Country. | | | For 12 Vols. in Town or 18 in the Country. | | |
|---|---|---|---|---|---|---|---|---|---|
| | £. | s. | d. | £ | s. | d. | £ | s. | d. |
| Yearly............ | 1 | 1 | 0 | 2 | 2 | 0 | 3 | 3 | 0 |
| Half-yearly ...... | | 12 | 0 | 1 | 4 | 0 | 2 | 0 | 0 |
| Quarterly......... | | 7 | 0 | | 14 | 0 | 1 | 1 | 0 |
| Monthly.......... | | 3 | 0 | | 6 | 0 | | 9 | 0 |
| Weekly.......... | | 1 | 0 | | 2 | 0 | | 3 | 0 |

Annual Subscribers of Two Guineas and upwards, have liberty of access to a commodious Reading Room, in which London and Dublin Newspapers, and the various Magazines, Reviews, Reports of Societies, &c., are always kept.

Books sent to Subscribers to all parts of the Kingdom, and in any quantities, by paying a proportionate Subscription.

Catalogues, and Boxes, with Locks and Keys, always ready.

Libraries purchased.

Country Libraries and Book Societies supplied at the shortest notice, on moderate terms.—Jan. 26, 1827.

*From The Dublin Evening Mail for 14 February 1827*

and quadrilles.

The *Cork Directory* for 1787 produced by Richard Lucas lists not one single circulating library although nine establishments calling themselves booksellers are listed, three of them also being lottery office keepers! The list of those dealing in some way with the book trade is as follows:

> James Cronin, Printer, bookseller and stationer at 12 Grand Parade
> Eugene Daly, Bookseller and stationer at Paul Street
> Robert Dobbyn, Printer at Batchelor's Quay
> Anthony Edwards, Bookseller and Lottery Office Keeper, 3 Castle Street (see Figure 3.2)
> William Flyn, Printer, bookseller and stationer, South Main Street.
> Daniel Hood, Bookseller and stationer, Grand Parade
> Sily McInerney, Printer, 12 Fishamble Lane
> Michael Mathew, Bookseller and stationer, 1 Castle Street
> Hannah Mayberry, Bookseller at Paul Street
> Richard Merrick, Stationer and patent medicine warehouse, 9 Patrick Street
> Jeremiah Sullivan, Bookseller and Lottery Office Keeper at North Main Street
> Thomas White, Bookseller, stationer and Lottery Office Keeper, 55 at The Exchange (see Figure 3.2)
> Thomas Whitney, bookbinder at Hanover Street

In Lucas's General *Directory of the Kingdom of Ireland on Merchants and Traders* in 1788 Limerick had four booksellers. Edward Flin in Mary Street, John Gloster in Broad Street, William Goggin in Mary Street, and Andrew Watson and Co. of Mary Street, booksellers and publishers of the *Limerick Chronicle*, agents for the Dublin Fire Insurance Company and the Irish Insurance Company for ships and lives! However by 1791 – 92 two circulating libraries are listed for Limerick, these being John Carroll of Bridge Street who had a bookshop and circulating library, and R. Hill who ran a bookshop and library near the Main Guard. In 1802 John and Thomas McAuliff were printers at the Pope's Head in Limerick and by 1803 they were advertising their circulating library 'near the Exchange' and the New Library at 14 Patrick Street, In 1810 the circulating library was still in existence.

In the 1824 Pigot and Co. Hibernian Provincial Directory, circulating libraries seem very thinly spread over the rest of the country. At Bray, Co. Wicklow, James Carroll ran a circulating library. At Dundalk James Parks is recorded as being a printer and

*Almanacks for* 1799.

A. EDWARDS has received,

| | | |
|---|---|---|
| Watfon's Gentlemans and Citizens Almanack, | 1 | 7h |
| Ditto, with the Englifh Regiftry, - - - | 3 | 3 |
| Irifh Merlin, or Gentlemans Almanack, - - 1 | | 7h |
| Ditto, with the Englifh Regiftry, - - - - | 2 | 8h |
| The Cork Book Almanack is. 1d. and Sheet, - | | 6h |

☞ Several new Books and Pamphlets on the Union.

December 27

**ALMANACKS FOR 1799,**

Juft arrived to THOMAS WHITE, No. 4, Caftle-ftreet, ☞ Watfon's Almanack, with & without the Englifh Regiftry; the Irifh Merlin and the Cork Almanacks.

WHITE, has on fale, an extenfive affortment of the beft Englifh and Irifh Writing Papers; Account Books of various fizes; Sealing Wax, Wafers, and Wax Candles, and has lately imported a fupply of Doctor James's Powders, and Analeptic Pills; Anderfon's, Scots Pills. and feveral other Patent Medicines of eftablifhed reputation—alfo Maps, Sea Charts, and 12 Inch Globes,

December 27

stationer who was also running a circulating library. Galway too had one run by Louisa M'Cartney in her bookshop in Shop Street. Carrick on Suir had acquired a bookseller, stationer and library operator in the form of Michael Boyle, and at Clonmel Richard Heuston had established a circulating library in Bagwell Street. At this time Clonmel is listed as having five booksellers in addition to the circulating library.

For the town of Cork is listed the Cork Public Library and Reading Room at the Minerva Rooms, 10 Duncan Street. Opened in 1819 it had a collection of several thousand volumes and was supported by subscriptions paid in advance. The rooms were open from 11 a.m. to 5 p.m. and a Mr Jas. Higginson is listed as the conductor. Also listed are the Cork Library at Pembroke Street with T.S. Carr as the librarian, Ellen Constant at 8 South Mall and Thomas Kingsford at 32 Patrick Street. Cove had also acquired a

A Collection of Manuscripts Sermons, Warranted Originals, remarkable for purity of Doctrine and neatness of stile, by a late eminent Divine of the Church of England, to be difpofed of by Robert Bell, Bookfeller and Auctionier, at his Book Shop, the Corner of Stephen-ftreet, oppofite Aunger-ftreet. — A few remaining Copies of Sir James Ware's Antiquities of Ireland may be had at faid Book-Shop : Where alfo may be had Propofals for printing the Travels of John Bell, Efq; through diverfe Parts of Afia.—Extracts from this Work may be feen in Wilfon's Dublin Magazine for Auguft 1763, page 499, and 511.—The Britifh Edition is fold for one Guinea. — Note faid Bell gives ready Money for Liberaries or Parcels of Books. He alfo fells by Auction for thofe who pleafe to employ him.

circulating library run by Catherine Geary at her stationer's shop at 5 Harbour Row.

Two circulating libraries are noted in Limerick, both organised by women. Mary Crips was a bookseller and stationer and also had a circulating library at her premises at 17 Patrick Street, while Eliza O'Shaughnessy operated a circulating library from her bookshop at 42 Patrick Street. In all nine bookshops are listed but it is well worth while to consider McGregor's remarks in his *History of the County and City of Limerick* published in 1827, where he states that there were only two or three respectable bookshops in the town. Pigot's Directory fails to mention the library attached to the Limerick Institution, although Brien O'Brien is listed as a bookseller at 101 George's Street, where he had moved to in 1820. It is therefore wise to question the veracity of the information in the Directory.

Moving into Ulster, Armagh had a circulating library run by Robert Graham in College Street. Belfast is quoted as having three circulating libraries, one at 63 High Street where Eliza Archer, bookseller and stationer, ran a circulating library and supplied books to the Linen Hall Library. John Hodgson had a slightly more exciting emporium at 9 High Street, from which he operated as a bookseller and stationer as well as dealing in patent medicine, acting as a lottery office, running a paper warehouse, and organising a circulating library. Hodgson had had an earlier circulating library originally at 116 High Street in 1808, and later at 4 High Street. The third bookseller running a circulating library was Francis Lamont at 78 High Street, where he also acted as a toy dealer. There is no entry for Robert Caldwell who in 1812 was supplying books to the Linen Hall Library. Mary Thomas ran a circulating library in the Market Place, Carrickfergus, and in Londonderry two booksellers ran libraries, William Boggs at Ferry Quay Street and Ann Kelso at 18 The Diamond.

In the first decade of the 1800s a circulating library was run by James Galland in Dungannon who started business in January 1810. Upon his death in 1811 his wife carried on her husband's business of hardware, stationery, glass and a circulating library. James Galland was also a poet and had his poetry published in the *Belfast Commercial Chronicle*.

A list of circulating libraries for Dublin in 1846 follows.

*The Dublin Almanac and General Register of Ireland 1846*
*List of Circulating Libraries in Dublin in 1846*
*Bellew, Gerald, 79 Grafton Street
Bourke, H. and stationer, 45 Lower Baggot Street
Browne, John, 21 Nassau Street

### FIGURE 3.4   ADVERTISEMENT J. GREENE'S PUBLIC LIBRARY

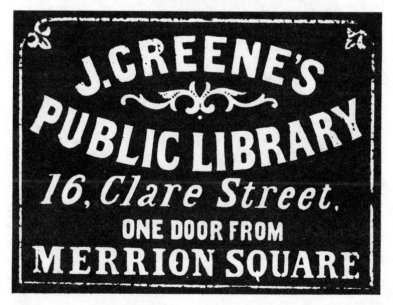

*Cardiff, Edw., 38 Charlemont Street Lower

Claney, James, and printer, 6 Bedford Row (also listed as bookseller)

Dyott, W.H., 24 King Street North (also listed as bookseller and printer)

Fannin, John, medical, 41 Grafton Street (also listed as bookseller)

Gerrard, Thomas, 3 York Row

Greene, John, 16 Clare Street (still extant in 1884) (see Figure 3.4)

Hall, Joseph, bookseller, stationer and circulating library, 9 Bedford Row

Hamston, Kate, 93 Britain Street

Kennedy, Patrick, 11 Cope Street

McCafferty, George, circulating library, 37 Gardiner Street

Machen, Samuel J., 28 Westmoreland Street

Mooney, Wm., 16 Arran Quay

Paine, Benjamin, 19 French Street

Percy, Jane, 11 Frederick Street N.

Scholer, Anne, and stationer, 34 North Strand

Slevin, Pat K., 50 Charlemont Street

Tyrrell, Gerard, 11 Lower Sackville Street (also listed as bookseller and newsroom)

Webb, Thomas, 47 Lower Sackville Street

Yates, John, 118 Grafton Street (also listed as bookseller)

*also bookbinders.

In addition there were 32 bookbinders and 81 booksellers and stationers.

# 4         Great private collectors and their libraries

The dearth of books and libraries in the Ireland of the late seventeenth and early eighteenth centuries led the new men who controlled the country to gather books together for their own use and to establish libraries for the benefit of others. Notable among these were the medical men whose personal book collections were bequeathed as the nuclei of famous medical libraries.

First the Worth Library at Dr Steevens' Hospital in Dublin. John Steevens, a Royalist, arrived in Ireland with his twin children Richard and Grissel to escape the wrath of Cromwell. Unfortunately Ireland was no refuge from the Protector but he was eventually rewarded for his loyalty to the Royalist cause when Charles II appointed him Vicar of Athlone. His son Richard was twice the President of the King and Queen's College of Physicians and enjoyed considerable success in his practice. He died unmarried on 15 December 1710 and in his will left his property to his sister for life, and after her death to trustees to build 'a proper place or building within the city of Dublin for maintaining and curing from time to time such sick and wounded persons whose distempers and wounds are curable'. Grissel Steevens determined to put her brother's intentions into effect immediately, and she gave £2,000 to build the hospital designed by her brother. Among the trustees was the physician Edward Worth. The building of the hospital started in 1720 and was completed by 1733.

Edward Worth came from an English family settled in Dublin and his father John was the Dean of St. Patrick's Cathedral. Edward was sent to Merton College, Oxford, later taking a degree in medicine at Utrecht. He was elected a Fellow of the King and Queen's College of Physicians in 1710 but little detail of his life has survived. He died just before the hospital was opened, leaving £2,000 to Merton College and £1,000 to the hospital to be spent on general purposes. He further left all his books 'Except the English books in the glass case of my present study, hereafter to be devised, and likewise those which did belong to my late father and are now at Rathfarnham'.

The books were left to the hospital for the 'use, benefit and behoof of the physician and surgeon of the time being' but were not to be removed from the room in which they were appointed to be kept. He further instructed in his will that three catalogues of the books were to be made. One of these was to be kept chained in the library of the hospital, one in the library belonging to the college of Dublin, and the third to be kept in the public library at St. Sepulchre's, known to us as Marsh's Library. In order that the library should not be a charge on the hospital he instructed that certain of his father's books were to be sold and the money paid to the governors to defray the expense of fitting up the library. If however his trustee paid £100 to the governors of the hospital the books need not be sold but could become his property. His executor adopted this latter method and later these books, which numbered about 1,000, were bequeathed to Trinity College Library in 1742. Out of the £100, some £30 was to be paid to some deserving person of the College of Dublin 'who shall digest and place the books in order', and £20 to some able clerk who shall 'transcribe the catalogue into three large books fairly written and engrossed'. The remainder of the £100 was to be spent on fitting out the room with shelves and chains.

His cousin and namesake Edward Worth did not delay in discharging the obligations placed upon him by his cousin's will and the books were delivered to the hospital quickly. But there was some delay in getting the library fitted out and there is a minute dated 14 January 1733/4 stating that the books 'do suffer greatly by their not being taken out of the boxes and aired'. In March 1733/4 Edward Worth was made a governor of the hospital and he then lost no time in getting the library put into order.

The library is chiefly interesting as a collection of books practically intact made by a cultured physician in the first 30 years of the eighteenth century. Edward Worth was a true bibliophile and he was extremely catholic in his tastes. Nearly all departments of literature are represented in his collection, except English literature because these books were probably bequeathed to Clotilda, Lady Eustace. Other subjects covered include medicine, surgery, chemistry, botany, pure and applied mathematics, history, topography, antiquities and books of reference, the ancient classics and theology.

The Royal College of Physicians is an old foundation which came into being in 1651 through the efforts of John Stearne, a grand nephew of James Usher, Bishop of Meath. Stearne had received a disturbed education, first at Trinity College, later at Cambridge, and later still at Oxford, all removals being due to the Rebellion and the triumph of the Parliamentary party of which he was not a supporter. Little use was made initially of the building known as Trinity College which Stearne had acquired from Trinity College, but witth the Restoration a grant was renewed from the Board of Trinity College and various medical men were elected Fellows of the College. On 8 August 1667 the College was incorporated by Royal Charter as the Royal College of Physicians of Ireland.

However, at this stage the College did not seem to possess a library and probably the members made use of the library at Trinity College. But this connection did not last long. In 1687 the Board of Trinity College refused to ratify the appointment of John Crosby as President of the Society on the grounds that the nomination had not been communicated to it by the Registrar and seeing 'that the person they had elected was not a Protestant of the Church of Ireland'. This dispute led to the complete separation of the two colleges and on 15 December 1692 William and Mary granted a new charter to the College as the King and Queen's College of Physicians in Ireland, naming Sir Patrick Dun as the first President. Patrick Dun was a native of Aberdeen and came from a medical family. He was sometime the physician to James, Duke of Ormond, and it must be supposed that this was the link that brought him to Ireland.

Patrick Dun occupied a prominent place in the social and professional life of Dublin. He served with King William in 1688 as physician to the Army in Ireland and was the physician and close friend of William King, Archbishop of Dublin. He was twice elected a member of the Irish Parliament. He died in 1713 devoting his fortune after the death of his wife to the foundation of a professorship or 'professor of Physick' in the College of Physicians, Dublin. In his will he gave his wife the use of his dwelling house on the Inns with one room set aside in the house for the preservation of his books. His will goes on to say:

> If the Society of the Inns would consent to grant the reversion of my house after the expiration of my lease from them for a Physic school and habitation for the aforesaid Professor he being obliged to keep the same in good order, I am willing to give my title and interest in my said house after the death of my dear wife for the said use and also for a hall for the King and Queen's College of Physicians to gather therein ... Likewise I would give my books for the lawful use of the said professors and College of Physicians ... and give bond and security to keep and preserve the said library and all and every book in it and if any should be lost or wanting to pay for or purchase another of the same kind.

It transpired that Lady Dun was not on the best of terms with her co-executor Dr Patrick Mitchell who was a Fellow of the Royal College which Stearne had acquired from Trinity College, but with relations between the College and Lady Dun became strained. In addition, the College became anxious to know the extent of the personal property of Sir Patrick Dun, apart from his estate, which would be conveyed to the College after the death of Lady Dun. They do not appear to have received a satisfactory answer to this enquiry and decided to prosecute in law to establish the title of the personal estate on the death of Lady Dun. This obviously was too much for Lady Dun who abandoned all intention of housing the College in her house and handed over the library to the President of the College. The collection, together with the catalogue, was delivered to Dr Henry Cope, one of the junior Fellows of the College. Although this departure of the library must have been a bitter blow for the College it was indeed a blessing in disguise for on the night of 1 September 1728 the house was burnt and during the fire the goods in it were looted by a gang of thieves. It was reported in a Dublin newspaper that the house was full of exceedingly valuable goods, as well as clothes, plate and linen, little of which was saved for the owner.

The disputes between the College and Lady Dun continued for several years and it was 1740 before the matter was finally settled. At this point the College decided to enlarge the scope of Dun's bequest and for this purpose an Act was passed in 1741 authorising the appointment of three professors instead of one – as soon as the Dun estates should fall into the hands of the College.

The care of the library was entrusted to Dr Henry Quin who was one of the professors elected under the Act of Parliament. In 1756 the House of Lords appointed a committee to enquire into the effects of the aforesaid Act and this enquiry disclosed a lamentable state of affairs. Anthony Relhan, the President of the College, stated that the remains of the books in Dun's library numbering about 300 were in the possession of Dr Quin, the College having no room for them. There were two copies of the catalogue 'in a chest of lumber with the old books', and he further stated that no security had ever been required for the forthcoming of the books. In spite of this damning evidence nothing appears to have happened to the books, and thirty years later they were still in the possession of Dr Quin and still in the 'chest of lumber'.

The ineptitude of the College in the administration of the library appears to have reached enormous proportions over the next thirty to forty years, and one begins to have a sneaking sympathy for Lady Dun who, when she was alive, must have felt on many occasions that the College was grasping and greedy. A further Act of Parliament, supposedly passed to strengthen the library, resulted in even worse administration. The Act of 1785 enabled the College to appoint five instead of three professors and limited their salaries to £100 a year, any surplus from the estates was to be used to purchase medical books amongst other things. This should have ensured the library of rapid development. Dun's estate at this time was producing nearly

£20,000, of which £2,575. 16s.5¾d. was paid to Dr Stephen Dickson, King's Professor of the Institution of Medicine, who in 1787 had been appointed as librarian with power to 'fix up a library'.

The regulations of the library allowed for the books to be lent out to Fellows or matriculated students of the school provided the librarian received a deposit which had to be at least the equivalent in value of the book lent, or the set to which the book belonged. The librarian had to attend in the library twice a week in the winter and once a week in the summer for the purpose of lending out the books, and to have certain other times when other students could consult the books which it was deemed inadvisable to lend. Given his far from arduous duties the sum paid to the librarian was extremely excessive. From the catalogue produced at this time there were 1,179 books in stock at Dun's library. However, Dr Dickson was not a success either as a librarian or as a professor, being deprived first of his professorship and two years later of his Fellowship.

He was succeeded as librarian by John William Boyton who kept the library books in his lecture room at Trinity College. While he was librarian the administration of Dun's estate was again the subject of consideration by a committee of the House of Lords. It was stated that the College had amongst other things squandered the money from Dun's estate, sometimes paying twice for the same books. It became obvious that the library had not developed as it should have, considering the large sums available to it. A manuscript catalogue of the library was made in 1800 and there are many entries noted against items 'lost by Dr Dickson'.

Given this mismanagement the power of spending any money on the library was removed from the College by the School of Physic Act 1800 which repealed the Act of 1785. Under this Act any money left over after the payment of the professors was devoted to the foundation and maintenance of a hospital called Sir Patrick Dun's Hospital. The administration of the library received special notice. A librarian was to be elected under the control of the President and the Fellows, his responsibility being to purchase books, to form a medical library, and to have care and management of the library. The librarian before entering office was to give a bond of security to the President and Fellows for the due care and preservation of the books. The librarian was to receive an annual salary not exceeding £70, out of which he had to furnish the necessary fuel for the library. When considering the vast sums paid to Dr Dickson this does not seem excessive! The books were to be kept in a room in Trinity College until the hospital was built. In fact the hospital was completed in 1818 when the books were transferred there in accordance with the Act. Successive librarians enriched the collection and produced various catalogues.

In the summer of 1865 the books were transferred from Dun's Hospital to the newly erected buildings of the College of Physicians and the decision was made to extend the library to the use of readers as well as borrowers. New catalogues were again produced and by 1920 there were some 13,000 volumes, excluding pamphlets, in the collection which was especially rich in runs of medical journals and transactions of medical societies. It is thought that only just over 90 of Dun's original books have survived.

After the train of disasters associated with the management of the library left by Sir Patrick Dun to the College of Physicians it is refreshing to discover the care and attention lavished on the library of the Royal College of Surgeons. This institution, founded in 1783, resolved to establish a library immediately and a subscription of one guinea annually was levied on each member for the purpose of defraying the expenses of the College and of forming a library. As the College had no property of its own it did not purchase many books before 1789, but its first investment was to purchase Dr Walter Wade's *Flora Dubliniensis* on 12 January 1787, and in the following year the *Anatomical Plates of D'Azyr*, published in Paris, was purchased. As soon as the College had its own property in Mercier Street the library began to grow. In 1790 the Physico-Chirurgical Society met in the College premises and founded their own library which, on the dissolution of the Society in 1816 became the property of the College.

By 1805 the College appointed John Armstrong Garnett as the first librarian. At the same time a library committee was set up consisting of three members of the College, and by 1811 an assistant librarian was needed and a Mr Todd was appointed to this post. Neither of these posts had any salary attached to them.

In 1817 a subscription reading library was formed with the annual subscription being two guineas, with life subscription at ten guineas. In the same year the committee resolved to spend £100 on books and to allocate an annual sum of £50 towards the maintenance of the library. Use of the library was not free, and an admission fee of three guineas was charged for members and licentiates. From 1 January 1818 this was increased to five guineas.

Activities in the library continued apace, with a code of rules being drawn up in 1821, and two years later an additional £50 was granted for the purchase of books, while some duplicate volumes were sold to raise further money.

In 1825 a Mr Courtney was voted a payment of £34.2s.6d. for looking after the library from 1819 when Mr Todd resigned his position, and his son was given £5 for preparing the first catalogue.

In fact his son became the first salaried official of the library when he was appointed a library clerk at the grand sum of £20 per annum. Book purchases over the years were quite generous, and in 1825 – 26 nearly £1,200 was spent on books, with outstanding orders amounting to another £524. Dublin did not have enough books to satisfy their needs, and in 1836 when allocating £300 for books they sent the librarian to London for book selection purposes and voted £25 to meet the expenses of his journey.

In 1835 it became a circulating library and an extra £100 was granted to buy more books. The assistant librarian at the time, a Mr O'Keefe, who was also the registrar, was requested to attend for duty on Mondays, Wednesdays and Fridays from 10 to 11 a.m. to give out and receive books, and for this increase in responsibility he received £10 annually.

By 1840 the number of books in stock had risen to 14,102 and there was insufficient room on the shelves to retain them all. Consequently the librarian withdrew 1,838 volumes and sold them to the medical bookseller Mr Fanin for £100. This neatly offset the £100 that the committee had given to the librarian in 1838 for cataloguing the library. It is interesting to study the salaries awarded to the librarians and assistant librarians over the years. By 1871 the assistant librarian's salary was £100 increasing in 1873 to £150 a year. Work on the completion of the catalogue warranted an additional payment of £50 in 1874. By 1885 the salary of the assistant librarian was £200. Although this does seem generous for the period, the work of the College librarian involved a fair amount of responsibility, including book selection and arrangement of the stock. Compared to the salary of the librarian of the Kilkenny Library Society, which amounted to £30 per annum in the late 1860s, the salary offered by the College was generous and reflected the pride and care which they lavished on their library.

The Protestant bishops and clergy also established great collections of books. The most renowned of these was that of James Ussher, Archbishop of Armagh from 1625 until 1641. As well as being a scholar, writing some 40 books in Latin and English, he was famed as a book collector. Ussher had wanted to bequeath his collection to Trinity College but the Civil War had reduced his circumstances and in the event he left the library to his only child to provide for her. Sir Timothy Tyrrell, her husband, put up the collection for sale. There was much foreign interest in buying the books, especially from the French Cardinal Mazarin, but the English Government intervened and prevented the collection from going overseas.

It was Oliver Cromwell and the Council of State that decided the collection should be purchased for a second college in Ireland, but not Trinity which already had a library. This college was to be primarily a Protestant seminary and Ussher's books being mainly theological in content were thought to be suitable for the library of the proposed second college. The money was hard to raise in the bankrupt Ireland of the day. It was popularly believed at the time that the library of Trinity College had been established by officers of the English army, who in thanksgiving for their victory over the Spanish at Kinsale in 1601 gave £1,800 to buy books for the library at the College of Dublin. This story has subsequently been found to be untrue but in 1656 there was clear precedent how Ussher's library could be bought for Ireland. The officers in the army, upon Henry Cromwell's recommendation, agreed to allow out of their pay as much money as would purchase the collection. Their decision was unanimous, the groundwork having been very well prepared by Henry Cromwell and two nephews of Ussher, Dr Henry Jones and Sir Theophilus Jones, both of whom had a vested interest in the collection returning to Ireland. As the officers' money was in arrears anyway it was a simple matter for them to waive part of the arrears due to them, and for the money to be paid directly into the Dublin Treasury, and thence to Tyrrell. Robert Wood, a member of Henry Cromwell's household in Ireland, stated that 'you see how well soldiers can be employed in time of peace', and in the seventeenth century a writer confirmed that the Cromwellian soldiers had acted 'out of emulation to the former Noble Action of Queen Elizabeth's Army'.

In July 1657 the books were shipped to Dublin, and as the future of the proposed college had not been finalised, the books were stored in Dublin Castle. At the same time Henry Cromwell was recalled to England and this led to the unfair charge that he had deliberately withheld the collection from Trinity. It was however the uncertainty about the second college that led to the storage of the books, and it was not until the Restoration of Charles II that the hope of the new college was finally abandoned. Thus it was Charles II who claimed the honour of bestowing the collection on the existing college – Trinity – thereby obscuring the earlier achievement of Henry Cromwell.

Ussher had collected both books and manuscripts. Cromwell had bought mainly the book collection, although some of the manuscripts did find their way to Ireland. Ussher was always lending books and manuscripts to his friends, so much so that after the purchase of the collection Cromwell had to chase up the return of many of the outstanding loans. Some manuscripts were even lent overseas to France, some to Christophe Justell, a secretary of Henry

IV of France and other scholars in France. Jacques Simond, the French Jesuit scholar sent manuscripts to Ussher (an example of international library loans).

Ussher was not particularly noted for his interest in the Irish language, but his collection did contain some Irish manuscripts as well as the *Book of Ballymote* and the *Book of Lecan* now in the Royal Irish Academy. His interests covered arithmetic, astrology and astronomy. He was also actively concerned with the acquisition of manuscripts from the Near East. His agent was Thomas Davies, a merchant with the Levant Company at Aleppo. Here in the 1620s Davies collected manuscripts in the Samaritan character, the Syriac tongue, Chaldean and Hebrew, and he employed men to copy those rare manuscripts not available for sale. Many transcriptions were made for Ussher from the great manuscript libraries in Paris, notably the Royal Library and the Library of De Thou. Despite religious differences his relations with the Franciscans seem to have been remarkably cordial, with Father Thomas Strange, Guardian of the Franciscan Order in Ireland having access to the Primate's library and Luke Wadding, an Irish Roman Catholic historian, having copied manuscripts in the Vatican for Ussher.

The Diocesan libraries are among the oldest lending libraries in Ireland. The earliest dates from 1692 – 93 and is the Ossory Diocesan Library founded according to the will of Bishop Thomas Otway. Evidence exists to suggest that the idea of a library had been mooted earlier by Bishop Griffith Williams who died in 1673 and who is credited with bequeathing money to build almshouses and a library. It is possible that the first floor of the library house had been erected but that Bishop Otway actually made it into a library by making provision for the books. Bishop Otway's will states that he gives his books and £200 for the beginning of a library for the Cathedral Church of St. Canice ... for desks, shelves and chains for every particular book. In addition he itemised that £100 owed to him by Agmond Cuffe of Castleinch and £97.10s. of Spanish and other foreign gold lent to George Thornton should be used to do it! He did however go further and state that the library keeper should always be one of the vicars of St. Canice's, chosen by the Bishop, and should be paid £5 a year, also that another £5 a year should be allowed for coals and weekly fires to be made in the library to preserve the books. This admirable will was not executed fully for the first librarian was left unpaid for nine years and in 1703 was owed £45 salary and £30 for the coals, nor were the books chained.

Bishop Edward Maurice, of Irish birth and educated at Trinity College, left to the library his books and bookcases of Danzig oak when he died in 1756. Under his will the librarian had to display the books at least once a year, neither to embezzle them nor deface them, and to attend at the library from 6 a.m. to the tolling of the bell for morning prayers in the Cathedral of St. Canice, Kilkenny. He also bequeathed to the librarian £20 a year. Bishop Maurice also wrote a condition into the will that enabled the library to survive until today. He ordered that if it proved impossible to form the books into a Cathedral library they should be sold, and that the money and the librarian's salary be used for raising and adorning the imperfect steeple of the Cathedral. 'And whereas a knowledge and practice of books is required to range them so they may be readily found', he desired his good friend Dr Lawson, Senior Fellow and first librarian of Trinity College near Dublin to lend a hand to transport, lodge and place them to advantage.

The library house contained on the ground floor accommodation for the library keeper and lodging for preaching dignitaries. This no doubt accounts for the interesting birth recorded on September 3, 1846 when the lady of the Revd. Draper had a son in St. Canice's Library, Kilkenny. The library collection is mainly theological, historical and classical. In 1929 the real threat of the projected sale of the library was prevented by the clause mentioned above in Bishop Maurice's will. At this time Sotheby's valued the books at £1,695 and arrangements were made to insure them. The idea of a sale was dropped and a Library Standing Committee was appointed to look after the collection. In order to make the library more attractive the Right Revd. H.R. McAdoo, when he became Bishop of Ossory, Ferns and Leighlin in 1962 initiated a scheme to buy a limited number of books each year so that the library has a small but expanding modern collection. Since 1960 nothing has changed except the addition of a few theological works to the modern section.

Glorying under the title of the first public library in Ireland is Marsh's Library, established in 1701 by Archbishop Narcissus Marsh. Few of these early Protestant clergymen were of Irish extraction and yet their contributions to Irish scholarship cannot be overlooked. The Duke of Ormond was instrumental in obtaining for Narcissus Marsh the Provostship of Trinity College Dublin. However Marsh was not happy at Trinity: 'I was quickly weary of 340 young men and boys in this lewd debauch'd town'. Under the statutes of the College thirty of the seventy scholars chosen every year had to be natives of Ireland but Marsh noticed that while these scholars could speak Irish they could neither read nor write the language. Marsh employed at his own expense a former Catholic Irish priest to teach Irish to the students and to preach a sermon in Irish once a month. For this promotion of the Irish language and his disregard for the Act of Parliament the object of which was to abolish the Irish language, Marsh was severely criticised, although his only concern was the instruction of the students in the Protestant faith.

Marsh also found the library at Trinity was much neglected. At this time there were no library keepers, only a junior Fellow who was paid six pounds annually. Marsh revised the library regulations and had tables drawn up and hung at the end of each division listing the shelves and the books on each shelf. One of the problems associated with the library was that only the Provost and Fellows of the College were allowed to study in the library. Should students wish to use the library they had to be accompanied by the Provost or one of the Fellows who then had to remain in the library with the student. Marsh was unable to get this regulation or the statutes of the College changed and it was for this reason that he began to think about building a library elsewhere. In a letter to the Lord Lieutenant of Ireland, Archbishop Marsh referred to this hope:

> seeing that the only library was inaccessible ... and that the booksellers' shops were furnished with none but a few modern English books, so that the clergy of the city ... and especially the poor curate who had no money to buy ... spent much of their time worse than ... if such a provision were made for them.

Marsh left all his Oriental manuscripts to the Bodleian Library and intended to leave all his books to the public library which he built on the site next to the churchyard of St. Patrick's. The library was designed by Sir William Robinson and consists of two galleries in an L shape. The ground floor was intended as a residence for the librarian with the library above. Having established it Marsh was keen to have the library and its government incorporated by an Act of Parliament. The Act of 1707 was called 'An Act for settling and Preserving a public library for ever'. The Governors of the library were the Church of Ireland Archbishop of Armagh, the Lord Chancellor of Ireland, the Archbishop of Dublin, the Lord Chief Justice of the Queen's Bench, the Lord Chief Justice of Common Pleas, the Lord Chief Baron, the Dean of Christ Church, the Dean of St. Patrick's and the Provost of Trinity College. The Act which incorporated the library exempted the building for ever from taxes such as the chimney money, hearth money, and lamp money, and from all other taxes hereafter to be imposed by Parliament.

The library building cost Marsh £5,000 and it was intended for the use of graduates and gentlemen. Marsh acquired some major collections such as the library of Dr Edward Stillingfleet who had been Dean of St. Paul's, London. This collection contained about 10,000 books and cost £2,500 to purchase. The range of subjects covered included theology, history, classics, law, medicine and travel. The Bishop of Clogher, John Stearne, gave his books to the library in 1745.

The first librarian Elias Bouhéreau donated over 2,000 of his own books worth £500, as well as depositing in the library a strong box in which were contained the archives of the French Protestant Church of La Rochelle. Elias Bouhéreau was born in 1643 into a prominent Protestant family of La Rochelle, and was educated at the Protestant Academy of Saumur. He became a leading citizen of his town and a church elder, but as the persecution of the Huguenots grew more intense he and his family fled from France to England. Before doing so however he went to the English Ambassador in Paris and begged him for a receipt as if he had purchased the library, which the Ambassador did and had the books sent to England, thus saving the collection from being burnt by the common hangman as being heretical. The family escaped from France and arrived in England in 1686 where Bouhéreau acted initially as secretary to Thomas Cox and secondly to Henri de Massue de Ruvigny, who later became Earl of Galway, travelling with him to Ireland. It was thus that Elias Bouhéreau came to the notice of Marsh and it was his notion that Bouhéreau should be appointed librarian at £200 per annum until such time as one of the dignitaries of St. Patrick's Cathedral should became vacant and when Bouhéreau should succeed to it. This proposal was rewarded by the issue of a Royal Warrant on 11 June 1701 with Bouhéreau now the first public librarian in Ireland, looking after his own books. The books in the library were chained at the request of Marsh himself in 1712, but the chains were put only on the two lower shelves of the bookcases.

The first catalogue appears to have been produced by Bouhéreau's successor Robert Dougatt, who was librarian from 1719 to 1730. Elias Bouhéreau's son John Bouhéreau eventually became the first assistant librarian of Marsh's Library and held this post until 1725.

The Revd. John Wynne was appointed librarian in 1730. Eight years later he was reporting to the Governors that a great many of the books had been stolen and many others abused and rendered imperfect by having tracts, maps and pictures torn out. The Governors' response was immediate. If any person was found to have stolen or defaced a book then he was to be prosecuted with the utmost rigour of the law without any expectation of pardon, and they recommended that an honest porter be employed to watch and search every suspected person admitted to the library. At this time for security reasons cages were erected so that the manuscripts could be deposited within them. Over the years the problem of lost books continued until eventually in 1779 the Governors ordered that no book should be taken down or read except in the presence of the librarian or his assistant. The first book thief was caught in 1828 and as a punishment was banished from the library. The librarian however was severely admonished and the public in future were only to be allowed to read the books at the public table in the librarian's room.

Although Marsh's Library was established with the very best of intentions it was never a particularly well-used library, its contents limiting its appeal to scholars. Edward Edwards of the British Museum library gave evidence to the Select Committee ordered by the House of Commons to report on public libraries in 1849, and said that the library had been completely mismanaged, with a loss of 1,200 books from the time of its foundation, but that latterly it was being well looked after and that 915 people had used the library in that same year.

In March 1856 the Governors of Marsh's Library nearly agreed to a Government proposal that the books in the library should be taken to form a new gallery of Painting, Sculpture and the Fine Arts. The only dissenting voice was that of Dr Robert Travers, the assistant librarian, who felt that the proposal was the result of a conspiracy by the Roman Catholic party to do away with an institution which had been founded through the generosity of a prelate of the Established Church. Benjamin Lee Guinness eventually came to the rescue with an offer to build a new road making access to the library more pleasant. He also offered £1,000 of Government stock to be put in trust for the purchase of books and the preservation of the building. It took the Governors nearly four years to decide to accept this offer!

However, in the Post Office Directory for Dublin in 1860, Marsh's is described as the Public Library of Dublin, with the number of readers ranging from 1,200 to 1,500 annually. It goes on:

> Readers are admitted gratuitously and without any religious distinction, the only request being a satisfactory certificate of respectability and good character; strangers and occasional visitors are admitted to see the library and to consult any books it may contain without any introduction on merely giving their cards of address to the librarian. Literary enquiries by letter are promptly answered, searches made, and extracts provided on the same conditions as at the Bodleian Library, the British Museum and the Archiepiscopal Library of the Palace at Lambeth.

However, Thomas Russell William Craddock, librarian of Marsh's Library in the nineteenth century, had little literary knowledge, resented people using the library and frequently prevented his assistant Dr Travers from getting into the library as he held the one and only key.

During the Easter uprising in 1916 Marsh's Library was in the direct line of fire between British troops and the IRA who had taken over Jacobs' Factory. The library suffered much damage as machine-gun bullets shattered the glass doors in the reading room and bullets penetrated many of the books throughout the library. By 1958 the fabric of the building had deteriorated considerably but it was successful in its restoration appeal, obtaining support from the Government and from many organisations in a number of countries.

Other important Diocesan libraries must include mention of the Clogher Diocesan Library. Although there is no firm date for its foundation, it had certainly not been founded by 1745 when John Stearne, Bishop of Clogher, died leaving most of his collection of nearly 3,000 books to Marsh's Library, and ordering the rest to be sold or given to the curates of his Diocese. With typical Irish gambling instinct the executors divided the books into lots and these were drawn for by the curates. The library was probably formed towards the end of the eighteenth century when gifts were received from four sources in order to establish a library. These came from the Hon. Charles Talbot, 8th Lord Blaney, Rector of Muckno, authors' copies of books presented to the Bishops of Clogher, theological works formerly belonging to the defunct local clerical societies of the early nineteenth century and the bequests of the Revd. Canon Benjamin Moffett, Rector of Carrickmacross. This collection, numbering about 3,500 volumes, was housed in the boardroom of the Diocesan Library at Clones, while some older books were kept at the Bishop's residence. Membership was not free and the clergy and laity of the Diocese could borrow books on payment of two shillings annually which enabled them to borrow three books at a time for a period of two months. A title catalogue was produced in 1916 called the *Clogher Diocesan Library, including the Moffett Library*.

Unfortunately the library fell into decline in the early decades of the twentieth century, the books becoming dusty and mildewed. By 1950 the Diocesan Council had decided to dispose of the library and to devote the proceeds to the poorer clergy. The sale took place over several months during 1953 – 54 raising very little, about £200 with £50 costs. Some 500 volumes were sold as waste paper, but fortunately many of the rare items were purchased by important Irish libraries as well as by the John Rylands Library in Manchester.

The zeal of these clergy in establishing libraries is evident by the number of Diocesan libraries set up during the eighteenth century when the Church of Ireland was in its heyday. The Diocesan Library at Cork, for example, was founded by Bishop Browne in 1720 as the Cathedral library at St. Finbarre's Cathedral, when at his instigation the Chapter made a grant of a piece of land for a library and a school. However, an earlier record of a library in the Cathedral is to be found in the Chapter Books where an entry for 1629 states that Richard Owen, Prebendary of Kilnaglory, presented £20 towards the erection of a library 'the said Richard to have use of the library during his life and at his death to remain for the use of the prebendaries'. There is no further record of this particular venture.

The eighteenth century library was further endowed by Archbishop Pomeroy who in 1725 bequeathed some of his books to form a parish library. The largest addition to the older part of the library was in 1727 when the committee purchased the library of Bishop Crowe of Cloyne for £115. In 1805 Bishop Stopford bequeathed his collection of books and in 1813 James McGrath presented a collection of music scores. In addition in 1785 £5 a year was voted to keep the library clean. In 1816 the library building was raised one storey and from this time used as a residence for the librarian.

In 1830 the library was opened every Wednesday and Thursday from 10 a.m. to 12 noon for the use of the clergy in the Diocese of Cork and Ross, and by 1857 the south end of the library had been fitted up as a reading room for visitors. In 1892 the parish library and the Cathedral Library were formed into the Diocesan Library. Currently it has 3,000 volumes, mainly theological works, but it also has some early printed books from the sixteenth century. In an effort to secure proper care for the future of the collection negotiations are in progress to house the old Cathedral Library in the new Cork University Library.

The Derry Diocesan Library was founded by Archbishop King in 1726. His own library consisting of just over 7,000 volumes was first catalogued in 1686. King was consecrated in January 1691 and although he assembled one of the great private collections in Ireland he was not a bookish man. He was determined to make his diocese a precedent to others and as such strove to restore buildings. He applied himself with the greatest possible industry to rectify the turmoil caused by the problems of the 1690s in Derry. His nephew was Robert Dougatt who, as we have already seen, was Precentor of St. Patrick's and Keeper of Marsh's Library at St. Sepulchre's from 1719 to 1730. Dougatt was an indefatigable cataloguer, responsible for the cataloguing of Marsh's Library in 1726 and also for the design of a catalogue and the writing of a large part of the catalogue of King's Library.

The Derry Diocesan Library consisted of the library of Ezekiel

Hopkins, Bishop of Derry from 1681 to 1690. Archbishop King bought the collection from Hopkins' executors, and later presented his own books to the library. The Derry Library was increased in 1834 by the addition of some 4,000 volumes in the Raphoe Diocesan Library, which had been founded in 1737 by Archbishop Foster and which had been housed in the Raphoe Royal School. During the eighteenth century the library suffered many losses and it was not until after 1870 that it was transferred to the Diocesan Synod Hall, Londonderry, and not until 1921 was a librarian appointed in the shape of the Very Revd. R.G.S. King. The collection is very strong in the Anglican Divinity of the sixteenth, seventeenth and eighteenth centuries, and has many books covering philosophy, history, Irish interests and biography.

King was a keen historian and in 1922 he started the Chapter House Library containing works relating to the history of Londonderry. Many rare books and pamphlets have been purchased and bequests received, particularly from Sir Frederick Heygate who gave the library some rare seventeenth century pamphlets on Irish affairs which were bound in four volumes shortly after the siege in 1689. Another benefactor was A.M. Munn who presented a collection of records relating to the history of Londonderry which he had gleaned from other libraries. Another special collection was bought from the executors of Tenison Groves who had started to collect material prior to the destruction of the Dublin Record Office in 1922. The collection is therefore of great importance since the original materials have now been destroyed.

Among the most famous of the Diocesan libraries is Cashel, modelled on Marsh's Library and founded by Archbishop Theophilus Bolton in 1730. Bolton was known as the best lawyer in Ireland and he frequently checkmated Swift with his command of the canon law at Chapter meetings when he was Chancellor of St. Patrick's Cathedral in Dublin. His own collection amounted to almost 6,000 volumes some of which had belonged to Archbishop King. In his will the Archbishop left his books, his library and his dwelling home for the use of his successors and for the clergy of the Diocese. The books remained in the same building for nearly a century. They suffered somewhat during the rebellion of 1798 when soldiers were quartered in the vicinity, but from 1801 to 1822 an annual stipend of £10 was paid to a librarian. With the amalgamation of the See of Cashel with that of Waterford and Lismore a new home was found for the library and a new building was erected beside the Cathedral. Here the library has remained, although the building is now in need of repair. In 1910 it was decided that the more valuable and interesting books should go to Dublin where they would be more accessible to scholars. About 600 books were selected by E.A. Phelps of Marsh's Library, and they were transferred there before being removed to the Representative Church Body Library at 52 St. Stephen's Green. In 1949 part of the manuscript collection was deposited with the Representative Church Body as well, but both books and manuscripts were returned to Cashel between 1965 and 1967. Following a serious theft the library is no longer open to the public but by arrangement with the Irish Tourist Board interested people may be admitted.

Other Diocesan libraries include that at Waterford which was founded by the Right Revd. Charles Este when he bequeathed his books in 1745 to start a library for the clergy. Together with other donations, notably from the clergy, from ex-librarians and from Mr Dobbyn, a member of a family some of whom were solicitors for several generations, and who presented a great number of Irish Statutes, there is much material from the seventeenth, eighteenth and nineteenth centuries. The collection numbers about 2,000 volumes, mainly theological and Biblical works, and although it still exists it is little used and consideration is being given to its future.

A Diocesan Library was formed in Lismore by Dr Henry Cotton in 1845. Cotton was a well-known book collector and had been sub-librarian at the Bodleian Library for about eight years. There are about 3,500 books but very few manuscripts in the collection. A catalogue published in 1851 is still current though the library itself is little used. Dr Cotton obtained over 2,000 volumes for the library for use by the clergy in the Diocese. The Chapter showed its appreciation for the gift by providing a room attached to the Cathedral, and arranged to pay a librarian £20 per annum and to provide £10 per annum to buy books. The librarian was a clergyman, resident in Lismore, nominated by the Dean, and the appointment was confirmed by the Chapter. The Dean and Chapter had powers to inspect the library and arranged an annual visitation for that purpose. The library was opened at least two days a week between 11 a.m. and 1 p.m. A copy of the 1851 printed catalogue was given to every clergyman in the Diocese and this contained a list of the library's rules and regulations.

When the Dean and Chapter were dissolved as a body by the Irish Church Act of 1869 the collection became once again the property of Archdeacon Cotton by whom it was presented to a Board of Trustees consisting of the Bishop of the Diocese, the Dean, the Archdeacon and the Select Vestry of Lismore. In the rules published by the Board of Trustees in 1879 use of the library had been widened to include the clergy and gentry of the Diocese of Lismore and the clergy of the neighbouring parishes of the Diocese of Cloyne. The

Trustees set up a library committee of three persons to meet not less than twice a year to exercise general superintendance over the library. An annual report on the library was made at the Easter Vestry. The incumbent at Lismore is the Honorary Librarian with a deputy to whom duties were delegated during the Honorary Librarian's absence. The sexton was paid a yearly salary of £5 for ensuring that the library was properly heated, cleaned and ventilated.

The Diocese of Kilmore, Elphin and Ardagh has a small library housed in the Kilmore See House. This was founded by the Right Hon. Marcus G. Beresford, Bishop of Kilmore, in the 1860s. Also in the Diocese of Down, Connor and Dromore a library was begun in 1854 by the Revd. Thomas Drew at the request of the Bishop. Housed initially in the old Clerical Rooms, Belfast the collection is mainly of clerical interest but included is the Bishop Reeves collection of manuscripts dealing with the history of the Diocese, and also the Reynell and Swanzy collection of historical manuscripts relating to the Diocese. The library was used for reference by the clergy and by people recommended by the members of the Diocesan Council. The managing committee is now developing the collection as a modern theological library with some 500 books having been added to stock between 1980 and 1982. The library is currently housed in St. Anne's Cathedral Belfast and is open on the first and last Thursdays of each month from 11 a.m. to 2 p.m.

Not to be forgotten is the Diocesan Library of Tuam founded as late as 1881 when the Right Revd. Joseph Henry offered his large and well-stocked library to the Diocese. This formed the nucleus of the Tuam Diocesan Library which now has about 3,000 volumes, mainly theological. In 1980 the library was catalogued by the librarian and students of University College, Galway, and work is to commence on the manuscripts. Plans are afoot to re-house the library but it will not leave the Cathedral precincts.

The most important Church of Ireland library is the Representative Church Body Library which was founded in 1932 by Rosamund Stephen and to which she transferred as many as 5,000 of her father's and her own books. The library has on deposit materials from the Diocesan libraries and in an attempt to repair the losses brought about by the destruction of the Public Record Office in 1922 the Ecclesiastical Records Committee set out to collect the manuscripts. Since 1969 the library has been housed in a new building at Braemor Park and it now has over 2,000 volumes, among which are important theological works and a large history section particularly strong in Irish history.

Membership of the library is open to all members of the Church of

Ireland. The Ecclesiastical Records Department contains Canon J.B. Leslie's printed and manuscript Clerical Succession Lists for every Diocese not otherwise covered and these lists are kept up-to-date. It is therefore possible to trace information about almost every clergyman who has served in the Church of Ireland. As a consequence of this the library therefore receives constant genealogical enquiries from both Ireland and overseas. The library's manuscripts cover many different aspects of life in the Church of Ireland, including its history, liturgy and architecture.

Foremost among the men of the Reformed Church was Richard Robinson, Archbishop of Armagh from 1765 to 1794. In 1770 he established a library in Armagh for the use of the town's residents and the clergy. He was a bookish bishop but one that had concerned himself with a variety of public works and the improvement of the ancient city of Armagh, as when he first arrived there the arts had been in decline for nearly two centuries. In 1771 he endowed the library as a public library and the building was erected at a cost of £3,000. An inscription over the front door reads in Greek 'the healing place of the soul'.

To assure his foundation with permanence an Act of Parliament was passed in 1773 entitled 'An Act for settling and preserving the Publick Library in the city of Armagh for ever'. Under this Act there was provision for annual inspections and meetings of the Governors and Guardians. The library is under the control of the Board of Governors and Guardians, and although it is not church property it has always had close links with the Church of Ireland. No layman was appointed to the Board until 1886 and the Act required that the Keeper should be an Anglican clergyman. The first librarian was the Revd. William Lodge, Chancellor of Armagh Cathedral, appointed in August 1785, and he and his successors were responsible for the day-to-day running of the library. In 1797 Dr Lodge was allowed to employ a deputy, whose salary was not to exceed £20 a year. The Governors and Guardians were not, however, authorised to appoint and pay a librarian's assistant out of the library funds, it being decreed that the salary should be paid out of the librarian's private income!

The Act had required the Governors and Guardians to draw up rules and regulations for the conduct of the library. These were described by Stuart, the Armagh historian, as being liberal and judicious. Books could be borrowed but had to be returned by the thirteenth day and not taken out by the same reader until after an interval of at least sixty days. Each borrower could take such books as he wished to peruse in his own habitation on depositing, *pro tempore*, twice the value as security for their return! The Governors and Guardians were also authorised to make rules for the better management of the Institution, which the librarian was bound to fulfil under pain of suspension, or in the case of seven days *obstinate disobedience*, total removal.

Lord Rokeby granted a liberal endowment for the salary of the librarian, repairs of the house and the purchase of books, and he also presented the library with a highly valuable collection of ancient and modern works in every branch of literature. The original building contained accommodation for the librarian and in 1819, according to James Stuart's *Historical Memoirs of the city of Armagh*, contained 12,000 volumes.

According to Stuart there were manuscripts in the great public rooms to which every reader had the right of access, but there were other writings and books in the library which under Primate Robinson's will could not be submitted to public inspection. These had been committed by him to the care of the Governors and the librarian for the use of each successive Primate for the time being, to whom alone he devised the power of perusing them. As may be imagined this singular and strange restriction excited conjecture amongst literary men and others who made various guesses as to the nature of these manuscripts thus withheld from public scrutiny. However, Lord Rokeby was a man of liberal mind and by no means averse to the general diffusion of knowledge. Stuart dismisses the idea of secretive documents and postulates that the manuscripts in question relate to certain title deeds and muniments of the See, and not to any other department of literature.

But in 1822 books were only being lent out at the discretion of the librarian, and by 1886 all the deeds, leases, maps and other manuscripts were retained in the possession of the Governors. Restrictive opening hours may have had something to do with the scant use made of the collection by the citizens of Armagh. According to a census compiled by William Lodge, they numbered only 1,885 people soon after the founding of the library. Of these there were 162 Church of Ireland families, 131 Presbyterian families and 209 Roman Catholic families. Primate Robinson, not an Irishman, nevertheless had a vision of Armagh as a centre for study and a possible site for a university. He hoped that the foundation of a second university in Ulster would encourage conciliation between the various sects in the north of Ireland annd bind them together in the common interests of the Empire. Indeed in his will he left £5,000 for establishing a university in Ulster, providing it be done within five years of his death.

The small use made of the library by the population of Armagh worried the different keepers over the years. In 1902 in an effort to serve the ordinary people as well as the scholars, thirty books a year were borrowed from Mudie's Lending Library. From 1924 the Times Book Club started to supply books for loan to the general public, but this service was discontinued in 1949. Armagh still retains its original concept as a library for the public and as such is unique from the Irish Diocesan libraries which were set up for the benefit of the clergy in the Diocese. But of all these libraries only those of Narcissus Marsh and Primate Richard Robinson sought to protect their establishment by legislation and it is noteworthy that both these libraries are still in fact open to the public.

In penal times it was impossible for Catholic clergy to indulge their taste for books which had been acquired on the Continent. For Catholic priests, constantly on the move, books would have constituted an unacceptable encumbrance and in such circumstances only a few small devotional works would have been carried around. The Archbishop of Dublin, Piers Creagh, had a sizeable library numbering some 99 works which he deposited in St. Isidore's in Rome for safe keeping until other arrangements could be made. This was on his promotion to the See of Cork in 1676. At the time of the Titus Oates plot a Protestant informer accused Piers Creagh of treason and he was brought to trial in Cork in 1682. Four witnesses for the prosecution failed to appear and Manus O'Keefe the chief witness confessed that all the information he had sworn against the Bishop was untrue. At this point the courthouse collapsed, burying officials, jury and onlookers in the debris. Panic and pandemonium followed with Catholics seeing this as a manifestation of the vengeance of God on a perjured witness! On the resumption of the trial Creagh was found to be not guilty.

The Franciscan libraries in Ireland and on the Continent had a lot to do with the preservation and dissemination of literature of the past in Ireland. The dissolution of the monasteries in the sixteenth century witnessed the destruction of a good many Franciscan libraries, with volumes either being burned, confiscated or stolen. Some manuscripts were hidden away only to come to light as late as the mid-nineteenth century. Others were smuggled out of the country to St. Anthony's Louvain. This Irish Franciscan library was broken up when the college was confiscated by the French Government in 1797. Some of the manuscripts were sent to the Burgundian library in Brussels, others to St. Isidore's at Rome. The library of the Franciscans in Prague met a similar fate when the college was suppressed in 1786 and the guardian, Father Thomas Hogan, was ordered to surrender the keys of the library and the catalogue of the books. Many of these books are still in different collections in Prague and Vienna. Happily some made their way back to Ireland and were placed in the Franciscan Library at Merchant's Quay and in 1872, when under the threat of war in Garibaldi's Italy all manuscripts of Irish interest were returned to Ireland from the St. Isidore Library in Rome. These manuscripts are now deposited in the Franciscan Library at Killiney, Dublin. From the time of the dispersal of the old library of the Franciscan Convent in Donegal in the mid 17th century until the return of the Isidorian manuscripts in 1872 there had been no important Franciscan library in the country. In 1644 Father Brown complained that 'the convents are so poor that we cannot continue studies in the country and our benefactors so poor that they cannot relieve us'. In the second half of the seventeenth century Father Brian Higgins requested the friars at Moyne, Co. Mayo to say 700 masses or more for his intentions and promised to forward books to the value of that number of stipends.

In the second half of the eighteenth century the penal laws were eased and Catholics began to acquire and retain the output of the prolific Dublin printers. One such Catholic gentleman Philip O'Brien of Ballyporeen, Co. Tipperary, left his notebook for posterity. This contained prayers in Latin, charms, contracts, mottos, wills, geographical data, accounts, genealogical details, farming notes, remedies and, of particular interest, a list of books in his possession in 1767. (see Figure 4.1). They are as follows:

1  The Holy Bible
2  Abridgement of Christian Doctrine
3  Secretary's Guide
4  Doctor Helen
5  Think well on't
6  The Life of King David
7  History of England
8  The Rosary of the B.V. (Blessed Virgin)
9  Wars of the Jews
10  Nine Worthies
11  The Life of Thadea ô Brien
12  A Tour through Ireland
13  Brown's Exposition
14  Hugh McCurtain
15  Lord Viscount Taaffe
16  The Compleat Brewer (Sic)
17  The Art of Husbandry
18  Battle of Aughrim
19  Joe Miller's Jests
20  Oliver Cromwell
21  The English Registry

22 Bolug an tLathair (Bolug an tsolathair – Miscellany or Commonplace Book)
23 An Gramathach Gaoilge (An Gramathach Gaoidhilge – The Irish Grammar)
24 Dowway's Cathecism (Sic) – catechism
25 Roman Catholic Reasons
26 Manuel
27 Pilgrim's Progress
28 Gardner's Almanack
29 An Act for Planting Trees

This collection is probably representative of a gentleman's library of the time and is fairly comprehensive, ranging from religious works to popular literature, practical books on brewing and husbandry, the standard Catholic works of the time, plus the two books in Irish, written in an antiquated form of the language and it is thought that number 22 was in manuscript form.

This library is small however when compared to that of Archbishop John Carpenter of Dublin from 1770 to 1786, who had a fine library of over 4,000 volumes in all branches of literature. After his death it was sold at a book auction by James Vallence.

One of the greatest book collectors during the first half of the nineteenth century was Dr John Murphy, the Roman Catholic Bishop of Cork, a very learned and industrious man. The German traveller Kohl described his library in 1842, reporting that Murphy had made his house into a library so that every room, including sitting rooms, dining rooms and bedrooms, was filled with books, including the staircases, corridors and garrets. His house contained the largest private collection of books to be found in Ireland at that time. The Bishop was a well-known character and a frequent visitor to the Dublin booksellers who regarded his coming with great excitement. He learnt Irish at the age of 40 so that he could instruct his flock in their own language. He employed the Irish poet and scribe Michael Og O Longain to make copies of Irish books and manuscripts. Dr Murphy hoped that his books would be bequeathed to the city of Cork provided that a suitable building could be procured. This unfortunately was not to be the case and while his manuscripts went to Maynooth, the books were auctioned by Sotheby's in London between December 1847 and January 1848. The collection of at least 75,000 books was so vast that in the end they were sold by weight. A few of his books remained in Cork as they were Diocesan property.

The love of books was non-denominational and a charming vignette of the library at Edgeworthtown has survived to show just

**FIGURE 4.1 LIST OF
PHILIP O'BRIEN'S BOOKS 1767**

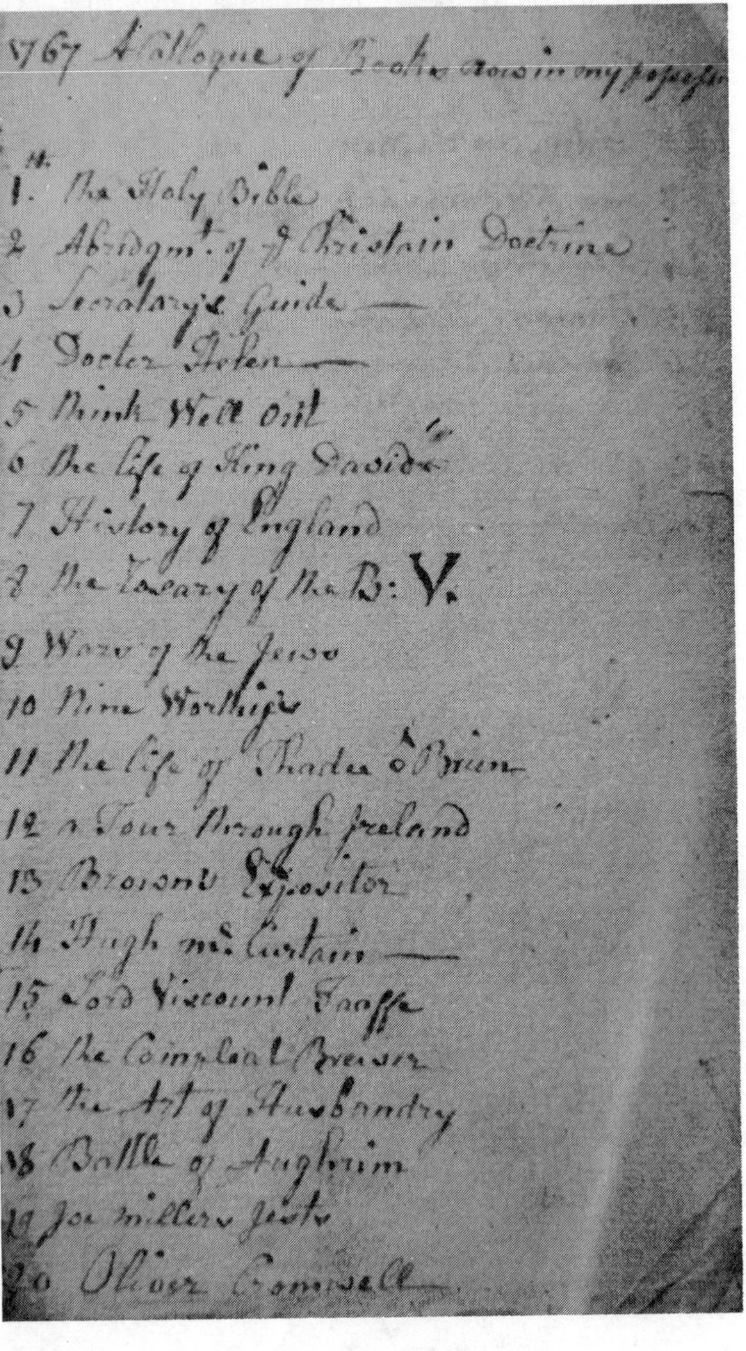

1767 A Callogue of Books now in my possession

1. The Holy Bible
2. Abridgmt. of ye Christain Doctrine
3. Secretary's Guide
4. Doctor Dolen
5. Think Well On't
6. The life of King David
7. History of England
8. The Rosary of the B: V.
9. Wars of the Jews
10. Nine Worthys
11. The life of Charles O'Brien
12. A Tour through Ireland
13. Brown's Expositor
14. Hugh mc Curtain
15. Lord Viscount Taaffe
16. The Compleat Brewer
17. The Art of Husbandry
18. Battle of Aughrim
19. Joe Miller's Jests
20. Oliver Cromwell

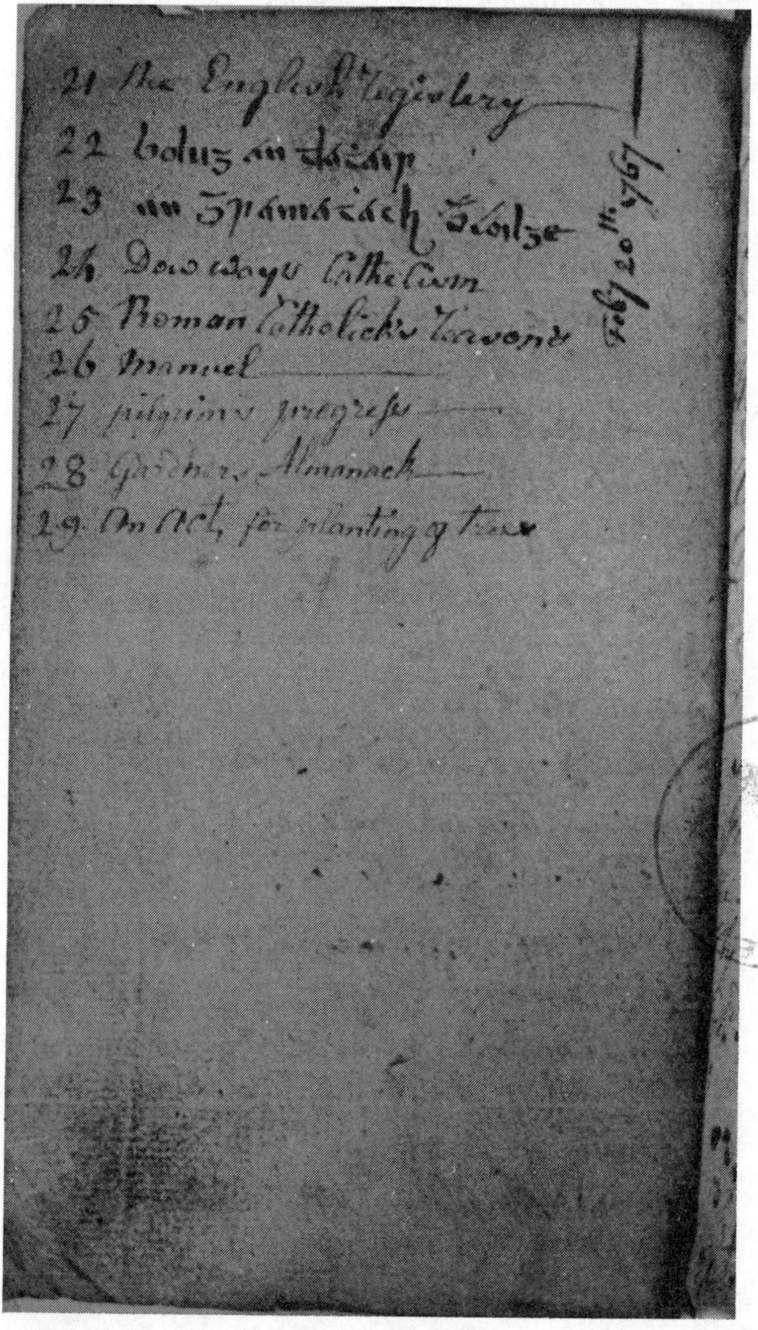

21 the English Registery

22 bolus an dóṡáiṅ

23 an ṡámáṫáċh Ścoilṡe

24 Douways Catheciun

25 Roman Catholicks reasond

26 manuel

27 pilgrims progress

28 Gardners Almannek

29 An Act for planting of trees

87

how much libraries meant in the lives of their owners, and illustrated the kinds of homes that the booksellers were selling books to in the late eighteenth and early nineteenth centuries.

"The library of the house was a large, spacious and lofty room, well-stocked with books. An oblong table in the centre was a sort of rallying point for the family who used to group around it to read, write or work. Quite often a large family party assembled daily in this charming room, young and old bound alike to the spot by strong cords of memory and love. Mr Francis Edgeworth, Miss Edgeworth's youngest brother, had a family of little ones who seemed to enjoy the freedom of the library as much as the elders: to set these little people to right ... to mount the steps and find a volume that escapes all eyes but her own and having done so to find the exact passage wanted are hourly employments of this most unspoiled and admirable woman. But of all the hours those of the evening in the library at Edgeworthtown were the most delightful, each member of the family contributes without an effort to the instruction and amusement of the whole"[1]

One of the most interesting collections started in the nineteenth century was that of Philip Evelyn Shirley, who was an antiquary, historian, herald and book collector. He died in 1882 after gathering together a unique collection of Irish books in his home at Carrickmacross, Lough Fea, Co. Monaghan. He began amassing his personal library in the 1850s when he acquired every possible book or ballad dealing with Anglo-Irish history and literature, and built a special library to house his unique collection. It contained about 4,000 items and was intended to be an illustration of the history and antiquities of Ireland. Although an author himself, his life's work was the production of a library catalogue. This was privately printed in 1872 as a memory of his splendid library which he thought should be on record somewhere, even if his collection was later dispersed. In the event the library has not been dispersed, with the exception of some books sold at Sotheby's in 1924. Though many fine Irish libraries perished in the troubles that swept the country in the 1920s the library at Lough Fea survived. In 1967 some of the books were rebound and more recently the house and library have survived a fire bomb attack.

# 5             The subscription and society libraries

In the late eighteenth century and at the beginning of the nineteenth century there was a revival of scholarly interests, not only in Ireland but in Britain and America, when despite the political and religious acrimony of the time, men of all opinions met together for scientific and literary pursuits. In Ireland, apart from a few exceptions, it cannot be said there was much interest in books, but the volunteer movement in the 1780s led to the mingling of people from different sectors of the community. Apart from the military pursuits, officers and men began to discourse with each other. Reading, at first a fashion, turned into being a favoured occupation. More books began to be bought and there was a renewed interest in literature.

Earlier manifestation of this desire for learning showed itself in the establishment of the Dublin Philosophical Society in 1684, based on the design of the Royal Society in London. At first just a few interested persons met together to discuss philosophy, mathematics and literature. As the company increased they forsook the coffee houses and, at the invitation of the Revd. Dr Huntington, the Provost of the College, met in his lodgings. Immediately after the formation of the Society contact was made with the Royal Society in London, to which abstracts of proceedings, experiments and discoveries were regularly transmitted. The Royal Society remitted half the subscription of those of its members who belonged to the Dublin Philosophical Society. The first President of the Society was Sir William Petty and he was succeeded by Lord Mountjoy and the Hon. Francis Robarts. The Society's meetings which, subsequent to November 1686, appear to have been few and irregular were brought to an end by the dispersion of its members and the start of hostilities between James II and the Prince of Orange. The Dublin Philosophical Society was reorganised in 1693 in Trinity College where it continued to assemble for some years after its revival.

Meeting at the rooms of the Philosophical Society were fourteen men who, anxious to improve the condition of the country, formed in June 1731 an organisation to be called the Dublin Society for improving Husbandry, Manufactures and other Useful Arts. The objects of this Society were to initiate and carry out useful experiments, and to exchange information with similar societies. The establishment of a library was discussed in December of that year, and the Society stipulated that all useful works, journals and transactions published by other societies and private individuals were to be purchased. The Society collected all the best books on husbandry and the useful arts, not only those in English, but also those from France, Flanders, Germany, Poland and Italy. Each member of the Society chose a particular subject in which to specialise, by reading, conversing and experimentation.

From the middle of the eighteenth century the Society began to receive grants from the Irish Parliament, additions being made to the library in agriculture, botany, mechanics and scientific and technical subjects. Booksellers were commissioned to attend auctions to obtain rare or out-of-print books, and members visiting the Continent were asked to purchase suitable books.

Many of the members of the Dublin Society were also members of the Physico-Historical Society which lasted from 1744 to 1754 and which researched into the ancient and topical state of the country. When this Society ceased to function the Dublin Society accepted the responsibility of collecting Irish manuscripts. In May 1722 an Antiquarian committee had been set up to gather information on the antiquities of Ireland. Lord Charlemont, Lord Moira, the Bishop of Cloyne, the Bishop of Derry and the historian Dr. Leland all sat on this committee, each paying £3.3s. annually towards the undertaking. They placed advertisements in the *Dublin Journal* and the principal Continental journals asking persons holding ancient Irish manuscripts to communicate with them. They thus established very useful connections with important Irish émigrés such as Charles O'Neill, Principal of the College of Lombards in Paris, but they were not always successful in obtaining copies of the manuscripts. The Antiquarian committee met for the last time in 1774.

The growing library was in the charge of the registrar of the Society but in 1795 the Revd. Dr John Lanigan was appointed as an assistant. He was ultimately recommended for appointment as assistant librarian in 1803 by which time the stock of the library had reached 10,000 volumes. Five years later he was appointed as the first librarian of the Society and the role of the library became more important. A committee was appointed to take stock of the books, manuscripts and maps, and to draw up rules and regulations for the use of the library. In the early decades of the nineteenth century the Society acquired the property of Leinster House and the library was transferred there under the supervision of Dr Samuel Litton who had succeeded Dr Lanigan as the librarian in 1815.

As the library grew in importance the library committee was reconstituted in 1812 as a standing committee charged with the control and supervision of the library which was now regarded as a national institution. By 1836 the library contained over 11,000 volumes, pamphlets and manuscripts, and with certain reservations was available not only to members of the Society but also to the public, if they were introduced by a member. But with the Act of Union in 1801 the generous grants from the Irish Parliament had ceased and the Imperial Parliament was parsimonious in its support of the Society. The religious and political rifts outside were reflected in the Society and in the 1830s Dr Daniel Murray, the Catholic Archbishop of Dublin, was refused admission as a member. The Government felt that the Royal Dublin Society (it has received the title Royal when George IV became Patron in June 1820) was not doing enough to justify the small grants it was now receiving, so a House of Commons Select Committee was set up under the chairmanship of William Smith O'Brien to investigate the Society and to make recommendations.

The Report of the Select Committee felt that the Society's library should be open to more people, and that it should be considered as a national library for people of respectable circumstances who wished to use it for research purposes, rather on the lines of the British Museum library. The Select Committee also suggested the abolition of the library committee so that the care of the library could be entrusted to the librarian, but despite this firm recommendation the committee continued to remain in being, although it was no longer a standing committee. The committee drew up plans for the additional rooms at the library including the provision of a new reading room for non-members, but the small funds available to the committee rendered the recommendations of the Select Committee almost inoperable. By 1841 the library was in such pecuniary difficulties that the librarian had to inform booksellers that under no circumstances should periodicals be provided to the library. The library was in fact trying to cater for two sets of readers, the members and the general public, and scarcity of funds was making its tasks very difficult. Many non-members were using the library, although a great many more were put off by the air of grandeur around Leinster House, and the fact that many of the members regarded their presence as an intrusion of their private club. The number of readers grew from a few hundred in 1836 to 4,860 in 1844.

In 1863 the library received the collection of Dr Jasper Joly, which numbered more than 23,000 volumes and was particularly strong in French material, but also contained some rare Irish works and manuscripts. The gift was to the Irish people, the Society was to be the custodian of the collection, and in the event of a National Library being formed by Act of Parliament the gifts should revert to it.

91

The National Library of Ireland owes it birth to the Royal Dublin Society. This transfer of library stock was envisaged over a number of years and it finally culminated in a series of proposals submitted by Lord Sandon, Vice-Chairman of the Committee of the Privy Council for Education, in 1876. He suggested to the committee the handing over of the library to the State and placing it under the control of a Board of Trustees as part of a Government scheme to augment and extend the facilities for science and art institutions in Ireland.

The Science and Art Museum Act received the Royal assent in August 1877 and the library of the Society including the Joly manuscripts and collections passed to the nation. Certain other works, to be adjudicated upon by the librarian of the British Museum, remained the property of the Society, especially the scientific serials, books and transactions of the Society making the Society the most important scientific library in Ireland. As a small concession members of the Society elected prior to 1 January 1878 were allowed to borrow books from the National Library. The librarian became both the librarian of the Society and of the National Library. A report dated 10 November 1880 stated 'that the present plan of having two perfectly distinct libraries mixed together on the same shelves is most inconvenient and gives rise to great complications and confusion. It appears utterly hopeless to attempt the proper management of the Society's library while this state of affairs continues'.

At a subsequent meeting of the trustees the committee asked that it should be made the duty of the librarian to discharge his duties with reference to the whole of the library housed at Leinster House so long as it included the library of the Society as well as the National Library. As soon as the Government could carry out the directions of the Act of Parliament and remove the public library, the Society would be perfectly prepared to provide for the custody of their own books. The situation was so unsatisfactory that the Government was appealed to by the Society to expedite the building of the new National Library.

The National Library building was opened in 1891, fourteen years after the Science and Art Museum Act. The transfer of the books gave more room to the Society for its own library. The link with the National Library has been maintained under an agreement of 1881 which provides that the National Library 'shall be under the superintendence of a Council of Trustees, eight of whom shall be appointed by the Royal Dublin Society'.

The funds of the Royal Dublin Society remained low and as most of the books that remained in the Society's library were of a technical nature there was very little in the way of general cultural reading or recreational literature. This problem was overcome by a subscription to Mudie's Circulating Library to provide light and popular reading materials. More serious works had to be acquired by purchasing second-hand materials.

Nevertheless the new library was gradually extended and this led to the appointment of a Society librarian in 1895. In June 1922 Michael Collins, head of the provisional Government, asked for the use of part of Leinster House for parliamentary purposes. This was agreed on the understanding that the rooms would be returned after one year. In the event civil war broke out and the housing of the Oireachtas (Legislature) in Leinster House was a matter of security. Eventually the Royal Dublin Society accepted an offer of £68,000 for Leinster House and moved to Ballsbridge. The removal of the books from Leinster House was an enormous task, but by 1925 the new library was ready with shelving for 40,000 volumes in the general library, and with more accommodation for periodicals around the balcony of the main hall.

At this time the Dewey Decimal Classification scheme and the Browne issuing system were introduced, changes which brought the Society library in line with the public library systems of the day. Continuing to move with the times, the committee agreed to make its books and periodicals available to research workers and students through the Irish Central Library and the National Central Library in London.

The library situation however did not remain static for very long and plans were drawn up for a new library with open access to some 30,000 books and reserve storage for another 100,000. The new library was opened by Eamon de Valera, the President of Ireland, in 1965. The Royal Dublin Society Library now contains over 200,000 volumes, some thousands of which are on all the branches of agricultural science, constituting the most important collection of works on agriculture in the country.

The Botanic Garden at Glasnevin was founded by the Society in the 1790s to provide instruction in botany and horticulture for the general public. The Botanic Garden remained under the care of the Society until 1879 when the Government took it over. From the beginning a library of botanical books was started. The collection was temporarily moved to the Society's headquarters in Hawkins Street in 1801 but by 1819 it was returned to the Botanic Garden and kept in a room used for lectures. In 1839 the librarian was Samuel Milton, a professor of botany. He was asked to keep in his house a collection of some 400 volumes bequeathed to the Garden by the botanist and horticulturalist John Robertson of Kilkenny, but he refused to do so. An old damp lecture room was not felt to be a suitable place but a new grate and two small stoves were put in to improve conditions. Here the botanical library and the Robertson bequest were kept until 1845 when the books had to be found temporary accommodation due to the fact that rain was pouring in through the roof of the lecture room.

In 1850 the library was transferred into glass-fronted bookcases in a lecture room in the gate lodge. After public lectures ceased the room was divided, half becoming a library and offices, the other half becoming a ladies waiting room. In 1891 the house was rebuilt and a special room on the first floor set aside for the library. At this time many of the non-botanical books were moved to the main library, and money was spent on completing sets of botanical journals. The library and the herbarium were rearranged in the 1950s.

Before leaving Dublin there are several more libraries worthy of mention. The first one must be that of the Royal Irish Academy. This Academy had been founded in 1785 and was incorporated by Royal Charter in the following year. The Royal Dublin Society catered well for the applied sciences but a group led by General Vallency and Lord Charlemont, feeling the lack of provision for the study of history, antiquities, literature and pure science, began to meet at the Neosophical Society and from these meetings sprang the idea of the Academy. Dublin itself was full of brilliant men, it had its own Parliament, and the city together with its intellectual life, flourished. This enlightenment and education were essentially Protestant and Protestant intellectuals from scholarly English families now established in Ireland developed an interest not only in establishing centres of learning and libraries in Ireland, but a desire to know more about the history of their adopted country.

Lord Charlemont was elected the first President of the Academy and it was through his intervention that premises were acquired in the form of Navigation House in Grafton Street, where the Academy met until 1852. The Act of Union in 1801 and the death of Lord Charlemont seriously affected the development of the Academy, but by the 1820s it was beginning to provide a brilliant forum for the learned men of the day. These included linguists, chemists, physicists, mathematicians, astronomers, naturalists, historians and antiquarians. From its earliest days the Academy received Government support as well as endowments. It began to publish Transactions in 1787 and Proceedings in 1836. These publications, containing much Irish research work, led to exchanges with other learned institutions in many other countries and by this means a considerable collection of serious publications was amassed. The Proceedings are now sent to well over 600 institutions and the library of the Academy contains about 1,700 sets of current serials and about 600 sets of non-current serials. The total number of volumes in this collection amounts to about 30,000.

The foundation of the library was one of the Academy's earliest activities and its objective of collecting early Irish manuscripts was begun immediately. The *Book of Ballymote* was the first acquisition when it was presented in 1785, followed by the gift of the *Book of Lecan* in 1787, and two years later by the *Leabhar Breac*. These three manuscripts formed the nucleus of what was to become the most extensive collection of Irish manuscripts in any library. In this endeavour the Academy was eminently more successful than the abortive Antiquaries Committee set up by the Royal Dublin Society. George Petrie, the founder of critical archaeology in Ireland, urged the collection of ancient Irish manuscripts and the Academy enlarged its collection from about 50 in 1829 to several hundred over the next fifty years, mainly by buying manuscripts as they became available at sales, but also by encouraging members and friends to contribute to the purchase of these materials, 227 of them coming from the Hodges and Smith collection to which the Government gave £600, a further £600 being raised by subscription, and a mere £100 being put up by the Academy itself.

The library of the Academy also received valuable bequests and gifts from William Smith O'Brien, who bequeathed 43 manuscripts and William Elliott Hudson, who left 80 manuscripts. The collection of the Galway historian James Hardiman was purchased in 1856. Collections from John Daly, the Dublin bookseller, Bishop William Reeves, President of the Academy and John Windele, the Cork antiquary were also acquired. One of the most important acquisitions was the Stowe Missal which came with 150 other manuscripts relating to Ireland in 1883 from the library of the Marquis of Buckingham at Stowe. More recent acquisitions are the papers of the Marquis Mac Swiney of Mashanaglass presented in 1946 which relate to Irish regiments on the Continent, and the papers of H.A.S. Upton which are concerned with family history and with Westmeath local history.

In Wright's *Historical Guide to Dublin* (1821) it is mentioned that the Academy was furnished with a tolerable lending library. The library was open every Monday for members 'but they cannot consult books at pleasure'. Books were, however, an important part of the library from the outset, despite the quote, and early in the 1830s the council voted the sum of £1,000 to buy books. This represented at least half the Academy's capital at the time. The renown of the library meant that it attracted many worthy collections from famous academicians, such as the library of about 1,000 volumes of Thomas Moore, presented by his widow in 1855. Mrs Charles Halliday also gave her husband's valuable collection of over 25,000 pamphlets and tracts, mostly of Irish interest, plus many manuscripts and printed books. The pamphlet collection has been added to since the acquisition of these materials and now consists of over 30,000 items. Book bequests have included a complete set of the publications of the Cuala and Dun Emer Presses. The book collection is particularly strong in relation to works about Ireland, including the Upton Bequest which consisted of 1,300 books of genealogical and archaeological interest. Lord Moyne donated 1,300 books of Irish interest in 1934.

Another association was the Gaelic Society which was founded in Dublin in 1806 for the preservation and publication of ancient Irish historical and literary documents. The principle people connected with this movement were Theophilus O'Flanagan of Trinity College, Denis Taaffe, author of the *History of Ireland*, Edward O'Reilly, compiler of the *Irish Dictionary*, William Halliday, author of a grammar of the Gaelic language, Revd. Paul O'Brien, author of *An Irish Grammar*, and Patrick Lynch, who wrote the *Life of St. Patrick* and also *A Short Grammar of the Irish Language*. Unfortunately the Gaelic Society only produced a single volume but the Society called forth the talents of scholars who achieved much when we consider the spirit of their time, and who exerted themselves for the preservation of native Irish literature at a period when it was greatly neglected.

Prior to 1791 several scholars were in the habit of getting together to read newspapers, new publications, memoirs and transactions of the various philosophic societies of the day, at the bookshop of John Archer at 80 Dame Street. The group thought it would be to their advantage to form a Society and Reading Room of their own and a preliminary meeting to this end was held on 10 May 1791. Dr Richard Kirwan, a Catholic and an eminent chemist, was one of the founder members. He came from a distinguished Connaught family, was educated on the Continent and was later elected a Fellow of the Royal Societies of both London and Edinburgh. He was also to become the President of the Royal Irish Academy. Dr Kirwan observed the want of a truly public library in Dublin, based upon popular principles rather than theological studies as was Marsh's Library.

Seeing this void, he decided to do something about filling it and it was his driving force that led to the formation of the Dublin Library Society. He put forward his proposals to found the Society, aiming to procure those great and expensive books usually beyond the reach of private individuals, whilst at the same time procuring smaller works of value and use on any branch of literature and science. His next step was to appeal to the city in a short address which was prepared and signed by him. Eleven days after this meeting, 45 members had joined the Society and the first general meeting was held at the Royal Irish Academy when the first committee of 21 members was chosen by ballot. One of the more interesting and patriotic rules of the Society was that no British copy of any book was to be purchased if an Irish edition of equal utility could be procured. There was obviously a strong desire to support Irish industry and trade.

This committee continued to meet at John Archer's until June 1791 when two rooms were rented in the house of Mr. Vallence, a bookseller, in Eustace Street. The first librarian, Mr Edkins, was elected in August of the same year. In March 1792 the committee chose the Earl of Charlemont as President with Dr Richard Kirwan as one of the Vice-Presidents. On the death of Lord Charlemont in 1799 Richard Kirwan was unanimously elected, without ballot or vote, to the office of Chairman which he then held until his death on 1 June 1812.

In his day Richard Kirwan corresponded with scholars in every civilised country, and in his own city he represented all that was connected with scientific and learned life. He bequeathed a collection of over 1,200 books to the Royal Irish Academy in 1813. In fact this was his third major collection of books. His first had been lost at sea travelling from France where he had studied for many years, and the second was captured in the Irish Channel in 1780 by American privateers and taken to America where it was bought by an association of gentlemen in Salem, Massachusetts.

Dr Kirwan once told Lady Morgan, authoress of *The Wild Irish girl*, that at Christmas and other great festivals he would throw open the servants' hall at Cregg, his ancestral home, to all comers, beggars, bards and storytellers, after the Connaught fashion and, taking his place amongst them, made each of his humble guests tell a story, recite a poem or sing a song in Irish. It was amazing how few of them could not recite or sing.

The pursuit of knowledge constituted the sole business and employment of Dr Kirwan. He died in 1812 and his demise cast a gloom over the entire city. The committee of the Society attended his funeral in a body, members assembling at the Rotunda without scarfs and hatbands as a tribute to the memory of their late President. Despite the intention of his family that the interment should not be a public one, Kirwan's status and popularity defeated this idea. Long before 7 a.m. numerous carriages had assembled near his home and continued to crowd the streets up to the time when the funeral was to begin. The hearse, followed by a long train of gentlemen on foot, members of the Society and others passed slowly down Sackville Street, Westmoreland Street, Dame Street, Capel Street, Dorset Street and Temple Street until it arrived at the churchyard of St. George's Parish where he was interred. After his death the Society commissioned a bust of Dr Kirwan to show their respect for his memory. He was returned thirteen times as President of the Dublin Library Society. On his death the President's chair was accepted by the Right Hon. John Philpot Curran, then Master of the Rolls.

But to go back to 1792. The extensive purchase of books planned by Richard Kirwan was prevented by considerable expenditure on English and Irish newspapers for the Conversation Room which had the effect of almost converting the Society into a political newspaper club. In December 1803 it appeared that great depreciations had been made to the stock of the library and that many valuable books had been stolen. A sub-committee was established to consider what was needed to protect the Society's property. Wire lattice doors with locks and keys were recommended for the book shelves and that no book be taken down except by the librarian. As this would have meant the employment of an assistant librarian these measures were not put into effect. It was also discovered that books were not the only items missing, the library funds having a shortfall of over £156. In fact £43 was spent trying to discover the culprit but to no avail.

On the foundation of the Society the annual subscription was fixed at one guinea, or ten guineas for life members. Additionally the donation of books worth fifteen guineas or payment of the one guinea subscription for a period of ten years would entitle sub-scribers to the full benefit of the library for life. Despite the admirable intentions of the founder of the Society, the organisation came in for much pungent criticism. The first appears to have come from anonymous sources and was printed in a booklet called *The Secret History of the Dublin Library Society*, published in 1808 by someone signing himself 'Melanctus'.

One of the main grievances was the repeal of the original terms of membership of the Society. Terms quoted later are similar but have one fundamental difference in that the subscription was £1 annually. Payment of ten guineas, or donation of books to the value of fifteen guineas gave exemption from subscriptions for fifteen years and not for life as before. This amendment may have been an attempt to bolster the depleted bank balance. In any case the measure was not without its opponents and at an extraordinary general meeting on 19 November 1804, when only eighteen members were present, the report of the sub-committee set up to investigate the missing books and the missing funds was received, and it was at this meeting that the qualifications for life membership were rescinded. The repeal was upheld at a noisy meeting on 11 March 1805, when a minority of 59 were ignobly defeated by a mere majority of 62. The member who had had the temerity to bring forward the question was so injured by the riotous expression of exultation that he had to remain at home for several days in order to restore his equilibrium!

Another complaint received from Melanctus was that the Society had acted contrary to a principle laid down on 25 August 1791 when it resolved that the introduction of newspapers would be a measure totally foreign to the design of the institution and destructive of the advantages to be derived from it. Notwithstanding the resolution the conversation room was soon well-supplied with newspapers which at this time swallowed up annually more than £140. This change was really extremely fundamental as it nearly converted what was intended to be a literary reading society into a political newspaper club.

In connection with politics the Society brushed swords on occasions with a newspaper called the *Dublin Evening Mail*. This paper first appeared on 3 February 1823 and was founded by William Saurin in order to attack the Marquis Wellesley for bringing to an end his fifteen years tenure of office as Attorney-General. It was a newspaper that sought to support the establishment, was rabidly anti-Catholic, and was against the repeal of the Union. An interesting article appeared in issue 127 of the *Dublin Evening Mail* on 21 November 1823, headed:

The Dublin Library

Some bigots in this sink of Radicalism, mean to propose the exclusion of two copies of the *Evening Mail* from the Reading Room. The asses! The fools! Surely if anything can incense them and induce them to discontinue these epithets will. We shall gain by their impotent malignity an increase to our circulation of a full hundred copies we are certain. Let these contemptible blockheads behave themselves well or not behave themselves at all. They are, at best, but food for our laughter.

What if we don't condescend to foreward them our paper? They will read nothing but what is written by the Bigot and the Dunce ... What nice paltes they have! What precious taste they have! O! the Monkeys! From what journal do they gather half as much information, or derive a twentieth part as much amusement as from ours! It is this that makes us independent of *them*.

The troubles of the Dublin Library Society didn't stop there however, as another report in the *Dublin Evening Mail* commented on 6 February 1824. The report does indicate a certain sense of humour amongst the membership!

Re the Dublin Library Society

The Rev. William Tighe Gregory is known as a firm supporter of the Constitution. The late proceedings of this Society induced the Rev. Gentleman to adopt a most Whimsical but at the same time a most happy mode of publicly conveying rebuke to this mean and liberal body styling itself 'literary'.

For ten days the following satirical notice has been posted in the room of the Society, in pursuance of which an extraordinary meeting was called for the purposes of taking it seriously into consideration. The Chair, gravely taken, and the following resolution solemnly moved and seconded, *sans badinage*.

– Resolved 'That to promote harmony in this Society and practical liberality each member be allowed as a matter of right to destroy or mutilate any newspaper not coinciding with his own private political sentiments and that the same licence be extended to the various books in the library.

– That animated fire screens be prohibited in these rooms.

– That no gentleman be allowed to occupy more than two chairs at the fireplace at the same time.

– That a portrait of Lord Chesterfield[1] of polite memory be placed above the chimney piece in the conversation room.

Upon these resolutions there was a long and animated debate but reporters not being permitted to attend discussion on questions so momentous, we are not able to ascertain whether they have been carried in the above form or one more modified; but the country will look forward with considerable anxiety to the result. We fear that the suspense in which so many remain is in a great measure attributable to us for it was proposed that the proceedings of the day should be published officially: but a *'friend'* of ours, whose name we have but which we do not think necessary to state, pulled the Mover by the sleeve and in an audible whisper said No! No! that d----d *Mail* will catch hold of it and be down upon us. We can assure our *friend* he need have no fears upon that score. As a literary body the Dublin Society is despicable and beneath our notice; as a political one it is dangerous and as such only comes within the line of our duty and is entitled to our remarks.

These attacks from the *Dublin Evening Mail* serve to illustrate the fervour and intensity of political feeling at this period. Catholic emancipation was in the air. The Union which many had seen as an advantage had turned out to be a fiasco both for the Protestant ascendancy and the Catholics alike. Feelings were running high.

Notwithstanding the hostility the Dublin Library Society did flourish during this difficult time. In 1808 the Society moved to a house on Burgh Quay belonging to a Mr Connolly, and in 1817 a circulating library was opened for the use of the members at an additional charge of one guinea per annum. The income must have been healthier than when Melanctus was complaining for in March 1819 the Society leased a site in D'Olier Street for 999 years and on this the Society erected a stone-fronted house into which it moved to take up residence on 18 September 1820. Here there was a library which cost upwards of £8,000 and a reading room stocked with English, Irish, Scottish, French and American newspapers. By 1834 the *Dublin Almanac and General Register of Ireland* recorded that the Society had spent more than £6,000 on books, and that many donations had also augmented the stock. Also listed in the *Directory* is the fact that a Chess Club was connected to the Society, composed exclusively of members who paid an additional subscription of five shillings a year.

In 1856 the Society changed its name to the Dublin Library Society and Hibernian Athanaeum. This title lasted until 1869. By 1880 directory entries merely record it as the D'Olier Street Club, late Dublin Library Society at 24A D'Olier Street. The demise of the Society took place in 1882 when the contents of the library were sold, the books and property being disposed of at Bennett's. Among the causes which led to its extinction were the gradual removal of the well-to-do professional classes from the city to the suburbs, and a change in the general taste of the readers towards light fiction. But probably the main cause was the conversion of the Society from a literary club to a political newspaper club.

Thomas Davis had written of a project to put Smith O'Brien, John O'Donnell, Gavan Duffy and five or six more on the committee of the Library at D'Olier Street. He stated that it had 13,000 volumes, a noble and well-situated house, and that it needed only vigour and control to become a great civic library and literary institute. It is probable that this project succeeded to some extent. Among the most notable names which appear on the membership lists over the years are Daniel O'Connell, who was a Vice-President in 1822, a factor which probably led to the outbursts from the *Dublin Evening Mail*, and William Smith O'Brien, who was a Vice-President in 1848. When Thomas Davis died in September 1845 the Dublin

Library committee sent a deputation to attend the funeral and accompany him to the grave, as did members of the Repeal Association, the Royal Irish Academy and the Corporation of Dublin.

During the period of intense intellectual force in Ireland from about 1780 to 1800 which saw the foundation of most of the big intellectual societies, small rural libraries became common, particularly in county Antrim. Arthur O'Connor who had aspired to Parliamentary honours for Co. Antrim and had participated in the Rebellion of 1798 stated that in all Europe the population of Ulster was the best informed, together with the Protestants of the Lowlands of Scotland. Each parish had its library and the journal *Northern Star* instructed them and regaled them in their evenings' recreation. The *Northern Star* was the organ of the United Irishmen in Belfast and was owned, edited and written by members of the Belfast Society for Promoting Knowledge.

People set up their own lending and subscription libraries and in Co. Antrim in particular these were spread over the county as early as the 1820s. Ballynure and Doagh had libraries, the latter being raided by the Yeomanry in 1798 and its books destroyed. William Galt, a freemason and teacher, had formed the book society in 1780 for the population around Doagh. The society was so successful that the members erected a building to serve as a community school, library and meeting place. There were similar societies in Newry and Portaferry, and a Society for Acquiring Knowledge in Newtownards.

Francis Joseph Bigger gives details of one such organisation called the Four Towns Book Club, which was essentially for the working classes. This club was situated in the parish of Templepatrick and the four towns concerned were Kilgreel, Ballynabarnish, Molusk and Craigarogan. The men who built the club were determined to provide themselves with every means of obtaining a liberal and extended education. These men included the poet and schoolmaster Samuel Thomson, the actor Luke Mallan, and the writer, Thomas Beggs. A frequent visitor was James Orr, a United Irishman and respectable farmer of Farranshane, who died on the scaffold at the age of 31. Orr had spent more than £50 on books for his own private library. He wrote the most popular ballad *The Irishman*.

The Four Towns Book Club had monthly social evenings where, once the ordinary transactions of the accounts, book circulation and the ordering of new volumes had been dealt with, there followed an evening of song, fiddle-playing and story-telling. A large bowl of hot toddy made of 'bright mountain' dew brought forth in a three gallon jar from the sonsy dame's under-press in the back closet' no doubt helped the evening convivialities along. Byron was quoted freely, Scott read by all, and Moore's songs were favourites. The toasts at these parties included 'The plough and the printing press', 'The book clubs of the north of Ireland', 'Ireland as it ought to be and freedom to those who dare to ask for it and are anxious to deserve it', and 'Lovely woman'.

At one time the library contained as many as 400 books which was no mean collection considering that it was a library for the working classes. The Four Towns Book Club had been preceded by the Lowtown Book Club in 1790 and the Roughfort Book Club which started in 1796. These two merged into the Four Towns Book Club in 1802 when the Club House came into general use. The entrance fee at this time was five shillings with a quarterly payment of one shilling as subscription. The Club elected a secretary, accountant, treasurer and librarian each January, and to raise money the Club room was let for dances at five shillings a time unless the dance was being organised for charity.

Bigger records that many of the people had not the rudiments of education in that they could not write or spell, but that the desire for learning and knowledge of literature was most pronounced. Every poem or essay as it appeared in print was criticised with acumen and delight, and when it appeared in a form too dear to purchase it was copied by someone and circulated in manuscript form. These libraries eventually passed away with the famine and the growth of city and industrial life in Ulster which led to the denudation of the rural population.

One of the most famous and enduring of the subscription libraries was that founded by the Belfast Reading Society on 13 May 1788, later re-named the Belfast Library and Society for Promoting Knowledge. The active merchant class of Belfast as well as doctors and lawyers gave generous support to philanthropic societies such as the Literary Society, the Belfast Reading Society and the Belfast Academical Institution, but there was already in the city a strong tradition of a library provided by 'the worthy plebeians of the town', and this may have been absorbed into the Society. As in Dublin the early meetings of the Society were held in the congenial atmosphere of local taverns such as Ireland's, Brown's or the Donegall Arms, each member being allowed to drink threepennyworth and no more. However the endroit of the tavern was discarded as soon as more suitable accommodation could be found.

The first objective of the Belfast Reading Society was the formation of a library which was to remain for ever the sole and undivided property of the whole Society and which therefore could not be disposed of unless by the unanimous vote of all the members.

Forty-five members, predominantly Presbyterian, signed the original rules of the Society, but Catholics were not excluded from membership. The subscription was one shilling a month, and the Society was to be managed by a committee of five, although this was later increased. Interestingly, one of the early rules which enabled the funds to be kept healthy was 'that a British shilling be paid by every member of the committee who shall be absent from any meeting of the Society'. This rule was strictly enforced. A candidate for membership could be excluded by 'six black beans' but every candidate had to be known to one or more of the regular members or come with strong recommendation from a person in whom the Society could place confidence.

Over the next few years the committee established an entrance fee of two guineas. Sometimes the entrance fee was waived on presentation to the Society of suitable works, on receipt of which the reader was given individual property rights in the Society. The management of the Society allowed lady members from the outset, as also did the Cork Subscription Library. The Dublin Library Society and the Kilkenny Library Society seem to have been all male establishments and not to have had such as enlightened attitude towardss the fairer sex. The library however was not intended for the reading of novels and the selection was to exclude 'any common novel, or farce, or other book of trivial amusement'. Book selection was done by the committee, with the secretary being given the power to purchase agreed titles.

At first only books in the English language were brought but this restriction was quickly rescinded. Books were to be acquired in Belfast if possible, or through Belfast booksellers. However, in 1812, complaints about delays in book supply led to orders being placed with Messrs Gilbert and Hodges of Dame Street, Dublin. This later changed as complaints were received of delays of up to three months in delivery and this time Morgan Yellett of Belfast procured the business.

The Society remained quite small at the beginning with only 89 members in 1789, but among these were some of the most eminent men in Belfast. In 1801 the Society was offered accommodation over the central hall of the Linen Hall, from which it acquired the unofficial title by which it is known today – the Linen Hall Library. It moved there in 1802 and remained until 1896 when it moved to a converted linen warehouse in Donegall Square North. Some of the early purchases indicate the intentions of the founding members to establish a worthwhile collection of reference books. Amongst the titles are Johnson's *Lives of the poets*, Pope's *Works*, Hume's and Smollett's *History of England*, Cook's *Voyages*, Gillie's *History of*

*Greece*, the Transactions of the Royal Society of London, the Transactions of the Royal Irish Academy, the Transactions of the Bath and Manchester Societies, of the Edinburgh Philosophical Society and the Royal Society of Edinburgh.

Art as well as literature occupied the thoughts of the members and in 1792 the secretary corresponded with Alderman Boydell of London asking advice about collecting books on the fine arts. In his reply the Alderman sent the Society an album containing 100 prints drawn and engraved by himself.

In 1794 £50 was remitted to London for the printing of the Irish music collected by Mr Bunting. Bunting had been employed to record the music of ten Ulster harpers at a festival organised by four members of the Society, in an effort to preserve from oblivion the few fragments of Irish music that remained. Supported by Dr James MacDonell, Bunting toured the north and west of Ireland collecting music that would have otherwise been lost. The Society was also keen to acquire and preserve books in Irish, and through the *Northern Star*, published in 1795 *Bolg an tSolair*, the first magazine in the Irish language ever produced in Ireland.

The first librarian was Thomas Russell, appointed in 1794, who hailed from Co. Cork. Russell was not only a radical but a founder of the United Irishmen which was set up to create a community devoid of religious rancour and a Parliamentary system representative of all the Irish people. As such it attracted not only Roman Catholics but the Presbyterian merchants who resented the indignities under which they had to labour. It was therefore not out of character that Russell should be appointed to this post and the committee, for example, unanimously supported Catholic emancipation. During the troubles which led to the rebellion of 1798 Russell was arrested and eventually executed in 1803.

With the establishment of the Queen's University of Belfast in 1849 the Society put its library at the disposal of the professors and students who were given free access to the books, pamphlets, journals and newspapers, but even so the Society began to decline after 1862. Subscribers fell off because of the difficulty in obtaining new books, the lack of popular literature, and the library was not sufficiently well-known to the public. To offset this problem the committee was empowered in 1863 to borrow books from the London Library Company, £7.15s. being allocated to obtain thirty books a year. However, this arrangement was evidently not satisfactory and in 1865 the subscription was placed with Mudie's Circulating Library at a cost of fourteen guineas. Mudie's subscription was discontinued in 1873 when the committee allocated £35 per annum to buy their own light literature, and by 1876 the library had more than 17,000 books.

The Committee also formed a small collection of early printed books, especially those printed in Belfast, and by 1886 the Society had produced a catalogue of Early Belfast Printed Books printed prior to 1751 and by 1887 a second volume had been produced taking the work up to 1830.

At the time of the possibility of adopting the Public Libraries Act it was mooted that the library should hand over its books to the Town Council in order to provide a public library at no cost to the ratepayers. This idea was however firmly quashed as the Society felt that there was room for both a public library and the Society Library. In 1885 under the Educational Endowment Act the Belfast Society for Promoting Knowledge ceased to be a private club for its members and under the law the Society held its assets 'upon trust for the promotionof knowledge in the city of Belfast and its neighbourhood by the maintenance of a library and by other such means as the Society from time to time deem it advisable to adopt'.

Since 1968 the Library has collected the political ephemeral material associated with the latest troubles in Northern Ireland. Much of this leaflet and pamphlet material has been run off on small presses and distributed on street corners – material that can all too easily be lost to posterity.

The Library has not escaped the bombing campaign in Belfast and its bookstore was damaged when the shop next to it was bombed. Losses were put at about 1,500 non-fiction books and about 8,000 fiction, much of it being late Victorian and early Edwardian material and some being of Irish interest.

The Library remains a subscription library. The membership fee in 1982 was £15 but severe financial problems are being experienced as the subscription income is less than double what it was in 1970 yet the running costs have trebled. In addition the fabric of the building is now in desperate need of repair. Membership stands at over 1,700 but to survive the Library must aim for a target of 3,000 members. Its stock is now about 200,000 volumes with a particularly valuable collection on Ireland, including the special collections of early Belfast printed books and a vast section on Irish history, literature and art, local studies and family history. It is specially rich in Ulster material.

Following a recommendation in the Hawnt Report of 1964 support was received from the Department of Education in the 1970s in the form of an annual grant but the Department indicated that this grant would not be renewed unless the Library could substantially increase income from within its own resources. Real efforts have been made to tackle the serious financial situation including a membership drive, introducing a corporate membership, covenanted donations, and the sale of some lesser used items, including the disposal of a collection of paintings by William Connor to the Ulster Folk and Transport Museum. The Library has also produced a series of prints for publication and has received an annual grant from the Belfast City Council. If the Library can survive until 1985 its financial situation will be considerably eased as leases on property which it owns will expire and thus create the opportunity to obtain higher rents.

In Cork in 1803 was founded the Cork Institution by the Revd. Thomas Dix Hincks of the Old Presbyterian Church in Princes Street. This institution gradually became the centre of the intellectual and cultural life of the city, and was the pioneer of adult education in the city of Cork, one of its stated aims being to lay the foundations for a university. It gathered together an extensive library which was particularly strong in medicine and law. Although founded by a Presbyterian minister the Institution was representative of all shades of religious belief.

Thomas Dix Hincks was a man who believed in religious liberty and he was a supporter of Catholic emancipation. Quakers, Dissenters, Catholics and Protestants all supported the Cork Institution. Hincks had earlier ran a school when he first arrived in Cork in 1790, pupils being accepted for fees of four guineas a quarter. The early lectures of the Cork Institution were based on his school lectures. By 1806 thirty gentlemen associated themselves with Hincks and the funds for the purchase of apparatus which had been secured by a subscription of ten guineas had grown to £2,200. On 20 March 1807 the Society received a Royal Charter of Incorporation and a grant which was afterwards increased to £2,500 annually. From this time the Royal Cork Institution modelled itself on the Royal Institution in London with the proprietors each paying an annual subscription of thirty guineas, and thirty managers being chosen from amongst them to administer the everyday affairs of the Society. Obtaining the grant from the government was a major achievement at a time when government investment in formal and adult education was virtually unknown.

The Institution was first housed in premises on the South Mall but later, thanks to government support, more permanent premises were obtained in the Old Custom House. In a report of 1808 it was stated of the library that there were few valuable works on chemistry, natural philosophy, mineralogy, botany or agriculture that were not available in it. A librarian had been appointed, a Mr P. Carey at a salary of £40 per annum, and there was a library committee of seven members. Later Richard Dowden the well-known nineteenth century philanthropist became the librarian as well as secretary to the Cork Mechanics' Institution.

The good work of the Cork Institution was threatened when the Parliamentary Commission of Enquiry into Education in Ireland issued its report in 1828. When the Commission reported it recommended the withdrawal of public funds from institutions and the establishment of a national educational system under the control of the state. This move affected the Royal Cork Institution adversely as the annual grant was withdrawn in 1831 as a result, and the Institution had to decide whether to carry on or to disband. It chose to carry on despite grave financial problems, and an indication of these difficulties is that the Ballyphehane site for the Botanical Gardens which they had bought in 1809 had to be sold in 1828 when it was acquired by Father Matthew of temperance fame, and became the first Catholic cemetery in modern times for the city of Cork.

In 1826 a request was received from Dr Lardner to use the library of the Royal Cork Institution during the course of lectures he was giving at the Cork Mechanics' Institute. The Mechanics' Institute was used by a different class of men than the more genteel users of the Royal Cork Institution, but the committee resolved that Dr Lardner could make use of the library during the course of lectures at the discretion of the secretary. By 1861 the Royal Cork Institution ceased to be the principal centre of learning in Cork, its place being taken by Queen's College Cork.

The Cork Institution was still flourishing in 1875 when it was reported that the library was extensive, consisting principally of scientific works, together with the proceedings of all the scientific societies of the world, a collection of over 400 oriental manuscripts collected in India, and a special room fitted out to contain the records of patents taken out in Great Britain, the United States and Canada. In addition it had a museum with a select collection of Egyptian, Irish, Indian and Chinese antiquities, as well as lecture and reading rooms.

Although no definite account of the fate of the library is available it is possible that many of the books went to the library of Queen's College, Cork. Dr Richard Caulfield became the librarian of the Institution in 1862, residing on the premises until his death in 1887. Dr Caulfield was also appointed librarian of Queen's College in 1878 and so was a direct link between the two organisations. It is also possible that parts of the library went towards forming the first Cork Municipal Library, as well as to the Crawford School of Art, both of which had made use of the premises formerly occupied by the Royal Cork Institution.

Still in Cork the Cork Subscription Library had its beginning as far back as 1792 when it was formed by a group of merchants. There can be little doubt that the Cork Library was the focal point of the brightest in the city, and that the intelligentsia were closely associated with it from its inception. The Cork Library with its commodious reading rooms and conveniently placed premises, first in Cook Street and later in the South Mall, catered successfully throughout a long period for the reading wants of many generations of Cork men and women. The Society was run by a committee chosen from among the subscribers. The earliest catalogue now extant is for 1801 and it forms a small octavo volume of 31 pages. It is prefixed by a list of subscribers which at that time comprised 143 ordinary members and eight life members. The library collection was not very extensive, consisting of 627 items. The majority of these were on history, antiquities and geography, closely followed by belles lettres, poetry and criticism. But there were quite a number of volumes on medicine, chemistry and the sciences generally. There were only 25 novels and romances.

No periodicals or newspapers are specified in the catalogue. Some of the material is early Cork printing including Leland's *History of Ireland* 1775, and Sir John Temple's *Civil Wars* 1766. The earliest printed book in the collection was an Irish dictionary compiled by McCurtin in 1732.

By 1820 the library membership had risen to 385, including five women. The collection had grown to over 2,000 items. Most of the books were published in London, but there were some printed in Dublin as well as a few European publications. A list of what is called Prohibited Books in the catalogue of 1820 is not quite as exciting as it sounds but merely means books not to be taken out of the library, or reference books of which there were 190.

Donations had been received from the Revd T.D. Hincks, among others. In fact there must have been cross-fertilisation of ideas for quite a few of the names which appear in connection with the Royal Cork Institution re-appear and are mentioned in the membership list of the Cork Library. Among these were Dr Charles Daly, N. Mahon and A. Lane, who were committee members for both the Cork Library Society and the Royal Cork Institution.

Would-be members of the Society had to be proposed by one member and have their names posted up in the library for five consecutive days. The applicant's name was then balloted for at the next committee meeting and if the majority voted for him he was allowed to join on signing the rules of the Society. The admission fee was half a guinea and the annual subscription one guinea. Lady applicants did not suffer the exposure of having their names posted in the library: instead they were recorded in a book specially provided for that purpose. Members who were three months late with their subscriptions automatically lost their membership. Interestingly a clause was added to this rule which stated 'unless he or she be absent from the country at the time in which case on paying up such persons shall regain the privileges of a member'. There was obviously a general expectation that people of this class would not be in Ireland for the entire year, and some of them may well have been absentee landlords or may simply have gone to London or to the spas for the season.

A ledger was kept in which requests were noted for books which were out in circulation. Once the book was returned it was delivered to the requesters in order of their applications, and only if a book was not requested would it be allowed out again to the same reader. Members lending Society books to non-members risks expulsion from the Society. A ledger was also kept for suggested additions to the library.

Fines for overdue books appear prohibitive. Any book detained beyond its time was charged at a rate of tenpence for every day the book was overdue. Five shillings was charged if someone borrowed a book without the knowledge of the librarian. Those members who refused to pay their fines were expelled.

In Guy's *Directory of Cork* for 1875-76 the library is listed as having more than 20,000 works on general literature together with some valuable books of reference. It is stated that a large number of newspapers and periodicals were also taken and that the reading room was spacious and well-kept. The subscription was still one guinea at that time.

By 1905 the restrictive membership rules together with the entrance fee had long been swept away. The stock was then listed as not less than 15,000 volumes which seems surprising given the number reported in the 1875-76 *Directory of Cork*. The Cork Library functioned until 1941 when its stock, then consisting only of some 4,000 volumes, was auctioned in 400 lots. Cork also had a Philosophical and Literary Society founded in 1819 which had similar ideals to those of the Institution. It failed after one year but was immediately replaced by the Cork Scientific and Literary Society.

Another group of gentlemen gathered together in Limerick to form the Limerick Institution in 1809. McGregor in his *History of the County and City of Limerick*, published in 1827, writes that Limerick numbered more than three hundred families of the gentry and that the city 'exhibits no ordinary ardour in literary pursuits!' There were two or three respectable booksellers' shops where works in the various departments of literature could be purchased, and perhaps another eight to ten more for the sale of books and school utensils.

The formation of the Limerick Institution which in reality was a subscription library was brought about by some public spirited citizens who desired to raise the character of the city by its formation. The library was originally at the house of Mr. Brien O'Brien, a bookseller in St. George's Street, and was started by each gentleman taking shares in the Institution at five guineas each. A respectable library was thus formed which was increased in size by the members' annual subscriptions of one and a half guineas each. The library was later removed to the house of Mr Seward at the corner of Glenworth Street. It was open from 10 a.m. to 4 p.m. daily.

This move was echoed in the city of Kilkenny where at a meeting of a number of gentlemen of the county and city held on 6 April 1811 at the Thosel it was unanimously resolved that the establishment of a library in the city of Kilkenny would be a highly useful and desirable achievement. Each proprietor was to pay twenty guineas which entitled him to a share in the library, the share money being paid by four successive half yearly subscriptions. Later in 1812 it was decided to insert the following into the title 'Founded as a permanent library of reference for the use of Kilkenny and its vicinity for the diffusion of scientific and literary knowledge'. As usual, a cursory glance at the committee of the Kilkenny Library Society shows a preponderance of the gentry and is littered with barristers, attorneys, architects, doctors and Church of Ireland clergymen. The Kilkenny Library Society appeared to have been pro-Union, judging from an attack on it in the press of 1812.

The committee, which consisted of the president plus four vice-presidents and eighteen members, was to be concerned with all management of the library and one of its first tasks was to compile a list of books suitable for purchase. The list included Bewick's *British birds and quadrupeds*; *Farming and husbandry*; Locke's *Essays*; Gibbon's *Decline and fall of the Roman Empire*; Ledwich's *Antiquities of Ireland*; Plutarch's *Lives*; Tighe's *Statistical view of the County of Kilkenny*; Scott's *Poems*; The *Letters of Junius*; all Dr Johnson's works, and various travel books. In all the committee selected 81 items though many of these would be in several volumes. The cost of the first batch of books came to £154.4s.4d. for 90 books which did not include the Bewick.

Two hundred copies of the rules and regulations were published in 1811 indicating the number of subscribers the Society hoped it would attract, (see Figure 5.1). According to the rules the property was vested in ten trustees. Persons wishing to use the library had to be recommended by five proprietors, two of whom had to be members of the committee, and new members were expected to pay

## FIGURE 5.1   LAWS AND REGULATIONS
## OF THE KILKENNY LIBRARY SOCIETY 1811

*Regulations were unanimously adopted and Ordered to stand as the fundamental Laws of the Institution —*

# Laws and Regulations
### for the Government of the
## Kilkenny Library Society

It is agreed that the Property of said Society shall consist of 175 Shares of 20 Guineas each, to be paid to Treasurer by four Successive half yearly installments of five Guineas, commencing on the 29th day of September 1811, and that the holders of such Shares shall be Vested the exclusive Property of said Society and all Dominion over the same; and that such Society shall be called the Kilkenny Library Society —

That the property of said Society shall be Vested in Ten Trustees, to be named by the Proprietors at a General meeting and as soon as the Ten Trustees so to be named, shall be by any means decreased to five, then at the general half yearly meeting of the Proprietors next following, five other Trustees being Proprietors shall be appointed in addition to the remaining five, and this regulation shall be always observed for the purpose of perpetuating the Trust —

That each proprietor shall be at Liberty to transfer or bequeath his Share provided the person to whom the same is transferred or bequeathed, assent to and sign the Laws of the Institution; each Share shall be deemed personal property, and transferable and Divisable as such —

That no Person shall be allowed to Vote on any Occasion but a proprietor nor by Proxy, nor be entitled to more than one Vote whatever number of Shares he may hold —

That the mode of transferring Shares shall be regulated by the Committee hereafter mentioned, and That no person shall ever be deemed a Proprietor until his Title shall be admitted by the Committee, and that the Title of Legatee or representative of any deceased proprietor, and also the transfer of every share, shall immediately be entered by the Secretary and Librarian, in a Book by him to be Kept for that purpose, and for the making of which entry he shall be entitled to a fee of 2. 6 —

That every proprietor shall pay one Guinea Subscription annually in advance a subscription of two guineas.

Initially the Mayor of Kilkenny was designated the President of the Library Society and could introduce as many of his friends as he liked to the library. This was no doubt a convenient measure since the corporation of the city of Kilkenny provided the Society with the use of rooms in the Thosel, and William Kingsmill, a member of a family of high Protestant pretensions and a popular magistrate who manifested great kindnesses towards the humbler classes, was the mayor. If William Kingsmill was not the mayor then another member of the family was, so much so that they seemed to regard this office as a family perquisite. Kingsmill was described by Hogan in his history of Kilkenny as a 'soft good-natured slob!'

At this time the library was intended for reference only. There were two rooms in the Thosel, one for the purpose of reading and the other for conversation, no conversation being allowed in the reading room. This regulation had to be reinforced according to an entry in the ledger records on 14 March 1812 when 'the former regulation of preserving the silence in the reading room be particularly attended to by the librarian'. Obviously some members must have complained of the noise of others and the usual flow of conversation inherent wherever Irishmen gather together!

The duties of the librarian are worth close perusal. The first librarian, Felix Byrne, was appointed on 20 April 1811 at the generous annual salary of £50. For this he appears to have acted more as a caretaker than as a librarian, except that he was expected to make two copies of an inventory of the books every half year. At these times, 21 March and 25 September, the committee examined the condition and number of all the books, manuscripts, prints and magazines which had been committed to the charge of the librarian. If any books or other properties were found to be damaged or not forthcoming the librarian was expected to make good the loss out of his own salary, unless he could give the names of the persons who had caused the damage or losses.

This was no idle threat, and at a time when books could cost from 2s.6d. to £22.15s. it was a rule that was calculated to keep the librarian on his toes. In fact an entry in the records for 1819 shows that the librarian was indeed charged for fifteen missing books. As the library was for reference only the librarian could not allow any book to go out on loan on penalty of his removal from office and ineligibility for future posts. Neither was he allowed to permit any gentleman to remove a book from the bookcases, but he was expected to hand it to them and make a note of the book and to whom it had been given. The librarian also had to report to the committee by entering in the memorandum book any and every infraction of the rules of the Institution, and the names of the persons infringing them under penalty of losing his situation. A catalogue was also to be prepared and laid on the table for the use of members of the Society. Among the librarian's other duties he was also expected to act as the secretary to the Society.

At the same time as the librarian was appointed a Joseph Cottrell was made porter. His salary was £18.5s. of which £10 was paid by the corporation. His duties involved attending the library rooms at the Thosel at such times as they were open and on ball nights until the rooms were cleared and shut up. He had to sweep and clear out the rooms every day, to make up the fires and keep them going while the rooms were in use, and he was also accountable for the fuel entrusted to his care. Another responsibility was to ensure that the candles were clean and in readiness for use. He also acted as doorman ensuring that no one entered the library rooms if they were not so entitled. He also had to gather the newspapers up and lodge them with the librarian.

Journals bought for the opening of the library were the following: *Courier, Correspondent, Patriot, Dublin Evening Post, Edinburgh Review, Quarterly Review, Annual Register, Philosophic Magazine, Repository of the Arts, Munster Farmers' Magazine, Monthly Review* and the *Gentleman's Magazine*. It is interesting to note that the two local newspapers produced in Kilkenny at this time do not appear on the list. These, the *Kilkenny Moderator* and the *Leinster Journal* were both printed in the High Street, Kilkenny. Tantalisingly, no criteria are listed in the records of the Society which can explain why certain newspapers were bought and others not.

Over the next few years the library stock grew apace, 465 volumes being added in 1813. By September 1815 the stock is reported as being 1,860 volumes, with 306 numbers of periodicals. In 1816 the number of volumes had risen to 2,203. This represented a very healthy growth in stock, but the library was not passing through easy times. The high esteem of the library is evident in a report of 1813 which stated:

> The number of readers amongst the youth of our city has increased since the last general meeting and we are encouraged to hope not only that there will be an increase of knowledge in the various branches of science and literature amongst those who at present enjoy the benefits of it but that information now received will be transmitted with increasing light to posterity so that future generations will look back upon this institution as one decidedly and admirably calculated to promote them.

Indeed the young received special privileges as any proprietor having paid his subscription could nominate any one youth under the age of 21 to use the library free of charge.

At the same time as these admirable statements were being issued the Society came under what it described as wanton and unprovoked attacks through the medium of the press. The committee lamented exceedingly that an institution that had made such rapid progress in the public estimation should be subject to any attempt which might check its growth. But, as the report goes on, 'secure in its intrinsic merit and steady adherence of its friends the Kilkenny Library will withstand the shock of its foes and outlive the vulgarity, prejudice and misrepresentation'. The Committee expressed its sorrow that any spirit should arise within their walls hostile to the Union.

Despite what appears to have been political hostility the Kilkenny Library did survive, but in a very few years it had run into financial trouble which is expressed in the minutes, when all kinds of economies were to be sought and observed in managing the financial concerns of the Society. Despite the restrictions under which he worked the librarian obviously valued his job and volunteered to take a cut of £5 in his salary. This was accepted, but as the economies were not proving effective the librarian's salary was again reduced in 1818 to £40 a year and the porter's wages reduced to a mere £10 a year. This probably represented the contribution paid by the corporation.

Why the Society should have found itself in financial trouble so quickly can only be a matter of conjecture. In 1812 the Society had an annual income of £150 which had risen in 1815 to over £187. The expenditure for the year was £169.19s.6d. none of which was spent on books. Out of this was paid the librarian's salary of £50 and a part of the porter's wages. Other expenditure must have included candles, kindling and coals or turf for the fires, but probably the major commitment was the cost of subscribing to newspapers and periodicals which were far from cheap at this period. The committee desperately tried to consider ways of making the library more useful and attracting more members by opening it to students of the literary and learned professions. This was countered in committee by a proposal to sell the library stock, valued at £409 and use the money for the relief of the poor. At the same time the committee came under pressure to lend books.

In the event salvation appeared in the form of a bequest from Alderman Joseph Evans. Joseph Evans of Belevans was descended from a Thomas Evans who had received large grants of lands in the liberties of Kilkenny and who had settled there at the end of the Civil War. Joseph died unmarried and by his will left his properties in trust to found a charitable institution known as the Evans Charity.

Other organisations to benefit from this extraordinary generosity, besides the Kilkenny Library Society, were the Charitable and Benevolent Society, the Dispensary, the Fever Hospital, the Penny Society, the Savings Bank, the Lees Lane Poor House and the Parochial School in King Street.

The receipt of the Evans Bequest enabled the Kilkenny Library Society to establish a circulating library which came into operation on 15 September 1820. The Trustees of the Charity of Joseph Evans are set out in an Act of Parliament dated July 2, 1819. These included the Dean of Ossory, the Mayor of the city, the Recorder, the High Sheriff of the Courts, and the Minister of the Parish of St. Mary in the city and the Vicar of the Parish of St. John in the city. Given the positions these men held it seems an extraordinary chain of events that began to unravel over the next fifty years. The money from the bequest saved the Library Society from financial collapse with a payment of £150 on 8 August 1820 and annual payments of £100 at later stages. Generously the librarian's salary was immediately raised to £50 in 1821. A Mr Leech was then the librarian. By the time the next librarian Mr Ryan was appointed the salary had again been reduced to £40 per annum in 1846 and the Library Society was owed £850 by the Evans Trust. The other beneficiaries of the Trust requested a meeting with the Kilkenny Library Society in October 1846 to consider jointly whether they should prosecute the Evans Trust. A total of £10,000 was now due to the charities and it did not appear to be forthcoming from the Trustees.

The finances of the Society were again in a dire state and the library was forced to discontinue some newspapers, among them *The Nation*, probably one of the most popular ever Irish newspapers, and to sell back runs of others in order to raise money. Still little money was being received from the fund, only £51.17s. in 1858, and they placed the matter in the hands of solicitors to see if they had to accept such a small sum. An order was made in their favour by the Lord Chancellor on 7 June 1858, and they immediately renewed the library's subscription to *The Nation*. The Trustees still owed the Library Society £1,605.7s.6d. and poor Mr Ryan's salary had been reduced to a mere £15 per annum for which he seemed to be working harder than ever as he also attended the Young Men's Society in Kilkenny to take charge of a class two or three times a week after he had finished his library duty at 8 p.m.

The Trustees, however, disclaimed all responsibility for the non-payment of funds and in their turn took proceedings against the Bank of Ireland. The position took a turn for the better with some funds being made available but the situation was so bad that when the long-suffering and loyal Mr Ryan died in 1866, to save him the indignity of a pauper's burial, the committee decided the least they could do was to make the funeral arrangements and to pay for his burial.

The next librarian was a Mr J. Power who was paid a salary of £30 a year, given firing and candles, and allowed to reside on the library premises, which from 14 April 1831 had been housed in the Coal Market, which the Society had purchased. The situation with the Trustees was never satisfactorily resolved as by 1869 the committee again had extreme difficulty extracting the bequest from the administrators of the fund. The property in the Coal Market had to be given up and some rooms in the Thosel were again rented at a peppercorn rent of one shilling a year. From then on the history of the library is one of moves to and from temporary rented properties, which included the Kilkenny Club and a house on St. John's Quay rented in 1893 for £20 per annum. In 1885 a deputation had been formed to ask the Trustees of the Evans Charity to investigate the position of the fund and the reasons for the falling off in the annuity paid to the Society.

The problems of the Society which had survived the vicissitudes of lack of adequate support and the mismanagement of the funds to which they were rightly entitled came to an end in 1911 when at a special meeting of the Kilkenny Library Society on March 14 the following resolutions were adopted:

1  That the Secretary of the Society be authorised to take steps to terminate the tenancy of the house at St. John's Quay in which the books are currently kept.

2  The Society shall in future rent a room in the Carnegie Free Library from the Kilkenny Cooperative and shall keep their books there, and that an agreement be reached between the Society and the Cooperative for carrying out this arrangement.

Earlier in 1904 when the Corporation had decided to start a Free Library an approach had been made to the Kilkenny Library Society. It had been decided that the books belonging to the Society were to be kept separately in a room in the Kilkenny Library and that the Kilkenny Library Society had to be kept alive in order to be entitled to the grant, such as it was, from the Charities of Joseph Evans.

In 1908 when the Corporation proposed to start building a Free Library at St. John's Quay, Mr O'Connell, the Town Clerk, suggested an amalgamation with the Cooperative and a transfer of the Evans Trust grant to the Corporation as in this way it would be

# FIGURE 5.2 NOTICE OF THE KILKENNY LIBRARY SOCIETY 1868

## KILKENNY LIBRARY SOCIETY.

GENTLEMEN,

In compliance with your instructions, and Resolutions carried at the Meetings held at the Tholsel, on the 2nd and 5th March Instant (the Mayor in the Chair), we have to report that we have examined into the Accounts and General State of this Society since the 21st March last, when the Accounts of the Society appear to have been audited. At that period a balance of £4 19s. 7d appears to have been placed to the credit of the Society; this sum, together with a sum of £1 1s. 0d., the Subscription of Dr. Kinchela, was carried forward and paid over to Mr. Michael Potter for his Salary up to 14th May, 1867, and a Pound additional on account of Salary due on 14th June, 1867. This appears to have closed the Account, and left no Assets at the disposal of the Society.

We find the Liabilities of the Society as follows:—

| | £ s. d. | £ s. d. |
|---|---|---|
| Smith & Son, Stamped Newspapers, to 31st March, 1867, ... ... | 9 0 0 | |
| Mr. Prim, "Moderator," to 1st January, 1868, ... ... | 1 6 0 | |
| Mrs. Maxwell, to 21st August, 1867, ... ... | 1 0 7 | |
| Mr. W. Nicholson, Newspapers, &c., to 30th September, 1867, | 16 4 9 | |
| Messrs. Coyle Brothers, Magazines, &c., to June, 1867, ... | 5 1 5 | |
| "Cork Examiner," to March, 1867, ... ... | 1 5 0 | |
| Kilkenny Gas Company, to 1st July, 1867, ... ... | 4 18 11 | |
| Grand Jury Cess, Summer Assizes, 1867, ... ... | 1 12 0 | |
| John Hogan's Account, ... ... | 0 5 6 | |
| Other small Miscellaneous Accounts, ... ... | 0 16 0 | |
| Mrs. Brenan, One Year's Rent, to 29th September, 1867, less Poor Rates,... | 28 0 0 | |
| Mr. Michael Potter, Salary, and all other Claims whatsoever up to this date, | 16 14 6 | |
| Total Liabilities ... ... ... | ... | 86 5 8 |

### MONIES DUE TO THE SOCIETY.

| | £ s. d. | £ s. d. |
|---|---|---|
| Trustees of the late Joseph Evans, now in Bank, ... ... | 59 9 5 | |
| George W. Kinchela, One Year's Rent, to 29th Sept, 1867, less Poor Rates | 11 2 0 | |
| Trustees of the late Joseph Evans, now due, ... ... | 59 9 5 | |
| | | 130 0 10 |
| Leaving to credit of Society ... ... | ... | 43 15 2 |

The Subscriptions of the Proprietors are now due; and we recommend that all the Proprietors be requested to pay a Half Year's Subscription in advance on 25th March Instant—amount 10s. 6d each—which would pay up to 29th September next.

We further recommend that a Meeting of the General Proprietors be called on 25th March Instant, for the purpose of electing a Librarian (at a Salary not exceeding £20 per annum), Trustees and Committees of the Society, when the Monies due to the Society should be applied for, and the above Liabilities discharged.

WILLIAM KEALY.
JOHN FEEHAN.
P. McDERMOTT.

Dated this 11th day of March, 1868.

Adopted at a Meeting held at the Tholsel 11th March, 1868:—

"A General Meeting of the Proprietors will be held at the Library Rooms, Parliament-street, on 25th March Instant, at One o'Clock in the Afternoon, to elect a Librarian, Trustees and Committees.

W. O'DONNELL, Mayor, President of the Society.

worth far more to the citizens of Kilkenny. This arrangement was eventually agreed to and on 4 December 1911 the Kilkenny Library Society handed over its collection to the Carnegie Free Library. They resolved that £10 be paid to the Free Library for the caretaking of the Kilkenny Library Society rooms from the date of the opening of the Free Library and that a sum of money be paid to the Carnegie Free Library for the purchase of books for the Society. Thus, after a chequered existence of exactly one hundred years the Society ceased to exist as a separate organisation and was taken under the umbrella of the public library.

# 6 University libraries and the National Library

Trinity College Dublin was founded in 1591 by Queen Elizabeth I and the first library dates from a time almost immediately after that date. In 1600 only 30 books and 10 manuscripts were listed but by 1604 the library had nearly 5,000 volumes.

The library of James Ussher was eventually given to Trinity via the circuitous route described earlier in this book and by courtesy of Henry Cromwell. The library at Trinity continued to grow mainly through donations, notably from the Countess of Bath, Sir Jerome Alexander and Provost Henry Huntingdon. Although the College was occupied by troops in 1689 the library was not damaged. The College received a grant from Queen Anne of £5,000 for the building of a new library in 1712 when the foundation stone of the Long Room was laid. The building was completed in 1732 and ready for occupation in 1734. The library at that time was a work of great vision and enterprise due mainly to the driving force of George Berkeley, the philosopher, who had been appointed librarian. He found the library bulging at the seams in its old quarters over the scholar's rooms, not only overflowing but damp, musty and the books in terrible disorder.

The new library was designed by Thomas Burgh who modelled the Trinity building on Wren's library at Trinity College, Cambridge. The two outstanding features of the building were that the books were to be housed on an upper floor which was raised over a colonnade to avoid damp from the waters of the Liffey which in those days came up to the walls of the College. The building was approached at one end by a grand staircase at the top of which was the Long Room 209 feet long and 40 feet wide. The main area of the Long Room would have been clear of furniture and used as a promenade and the library for those of graduate status only. No fires or lights were available for fear of setting the library on fire. This accommodation was adequate until the 1850s when the roof of the Long Room was raised.

Since 1801 Trinity College has been a copyright library entitled to receive all British publications and this right has continued since independence with an average of 35,000 additions being received annually in this way. The 1801 Act, made at the time of the Union, also added the King's Inns, Dublin to the list of libraries entitled to receive free copies but this right ceased in 1836, with Trinity remaining one of the copyright libraries. The Industrial and Commercial Property (Protection) Act of the Irish Free State 1927 and the Copyright Act 1963 have ensured that the copyright privilege has continued in respect of books published in Ireland.

The alterations to the building were sufficient until 1890 when the colonnades were enclosed with half the space being used for storage and the rest for a reading room. This proved adequate for some considerable time but plans went ahead to erect a separate reading room prior to the store becoming full. By 1937 the new reading room was completed and the remainder of the colonnade converted into a book store. In 1957 the manuscripts were removed from the manuscripts room in the old library and moved to a stone pavilion in the Fellows' Garden which had been refitted to house them. The space thus released in the old library provided additional office and workroom accommodation. By this time the library contained some 850,000 books and 5,000 manuscripts and again threatened to outgrow the space available, particularly as the library was active in asserting its right to legal deposit. Overcrowding became a real problem and affected the efficiency of the library. Periodicals were housed in the basement and maps were kept in the cellars underneath the chapel. Working space for the staff was practically non-existent. Materials not frequently asked for were housed in an attic at the other end of the College and even when located had to be taken to the separate reading room outside the library. With these problems in mind an appeal was launched in 1958 to raise money to build a new library which would provide an administrative centre, storage space, a large reading room, special rooms for research workers, a staff reading room and a bindery.

Trinity College did not have the means to finance this enterprise itself as it received only one-third of its income from government grants, unlike other universities in the British Isles which received about 73 per cent of their income in this way. Another third of Trinity income is from endowments and the remaining third from fees. Payment for a new library from capital funds would have crippled the service. Though short of money, the government was sympathetic and agreed to contribute on a pound for pound basis to the appeal for the new building. The money was raised through generous support from many directions, including the Ford Foundation which gave £100,000, the family of the then Chancellor, Lord Iveagh, gave £50,000, and Mr Jack Morrison £30,000. The Trinity College Dublin Endowment Fund and the graduates contributed £65,000, various trusts and similar organisations gave £35,000, and Irish firms contributed, by covenant, over £20,000.

In 1960 an international architectural competition was held which

121

attracted over 200 entries from all over the world. The winning design came from the architect Paul Koralek who produced a building which, while being modern, harmonises with the older buildings around it. The new library, now known as the Berkeley Library, was opened by Eamon de Valera, the President of Ireland, on 12 July 1967. The building consists of a basement bookstack, ground floor with administrative and staff rooms, catalogue and reference rooms, with the first and second floors being used as reading rooms (one of which is the Morrison Reading Room), and open access book storage areas. The library has space for 500 readers and over 800,000 books. The main information desk is in Iveagh Hall, and the building is linked to the Old Library by an underground passage.

The Old Library had the interior of its East Pavilion altered in 1967 to house a library shop with the Department of Older Printed Books above it. The interior of the West Pavilion was re-designed in 1971 and now houses the Department of Manuscripts and the Conservation Laboratory. Even this addition of space was not adequate and the Lecky Library, housed on the upper and lower ground floors of the Arts and Sciences building was opened in 1978 for the use of the growing number of undergraduates.

The library was fortunate during the nineteenth century to have as librarians men who were able to rescue the library from earlier neglect. J. Henthorn Todd, the antiquary, was appointed librarian in 1852. He is listed in the *Dictionary of National Biography* which said of him: 'No man in Ireland since Archbishop Ussher has shown equal skill in bibliography ... or devotion to the development of Irish literature'. It was under his care with the help of John O'Donovan and Eugene O'Curry that the books and manuscripts in Trinity's library were arranged and classified with many of its riches being brought to light. John Kells Ingram was in charge of the library from 1879 to 1887 and served as President of The Library Association in 1884.

No entry about Trinity College Library would be complete without reference to the Fagel Collection of some 20,000 books and manuscripts bought for the library in 1802 for £9,000. Greffier Fagel was Pensionary or Chief Minister of Holland and came from a family of distinguished scholars and statesmen. The collection contained books in nearly all branches of European literature and science, but was also strong in history and politics. William Palliser, Archbishop of Cashel, bequeathed 4,000 volumes in 1726 and Claudius Gilbert gave the College 13,000 volumes ten years later. John Stearne, Bishop of Clogher, Vice Chancellor of the University, and founder of the University printing press bequeathed his collection of manuscripts and historical records of the seventeenth century. The College also has an important collection of Celtic manuscripts presented in 1786 by Sir John Sebright, some of these having been collected by Edward Lloyd during a tour of Ireland in 1700. In 1805 Henry George Quin left the library 127 exquisitely bound editions of the classics and the great Italian poets. Other treasures of the library, perhaps better known, are the *Book of Kells*, an eighth century illuminated manuscript of the Gospels in Latin, and other early Irish manuscripts such as the *Book of Durrow*, presented by Henry Jones, Bishop of Meath and Vice Chancellor from 1646 to 1660, the *Book of Armagh*, and the *Book of Dimma* and the *Book of Molling*, two Irish copies of the Vulgate version of the four Gospels. Other valuable possessions are the *Book of Leinster*, probably dating from the eleventh century, and the *Annals of Ulster*, compiled in the fifteenth century.

Trinity College was vested with the powers of a university from the beginning and remained the only institution of its kind in Ireland for two and a half centuries. A charter of 1613 which gave it a representative in the Irish Parliament stated that the said college was and was esteemed a university. Over the years there were many projects to add more colleges, all of which came to nothing, and in effect Trinity College and the University of Dublin were one and the same thing. Trinity had been founded for the education of youths that they 'may be better assisted in the study of the liberal arts and in the cultivation of virtue and religion'. The religion to be cultivated was that of the Established Church and a primary function of the College was to ensure a supply of educated clergy for the service of the Church. Although admission to the College was never explicitly denied to Catholics and Dissenters, in the reign of Charles I all students were required to attend Anglican services and all candidates for degrees had to take the oath of supremacy and other anti-Catholic declarations, so in effect Catholics and Dissenters were excluded until 1793-94. Then a section of the Catholic Relief Act and letters patent granted to the College in 1794 enabled Catholics legally to enter and to graduate at Trinity. They were still excluded, however, from fellowships, scholarships, professorships and prizes, which meant that in fact few could afford to attend. Most Irish families had continued to send their sons to be educated on the Continent but when the French Revolution closed these establishments in France and Flanders the whole question of the education of the Catholics was raised again in Ireland, especially as the time appeared to be more conducive with the gradual dismantling of the penal laws from 1770 onwards.

The government of the day, at war with revolutionary France, looked with increasing sympathy at the request of the Catholic prelates to found a college for Catholics in Ireland where the students would be safe from the influence of the revolutionary ideas then rife in France. The Maynooth Act of 1795 set up a college for Catholics which ultimately became St. Patrick's College Maynooth, the national ecclesiastical college for the education and training of priests. The Act allowed for the governing body of the College to consist of trustees, mainly Bishops and Archbishops.

An account of Maynooth no doubt rather bigotted, is recorded by Mr and Mrs Hall in 1843 soon after the founding of the College. They give a rather one-sided view of the Maynooth priest:

> Generally he is of humble birth and connections, his school fees and college fees are liquidated by contributions amongst his relations; being at his outset utterly ignorant of society of a better order than his native village supplies, and having as a matter of course contracted the habits of those amongst whom his boyhood has passed; reading, not to enlarge his mind, but to confirm his narrow views of mankind – he enters the college where he mixes exclusively with persons under precisely similar circumstances. Here, it is reasonable to believe, all that is objectionable in his previous habits and education will be strengthened rather than removed ... his studies extend no further than the books authorised by his church.

The Halls go on to describe the library at the College:

> At Maynooth there is an excellent and rather extensive library formed chiefly by presents and bequests: containing the choicest works in History, Belles Lettres, the Arts and Sciences etc. But they are closed books to the students. The assistant librarian who conducted us through it stated frankly that he was not permitted to peruse any volume he was pleased to select, that the majority of the students were not allowed even to enter the room, and those that have the entrée must apply for express leave to read any particular book, explaining for what object they desired to consult it: the restriction, as we understand our informant, applies to every general history.

The Halls go on to quote a Mr. Inglis who has written about the library:

> the course of studies at Maynooth is arduous ... and very extensive but I learned that the course was not adhered to, but only as much of it as can be accomplished is followed. I glanced over the shelves with some attention and saw no work

improper by its levity or character for the perusal of a minister of religion and yet I was informed that a strict watch is kept on the studies of students and it is soon discovered if their studies be improper! I only saw standard histories, most unexceptional works of Christian philosophers and discovering – that all books not strictly theological – in short by which the mind can be informed and enlarged, are considered improper studies. Indeed upon this subject we have the testimony of the Commissioners of Irish Education who expressly state (Eighth Report) 'And if any student should read any book prohibited by the president or Dean, he is by the statutes of the College liable to expulsion'.

Those days are obviously long gone. St. Patrick's College, Maynooth is now to have a new library to be known as the John Paul II Library which is to be erected at a cost of 3½ million Irish punts and to be completed by 1984.

The Halls' description of the library rather belies its true value. The first librarian was the Revd Andrew Dunne who was appointed in 1800 with the power to appoint a deputy at £20 per annum. Dr Dunne already possessed a large collection of books which became the nucleus of the library. In 1815 £500 was paid to Dr Dunne for his books in the College and those he had taken from the library on quitting the College – the whole amounting to over 3,000 volumes. The oldest catalogue, produced around 1814, contains nearly 5,000 titles. The College, being in pecuniary difficulties, had allowed a very small sum of about £20 per annum to be set aside for the purchase of books. Yet when private collections were put up for sale great efforts were made to buy them.

The majority of the books naturally deal with the professional studies of the ecclesiastical students but the library also contains some rare and early printed books, some dating from the fifteenth century, books of Irish interest printed in St. Anthony's College, Louvain, and St. Isidore's College, Rome, kept not for their beauty of print but for what they contain, and usually smuggled into Ireland during the penal times. Could it be that the Halls did not see these materials? There are also in Maynooth manuscript copies of Irish books printed in Louvain showing how the Irish were dependent on the scribes long after printing had been established elsewhere. These manuscript editions actually follow the form of the printed book showing how the Irish scribes of the eighteenth and nineteenth centuries were consciously trying to emulate the printers. Maynooth library was able to repay its debt to the Continent by making a valuable contribution to the re-stocking of the University of Louvain library damaged during the First World War. The library at Maynooth was totally re-organised in 1930 and duplicate volumes were removed andd the whole library re-catalogued. It now contains about 200,000 books and periodicals. Maynooth is now, under the last Copyright Act, a legal deposit library for Ireland in common with the other university libraries.

In Ulster the Belfast Academy had been founded in 1785 as a combined grammar school and college. The Presbyterians had petitioned the government to establish a university in the north under the patronage of the Presbyterian clergy, but the government had no wish to create a Presbyterian Maynooth, and whilst the Belfast Academy was a great success as a school it had failed as a college. The well-to-do merchants and the enlightened liberals set about founding a new academy which would fulfil the original aims of 1785, but it was not until 1814 that the Belfast Academical Institution opened with both a school and collegiate departments. The latter issued a certificate recognised by the Presbyterian Synod as the equivalent of the MA degree at a Scottish university, which was where traditionally the Ulster Presbyterians had sent their sons to be educated. The title Royal was added after 1831 when Peel restored the grants which had been withdrawn between 1816 and 1827. The grants had been withheld because some of the managers of the Academy had been present at a dinner when objectionable political toasts had been proposed. Dr Coombie, the first Principal, was a Presbyterian minister in Belfast, and it was hoped that the Academy would furnish candidates for the ministry without them having to go to Scotland. However, one of the main principles of the Academy was to recognise no religious differences, and there were many arguments over the years that as a national seminary it should not become the property of one particular sect.

From the beginning a library and a museum were planned and incorporated into the architectural plans, although of necessity these had to be used as classrooms due to pressures on the other accommodation, with the loss of the government grant making expansion impossible. The use of the library was not free, and after matriculation students were invited to pay subscriptions of 1s.6d. for its use. Even so, the library was not adequate for the students' needs, being open for only two hours each day, and the Academy tried, unsuccessfully, to get permission for them to use the Linen Hall Library. When a North Wing was built in 1835 a large and spacious room was set aside for the library. A student librarian was appointed at a salary of £25 per annum, which represented a considerable advance on the £5 a year previously shared by two students who had undertaken the duties of librarian. The library opened daily from 10 a.m. to 3 p.m. during session, and on three days a week out of session.

Students' fees were raised to 5s. a year, but when it was found that many books were missing a deposit of 10s. was demanded. It turned out however that the main culprits were not the students but the teaching staff – a familiar problem in educational libraries even today. Because of shortage of money to stock the library the Academy bought second-hand books whenever possible. When the Collegiate department came to an end, many of the books were transferred to the new Queen's College, but the others were stored.

The school had never had a proper library, but in 1865 such books as remained from the collegiate library which were suitable were made available for loan to the senior boys, with a charge of 1s. a quarter being made for using the library. Only one volume could be borrowed at a time and fines were charged for the late return of books, thus raising money to purchase more books. Two boys acted as librarians, having to maintain a proper catalogue and borrowers' register. A proper school library was provided in 1928 and a librarian appointed, although this duty was combined with teaching practice. The governors made an initial grant of £100 with an annual grant of £25. Many donations were received including a bequest of £650 from a previous chairman of the board. Thus the library became a valuable amenity for the school.

There was indeed scant encouragement for the Presbyterians in Ulster for further education, excluded as they were from using Trinity, but they did endeavour to form their own libraries. As early as the beginning of the eighteenth century the Ministers of the Synod of Ulster at meetings of Presbytery were expected to produce catalogues of books in their possession and in this way small circulating libraries were set up.

Revd James Mackay, Minister of the first Belfast congregation in the mid-1760s decided to establish a library and spent a small sum of money on books and solicited others from both Ireland and England. The library was known as the Belfast Library. It was located in a room in his church and remained there until 1783 when the books were transferred to the first and second vestries. These books were eventually transferred to the Belfast Academy on the recommendation of Revd Dr Bruce so that they would be more accessible. Here the library grew in size and importance, receiving many donations of second-hand books. The Presbytery of Antrim met at the Academy every alternate month in order to have the opportunity to change their books. On the death of Dr Bruce the books had a temporary home for six months in a room rented in the Linen Hall, but soon found a more permanent home when the Revd William

Bruce, son of Dr Bruce, proposed to the Presbytery of Antrim that the library be transferred to his own house. Here it remained for six years but in 1829 presses were fitted up in the vestry of the Second Belfast Church at a cost of £28 and the books moved there. Books had been borrowed not only from Antrim but from the Presbytery of Derry whose ministers and students on payment of a small subscription were able to use the library. Under Dr Bruce a catalogue had been produced and he had been authorised by the Presbytery to deduct from each member a portion of the Regium Donum, 5s.5d. which was to be used to buy books.

In 1873 the library of about 1,800 volumes was transferred to Queen's College, Belfast with a special room set aside for it, and where it was known as the Antrim library.

A Divinity library had been founded for class use by the Revd. Samuel Hanna, who was appointed professor of Divinity in the Academical Institution in 1817. The library was never very large and in 1827 steps were taken to improve and develop the collection. This meant discarding over sixty volumes which were found 'not the best calculated to improve the students or forward them in their theological studies'. There is no indication of what the books were but the students contested this move vigorously and took strong exception to the cavalier methods of the College committee, successfully challenging the committee's right to make such decisions. By 1830 the fees formerly paid towards the support of the professor of Divinity were appropriated for the purchase of new books for the library. This idea, however simple, failed because fifteen out of the sixteen students refused to pay their fees to the treasurer, and although they paid up ultimately there was similar trouble in 1837 when no books were bought.

Other class libraries were established. Samuel Davidson set up a class library when he was appointed professor of Biblical Criticism in 1835 and Secession students had a class library under Professors Edgar and Wilson. At the Union of the Synods in 1840 all these various libraries were amalgamated but even so the total number of books were accommodated in a single bookcase in a corner of Dr Edgar's classroom. The students of course had access to the general library of the Institution. The libraries in the Academical Institution were solely for the use of students and after 1829 when the Antrim Library was no longer available for ministers of the Synod of Ulster it was felt quite strongly as early as 1830 that a new library should be founded. However it was not until 1840 that the newly constituted General Assembly appointed a committee to raise subscriptions for the founding of a library. A circular prepared by James Seaton Reid and sent out in the moderator's name set forth the advantages of the proposed library, which was to be chiefly one of reference. Reid's appeal was badly timed coinciding with other more pressing appeals for money. He received only about £200 and with this bought the first books for the new library. By 1845 there were 300 volumes, housed in a room in the Fisherwick Place Church.

However in 1845 a rare and beautiful copy of the Koran was acquired and in 1850 the library committee was instructed to expend its available reserves, amounting to some £300, in the purchase of more books for the collection.

When Reid died in 1851 he left instructions that his personal library of books and pamphlets should be offered for sale to the General Assembly of the Irish Presbyterian Church. The Church bought more than 600 volumes for £150 and transferred them to Belfast.

When the Presbyterian College was opened in Belfast in 1853 the students' library and the Assembly's library were transferred there, but maintained as separate collections, the Assembly's library being one of reference only until 1862. The students' library grew quickly but not without mishaps. Prior to the Union of the Synods in 1840 certain government monies paid to the Secession Synod had been set aside to establish congregational or circulating libraries. In 1850 the treasurer assuming in error that there was no longer a Secession Synod returned the balance in hand of £430 to the government, and when the error was discovered the College could not prevail upon the government to relinquish this money!

However in order to make the library more viable and useful a student was appointed in 1854 as sub-librarian at a salary of £10 per year, and for the next 55 years until 1909 some twenty students were to act as sub-librarians under one of the members of staff.

In 1863 the College committee instructed that the Assembly and College libraries which had remained independent should be merged into one. The library however suffered from inadequate financing and was not rescued until 1872 when Mrs Henry Gamble offered to found a library as a memorial to her late husband. For this purpose she gave £1,500 requesting that a room should be set apart for the new library and be called the Gamble Library. The Common Hall in the College was appropriated for the library, opening in 1873 with new doors, bookcases and platforms being erected, and with library chairs and oak tables covered with morocco. £1,200 was spent on acquiring 2,500 volumes, and Mrs Gamble herself donated some rare and valuable volumes. Ministers who had been students in the College could have access to the library on payment of a deposit of £1. Other ministers could enjoy the same privilege on payment of £2.

The library began to attract many donations, so that by the late

1880s its stock was estimated at nearly 17,000 volumes, although many useless or obsolete volumes were later disregarded.

In 1909 following a bequest of Miss Isabella Brownlee of Lisburn which brought in £125 a year, a permanent librarian could be appointed. The first such person was J.W. Kernohan who catalogued and re-arranged the library. With the setting-up of a separate government for Northern Ireland the Gamble Library was taken over by the Northern Ireland Parliament as a Commons debating chamber, and for eleven years the library was not available to students although ministers still had access to it. Since then the stock has increased, largely through donations and bequests. It is a collection of theological works almost exclusively, being particularly strong in relation to Presbyterianism in Ireland.

But to return to the early nineteenth century when the provision of education was a continual theme of various campaigns in Ireland. Thomas Wyse led a movement for educational reform and was largely instrumental in introducing to the government a scheme for a national system of education. In 1831 the Irish Chief Secretary announced that the government was to withdraw support for the Kildare Place Society and to assume direct responsibility for primary education, and although no reference was made to Wyse it was his scheme which was adopted. Lord Melbourne appointed Wyse chairman of a Select Committee to look into the possibility of extending and improving academic education in the country. The report, presented in 1838, laid down an organised and systematic approach to all stratas of education, recommending elementary schools in every parish, at least one secondary school or academy in every county, agricultural and professional schools, four provincial colleges, and in addition the provision of supplementary education through the literary and scientific societies, Mechanics' Institutes, libraries, museums, art galleries and botanical gardens.

The government took scant notice of the report and a system of secondary education was not introduced into Ireland until 1878. As far as university education was concerned there was still only Trinity College to serve a population of eight million. At the time of the Repeal agitation Peel attempted to win over the agitators by giving due thought and consideration to the problem of education, and by doing so he hoped to win over the great body of wealthy and intelligent Roman Catholics from the idea of repeal. First a Bill for the adequate state support of Maynooth was put through Parliament in April 1845, and secondly the College Bill received Royal assent on 31 July 1845. Three Colleges were proposed, one for the South at Cork, one for the West at either Galway or Limerick, and one for the North at Belfast. The Colleges were formally brought into existence by charters of incorporation on 30 December 1845 and in 1850 the Colleges at Cork, Galway and Belfast were constituted as the Queen's University of Ireland. Libraries were envisaged from the first, and the starting salary for the librarian at all three Colleges was to be £150 per annum. A capital grant of £4,000 was made by Parliament to each College for books, apparatus and specimens.

In Belfast the College reached agreement with the Belfast Society for Promoting Knowledge to avoid duplication of costly books, especially reference works. All the libraries began in conditions of some austerity but particularly in Belfast where the library had been placed in the Great Hall of the College which could only be heated when the supply of hot air was cut off from the lecture rooms.

Apart from the initial grant of £4,000 no financial provision had been made for the libraries, museums or laboratories. Consequently the Presidents of the Belfast and Galway Colleges in a joint statement to the Lord Lieutenant on 3 May 1852 argued that it was an unwise and unthrifty policy to spend public money in building and endowing colleges without providing the additional resources needed to enable them to discharge their functions properly. The matter was referred to the senate of the Queen's University which recommended an annual grant of £1,600 to each college for the maintenance of the library, museum and apparatus, but this sum was also to cover the cost of stationery, postage, printing, office expenses, advertising, heating and lighting, as well as to enable the college fees to be redevised. The government accepted the scheme in November 1852 and it was approved in October 1854.

In Belfast the librarian was expected to run the library single-handed, although in Cork and Galway library porters had been employed from the beginning. Revd. George Hall, who was appointed librarian at Belfast in 1850, paid a senior student £40 to act as his deputy when he was on sick leave. On resuming his duties in October 1852 he had to employ an assistant at £35 a year paid out of his own salary. He was very aggrieved at his situation and his demands became more and more militant until his grievance was acknowledged in May 1864. From then on he annually petitioned the College for recoupment of the salary of his assistant, but the College whilst not disputing his claim held that they had no power to satisfy it. It was, felt that Hall exaggerated the duties of librarian, and when he resigned in 1872 the College tight-fistedly appointed Samuel James MacMullen at a salary of £50 per annum. When in due course MacMullen resigned in 1878 his successor was granted a salary of £80 a year. Although Hall was rather morose, under his care the library grew into a sizeable collection of about 30,000 volumes well-organised and well-catalogued. From the initial £4,000 grant about two-thirds had been spent on books, and from 1854 the annual grant usually allowed about £500 to £600 for new books. In 1869 the library at Belfast was housed in its own building which was designed on distinctly ecclesiastical lines, with a high rectangular nave and steeply pitched roof, flanked on either side by five gabled bays.

The Irish Catholic prelates however, denounced the non-sectarian nature of the Colleges and it was agreed that no bishop would cooperate in the administration of the Colleges. The prelates were determined to found a college of their own and this eventually came into being in 1854 as the Catholic University of Ireland in Dublin with John Henry Newman as the first Rector. There was an enormous problem however, recognised in both the north and south of the country, as the national schools had inflicted a serious loss on Ireland by destroying the teaching of the hedge school masters, who had at least provided classical scholars capable of higher education. The National Board system of education set up in 1831 had in fact departed from the fine tradition of classical learning and was not providing scholars with the background necessary to become undergraduates. The numbers enrolling in the Colleges were small, for example in Galway in 1849 it was only 68, though this had risen to 131 by 1908.

The Irish University Education Act of 1879 left the three Queens colleges intact. Trinity College and the University of Dublin were also untouched. It did, however, replace the earlier Queen's University by a University Senate of the Royal University empowered to examine for degrees candidates from any institution inside or outside Ireland. Its considerable endowments allowed it to give financial aid to the Catholic University College, Magee College Londonderry, founded in 1865, and the three Queens Colleges.

In 1906 Sir Edward Fry was appointed chairman of a Royal Commission to investigate the growing discontent with the Irish university system. About the same time the library at Belfast was rapidly outgrowing its accommodation and an appeal for help to extend the library building was referred to the board of works and the government. The government's attitude was not encouraging as the University question was shortly to be discussed by Parliament. In any case no further grants would be made to Belfast unless something was done at the same time for Cork, where the needs were also urgent. The question of giving assistance to Cork had a special connection with the larger question of university education as a whole, especially as it affected the Roman Catholics of Ireland. Political problems were once again threatening to stifle the development of the university libraries.

Eventually an Irish Universities Act of 1908 restored the idea of a teaching university rather than an examining institution which gave external degrees, and it set up by Royal Charter three constituent colleges at Dublin, Cork and Galway as the National University of Ireland. Queen's College Belfast was transformed into Queen's University with its own senate. Maynooth was recognised as a college of the National University of Ireland in 1910.

The senate of Queen's University Belfast proposed as one of its most urgent tasks the enlargement of the library, encouraged by a government promise of £60,000 for purchasing lands and providing buildings for the University. Plans for the library extension were approved in 1911, involving a new reading room with a high roof to match the ecclesiastical style of the earlier building, and the work was completed in 1914.

The establishment of the six counties as a separate political unit had considerable importance for the future development of Queen's, for this was the area from which the University drew the great majority of its students. Queen's University Belfast was now a university in a separate political area and from 1920 onwards its expansion depended upon financial support from the people of Northern Ireland, whether from private benefaction or from Parliamentary grant.

The library was perhaps the most important unifying force in the intellectual life of the University and it developed in two ways. The first was physical expansion. The need for more shelf space was urgent and to meet this, without incurring the cost of a new building, the senate sanctioned the erection of a metal stack, five storeys high, inside the old library. This virtually turned the whole of the old building into a bookstore, but left the great reading room untouched until 1952. Work began on the stack in May 1926 with the idea of completing it during the Long Vacation, but supplies were held up by the General Strike in Britain and library conditions were not restored to normal until January 1927. In 1952 the great reading room was divided by a floor at gallery level, the upper storey being used as a reading room, the lower for storage and offices. Another change was the appointment of a librarian. Since the resignation of George Hill in 1880 the post of librarian had always been held by one of the professors, but in 1930 Kenneth Povey was appointed as a full-time librarian.

In 1929 the pro-Vice Chancellor R.M. Henry had presented to the University Library over 1,000 volumes about Ireland and he continued to donate books from time to time. After his death in 1951 the University purchased the greater part of his library and the total now forms the R.M. Henry Collection. With increased government grants it became possible to expand the library's resources and by

1952 a major reorganisation of the library building was completed. This reorganisation did not remain adequate for very long, and it soon became necessary to plan a new building programme to house the ever-increasing stock, consequent upon the expansion of the University. The first stage of the new main library complex, known as the 'Tower Stack' was completed in 1967. The second stage, involving the rehabilitation of the original nineteenth century building, was completed in 1983. The two buildings are connected by a bridge at first floor level.

In 1977 a feasibility study was undertaken to consider ways of automating the library. So far the Telepen Book Circulation system has been installed in the Undergraduate Collection in the Main Library and in the Biomedical Library. There are several departmental collections of which the most notable is the Medical Library. The latest figures of library holdings are approximately 844,500 items, which includes books, manuscripts, theses and microforms.

Stanmillis College is part of the Institute of Education at Queen's. It has a purpose-built library capable of holding 100,000 volumes. The library, completed in 1969, is an integral part of the main lecture block. There are three sections, one covering all major academic subjects with a special reference to education, a teaching practice library complete with children's books, and a non-book collection.

Magee College had opened in Londonderry in 1865 to provide courses at university level for entrants to the Presbyterian Ministry. The library opened a year later. It became Magee University College in 1935 and developed rapidly from 1951 onwards when government grants were made available. The stock numbers about 75,000 items and is rich in sixteenth and seventeenth century material.

The New University of Ulster opened in Coleraine in 1968 starting with a small stock of about 5,000 books. Phase two of the building was ready in 1973. Almost from the outset the library of the New University of Ulster became deeply committed to automation. Between 1972 and 1975 an evolutionary automated system for ordering, for periodicals circulation and for cataloguing was established, with the first steps towards an integrated system being takenin 1975. The University library was one of the first to employ the Plessey light pen system, and it remains the most comprehensive exponent of library automation in Ireland. The library at Magee is also an integral part of the University Library, but it is now principally concerned with the activities of the Institute of Continuous Education.

The library of University College Dublin possessed about 70,000 volumes by 1932, and it included the library of the Catholic

University of Ireland, the library of the Royal University, and about 6,000 volumes in a collection on Celtic languages and literature formed by Professor Heinrich Zimmer of Berlin. Over 2,000 volumes of the law library belonging to Chief Baron Palles were purchased and donated to the library by Dr William J. Walsh, Archbishop of Dublin, and a large collection of historical works belonging to John Richard Green was also acquired. James F. Kennedy bequeathed a collection of books on Celtic and mediaeval Ireland, and the library also received the John McCormack library containing the singer's music. In its early days the library and the various faculties were scattered on sites around Dublin. The main library was housed at Earlsfort Terrace with four main reading rooms, but the Engineering and Science faculties had their own separate libraries with a centralised union catalogue listing all the stock.

In 1964 the College moved from the city centre to a new campus at Belfield where the faculties of Arts, Commerce, Law, Agriculture and Science are located with the library. Some faculties remain in other older buildings but it is planned to move these to Belfield in due course. The College library consists of a main library and five branch libraries serving a population of approximately 10,000 students and 700 academic staff. The main library at Belfield houses the central services and administration.

The main library occupies phase one of a two-phase development and was opened in 1972. When phase two is completed there will be accommodation for 900,000 volumes and 3,200 readers, providing a central library for the College. The library system now has a stock of over 600,000 volumes, including some 30,000 early printed books and special collections. New acquisitions average about 21,000 items annually and 9,000 periodical titles are currently taken.

Some progress has been made in the computerisation of library procedures. Loans from the main and Science libraries are controlled by the Plessey light-pen circulation system. Records of the periodical holdings are computer-based and have been used to produce a union catalogue and various subsidiary listings. A limited on-line retrieval service from data bases is offered using ESA/IRS Information Services through the Institute for Industrial Research and Standards. There are plans to extend the scope of this service using EURONET.

The library is a depositary library for EEC material and a national centre for publications of the US Department of Energy. It also receives, under Irish copyright legislation, titles published in the Republic of Ireland, and an annual bibliography of these and of items from Northern Ireland is prepared in the library under the title of *Irish Publishing Record.*

The library of the University College, Galway dates from the opening of the College in 1849 and had as its first librarian James Hardiman, the Galway historian and antiquary. The College has long specialised in Irish and Gaelic culture and by the University College Galway Act 1929, the government ensured by means of adequate financial provision that the fullest use be made of the Irish language with lectures in most subjects being presented in Irish.

The library was officially without a librarian from 1936, the duties being discharged by the assistant librarian who also represented the governing body of the University on the Library Council. The original library was placed in the Hall which was still being used as a reading room in the mid-1960s with seating for about 100 students. As the library expanded additional reading rooms opened in other parts of the College, notably on the ground floor of the library, the Aula Maxima and the Department of Anatomy for the first and second year medical students. Some of the library's medical stock is accommodated in the Regional Hospital.

The stock numbers about 170,000 volumes with over 1,000 periodicals. As with other Irish university libraries in the Republic, Galway is an Irish legal deposit library, but its more interesting holdings include manuscripts belonging to Dr Douglas Hyde, the first President of Ireland. These either relate to the Irish language or are in Irish. Also in the collection are the statute books and minute books of Galway's ancient corporation, and a map 6 feet by 5 feet of the town of Galway, made shortly after 1651. There is also a collection of audio-visual materials.

A new library known as the James Hardiman Library opened in 1974 and is capable of seating 800 readers. This new building is only the first phase of a programme intended eventually to double the capacity of the library, but the second stage is not planned in the near future. University College Galway is a Euronet subscriber, although for the present the terminal is not housed in the library. Both the circulation and the cataloguing system are automated, using Plessey and LOCAS respectively. The Higher Education authority has recently set up a feasibility study to consider a cooperative agency amongst the universities for automated cataloguing.

At one time the library of the University College of Cork was the only library of any importance available for students in the whole south of Ireland. In the very beginning from 1845 to 1850 it possessed about 4,500 volumes. The governing body appointed the registrar as librarian and increased the grant, giving him free rein to develop the library. In Guy's *Directory of Cork* for 1875-76 the library is described as a handsome room containing a large collection of the best editions in every department of science and literature.

The growth of the library was gradual from 1849, when the original library was built, until 1921 when Dr A. O'Rahilly became a member of the library committee. Ten years later he became director of the library. He was a true bookman and under his care the library steadily grew into a worthwhile collection. In 1928 a separate history library had been established and this now has a valuable collection of printed source material as well as microfilms and photocopies. The Music library is an important collection and has received a Gulbenkian grant to aid its development. Notable private collections include d'Arbois de Juboinville's Celtic library and the historical collection of Sharman Crawford.

In the 1960s there was considerable growth in student numbers in the Republic and the 1849 library became totally inadequate but served as the main access point for staff and students with some other minor collections in different locations. There was a large secondary store in a disused brewery holding the reserve stock. The library now contains 280,000 volumes and takes 2,500 current periodicals. It is divided into the Main library, Science library, Medical library, Dairy Science and Documents library, and Music library.

In response to space and catalogue problems a comprehensive development plan was devised which included projects for a new central library building and for automating the cataloguing system utilising BLAISE. In the event the University College Cork used DOBIS (Dortmund Library System) for the enormous task of re-cataloguing the library, and LIBIS (Leuven Integral Biblioteck System) for an on-line circulation and acquisition system. An older printed books collection has recently been established consisting of material withdrawn from the library's general holdings on the basis of a pre-1951 date of publication. There is also a collection of Munster printing. The new library, named the Boole Library, should have opened in 1980 but was considerably delayed. It is a five-storey building capable of housing 600,000 books and seating 1,900 readers. Additional accommodation will provide for binding, cataloguing and inter-library loans. There is special provision for archives, seminars, audio-visual and microfilmed records. Four lecture halls have also been built into the library. In common with other college libraries, under the Irish Copyright Act 1963 the library claims a free copy of all new books published in the State.

University College Cork and the Southern Health Board have agreed to provide a medical library at the Regional Hospital, Wilton. The accommodation will be provided by the Board but the library will be staffed by the University College. The funding of staff, books and periodicals is to be on a joint basis.

The emergence of the National Library has been dealt with in a previous chapter. The present National Library building in Kildare Street, Dublin was opened in 1890 and was planned to contain 500,000 volumes. The National Library is the State reference library and aims to collect all material relating to Ireland, and works by Irish authors in Ireland or abroad, but it has a general collection on non-Irish works covering all fields of knowledge. In its early years the National Library fulfilled the role of a large municipal reference library in Dublin as the public library was slow to provide an adequate service. The general reading room, which has hardly altered, seats about 80 people, with a newspaper reading room and a manuscript room adjoining it. There are three divisions of the National Library – the Department of Printed Books, the Department of Manuscripts, and the Genealogical Office in Dublin Castle. In 1943 the library took over the Ulster Office of Arms with its large collection of Irish genealogical manuscripts and its Heraldic Museum. The functions of the Genealogical Office are carried out by a Genealogical Officer and a Chief Herald.

The first librarian of the National Library was William Archer who was also joint librarian of the Royal Dublin Society. He introduced the newly available Dewey Decimal Classification scheme into the National Library which was the first library in Europe to adopt it. He was succeeded as librarian of the National Library by Thomas William Lyster in 1895. Later librarians were Robert Lloyd Praegar and Dr R.I. Best who became the first director of the National Library. In 1940 R.J. Hayes took over as director and to him must go the credit of the monumental work *Manuscript Sources for the History of Irish Civilisation*, which lists all known sources for Irish materials not only in Ireland but also materials held in libraries overseas.

The National Library became a legal deposit library in 1927 for items published in Ireland, including Irish newspapers. It is also a deposit library for United Nations publications. The Kildare Street building is now seriously overcrowded with over 500,000 printed books, 10,000 bound volumes of manuscripts, and over 6,000 reels of microfilm, much of it being copies of manuscripts of Irish interest preserved in overseas libraries. Included is the Joly collection of more than 23,000 volumes received from the Royal Dublin Society, and a collection of early Dublin and provincial printing which had belonged to E.R. MacClintock Dix. Other special collections include the Ormond Archives from the twelfth to the nineteenth centuries, the Lismore Castle papers and the Fitzgerald-Lennox correspondence. The Department of Manuscripts has over 1,000 Gaelic manuscripts including the *Book of Magauran* from the fourteenth century, the oldest known book of bardic poetry. The Library houses a large collection of topographical prints and drawings as well as Irish historical prints, cartoons and portraits. There is also a large map collection. The Irish Architectural Record Association, founded in 1939, is based in the National Library and maintains a collection of architectural drawings.

The National Library has a Board of twelve trustees, four appointed by the government and eight appointed by the Royal Dublin Society, but all matters relating to finance and policy are controlled by the Department of Education.

Coming under the heading of a special library, if not strictly academic or national, is the collection of the Chester Beatty Library and Gallery of Oriental Art, left in trust to the Irish people in 1968 by Sir Alfred Chester Beatty. The collection first came to Dublin from London in 1953, and it reflects Chester Beatty's interest in the Orient. The oldest of the library materials are Babylonian clay tablets and Greek Biblical papyri from the second to the fourth centuries. The collection contains about 5,000 rare books and 10,000 manuscripts, some of which are European but most are Oriental from Chaina, Persia, Arabia and Armenia. There are also Japanese colour prints and miniatures from India, the Far East and Islamic countries.

Mentioned earlier in this chapter was the King's Inn Library which was in receipt of copyright books from 1801 to 1836. This library, founded in 1787, surrendered its right to legal deposit in return for an annual grant of £300. It is primarily a reference law library, but is particularly rich in Irish historical materials. The library contains well over 100,000 volumes, including the papers and manuscripts, of the Irish historian Prendergast and a very large number of rare eighteenth century pamphlets.

# Repeal reading rooms and *The Nation*

The Catholic Association was first mooted as an idea in Dempsey's Tavern in Sackville Street, a well-known retreat of Dublin citizens who loved a good glass of wine and a well-cooked chop or steak. In addition to these culinary attractions it possessed a large and lofty room which, when the Tavern was succeeded by Tyrrel's Library, formed the reading room of that institution. It was here and in Coyne's back parlour in Capel Street that Daniel O'Connell and his friends gathered in 1824 to found the association that was eventually to wrest Catholic emancipation from the English government. The Catholic Association was one of the most effective modern political mass movements. Membership of the Association was a fee of one penny a month, known as the Catholic rent. In order to collect this weekly rent of ¼d a week, O'Connell suggested the appointment of two Catholic churchwardens in each parish, and to stimulate interest in the progress of the movement a *Weekly Register*, containing reports of speeches and resolutions of the meetings of the Association, was sent to these churchwardens every Saturday.

When the Catholic Association began to address Ireland in this way newspapers were scarce and dear, never penetrating lower than the middle classes. The day's wages of a labouring man would hardly purchase a single copy. In its heyday about 6,000 copies of the *Weekly Register* were sent out to the country area and the church-wardens read it out aloud each Sunday after Mass at the church door. Back copies were then kept on file.

Once Catholic emacipation had been achieved by political agitation in 1829 the people began to feel confident in the possibility of combined but peaceful political action. O'Connell, who had long been the idol of many of his countrymen, in 1840 suddenly invited the Irish nation to unite with him in the enormous tasks of repealing the legislative union between Great Britain and Ireland. This union had already lasted for more than one generation of Irishmen and had been repeatedly assailed by both the Protestant ascendancy and the Catholic sector of the population, many of whom felt that national and individual property had declined under the union. The Act of Union had come into being on 1 January 1801 to unite the two kingdoms of England and Ireland for ever, and it had abolished the independent Irish Parliament. It was the restoration of the right of this Irish Parliament that O'Connell sought to achieve, an Irish

Parliament no longer dominated by the Protestant ascendancy but one reflecting the aims of the Catholic majority. O'Connell's initial call met with but little response, for at the inaugural meeting in the Great Room of the Corn Exchange capable of holding 500 persons, the room was not one fifth part filled. However, the movement called the Loyal National Repeal Association of Ireland rapidly gained support from the submerged Catholic masses, most of whom were so poor that the wages they received only enabled them to buy enough potatoes and salt on which to survive. But in the Catholic struggle they had learnt self-reliance and the secret of their own power. From O'Connell they had received a political training which in some degree compensated for their want of culture and knowledge.

Every week brought fresh recruits, Protestants as well as Catholics, and the clergy sent in their adherents in droves. Father Mathew's Temperance movement was essentially useful to the Repeal Association. The Temperance movement was apart from the repeal agitation but auxiliary to it, for by encouraging men to take the temperance pledge Father Mathew was freeing them from the degrading influence of drink and enabling them to think and reason for themselves. The temperance movement was indeed seen in some quarters as a threat, and the *Protestant Magazine* for June 1841 quoted from the more congenial *Times* the following passage: 'We cannot but suspect that this temperance movement is substantially a sort of Trojan horse, within whose ribs there lurks an overwhelming phalanx, which some of these nights will sally on the sleeping sentinels of Ireland and make it an easy prey'. Words which were indeed destined to come true.

The temperance movement was also instrumental in the establishment of the reading rooms. In J. D'Alton's *History of Drogheda* published in 1844 the Total Abstinence Society had set up a public reading room and newsroom in West Street to which a circulating library was attached. This, it was hoped, would be the means of:

> recommending to the working classes such popular treatises as will best instruct them in the capabilities and chemistry of the soil, the improvement of long mismanaged farms, the cultivation of untenanted and unwholesome wastes, and other available resources for the manufacture of native produce. With the main objects of this Society have also been united, in the last year, useful and desirable efforts for the revival of the Irish language, literature and music.

Several young Irelanders on a tour through Ireland in the early 1840s visited schools, reading rooms, teetotal societies and bookshops everywhere. They record 'the books are detestably

English, no Irish novels, poems or plays except by accident. There are 630 teetotal bands alone in Cork set up at a cost of £50 to £100 each but the teetotal rooms are a melancholy spectacle'. But Father Mathew and the Temperance movement did enable the repeal meetings to have a moral and temporal significance that they might otherwise have lacked.

Thomas Davis was to write to Charles Gavan Duffy who was staying with O'Connell: 'For God's sake get O'Connell to undertake, or allow others to undertake, a plenipotentiary mission to establish Repeal Reading Rooms, and give them books and good advice. Damn the ignorance of the people; but for that we should be the lords of our own future'. Davis saw this as a splendid opportunity for the establishment of parish libraries and he advocated the lines on which the movement should run; how maps and books should be distributed, suitable for each centre and how Irish grammars, dictionaries and general works in Irish should be sent to Irish-speaking districts. He was a man who lived half a century before his time.

In 1842 repeal missions were sent to the provinces of Munster, Leinster and Connaught to organise repeal agitation and to inculcate the principle of nationality into the various districts. No mission was sent to Ulster where opposition to repeal was strong, although eventually Protestant Repeal Associations were instituted in Dublin, Drogheda and Lurgan. There was also one in Belfast, for which a respectable physician, Dr Beck, was the honorary secretary. Thomas Mathew Ray, the secretary of the Association, was allocated Munster and he proceeded to Limerick. Mr Ray was in fact the originator of the repeal reading rooms and he established several of them on his Repeal mission in 1842. The first of these was at Newcastle, Co. Limerick.

The Repeal Association with the repeal rent, similar to the Catholic rent earlier, had in 1843 a staff of 12 to 15 people, this number increasing to 48 by 1845. Repeal wardens were appointed to supervise districts, to gather in the repeal rent, and to run the repeal reading rooms, ensuring that the repeal newspapers such as *The Pilot* had as wide a circulation as possible. Additional duties were to promote the use of Irish manufactures as opposed to foreign imports and to organise local meetings. This they did very effectively.

By December 1844 rules for the repeal reading rooms were adopted on a motion put forward by O'Connell. These reading rooms were established to diffuse amongst the people useful information and early intelligence on all subjects of public interest, especially on the great national question of repeal. It was an attempt to establish reading rooms in every populous parish in the country, but the aim was quite openly political.

A reading room could be opened in any district where there was at least 2,000 members of the Repeal Association who regularly subscribed at least one shilling in the year. Repealers who paid this amount were to be allowed access to the reading room and its contents. The rooms were under the direction of an inspector, a committee of wardens, and the local clergy, but were to be subject to the control of the Repeal Association on all accounts. The Association defrayed the expenses of firing and lighting, and also gave £1.6s. for the purchase of newspapers. These newspapers were carefully filed for future reference, and all books and tracts carefully preserved. Books supplied by the Association to the repeal rooms included O'Connell's *Memoir of Ireland*, John O'Connell's *Argument for Ireland*, *Repeal State Trials* (accounts of the trial of O'Connell himself), and the *Life of Grattan* by his son.

The reading rooms were used also to house the local meetings and as venues for the collection of repeal rent. At the regular meetings after the transaction of business a reader was appointed to read out aloud from the newspapers, books or tracts anything that related to the cause. The adherance to the temperance movement meant that the Association refused to allow any repeal reading rooms to be housed in a public house. As the reading room system extended these local centres became rallying points where the intellect of the provincial repealers was exercised and political information acquired. Morality was strengthened by the inducement afforded to the people to employ their leisure hours in mental recreation instead of sensual indulgence. Through the reading rooms it was hoped to increase patriotism, temperance and virtue, especially amongst the young.

Mr Ray kept a quarterly record of the returns sent in by all the reading rooms. These parochial registers were arranged alphabetically for each county, and related to wardens, committees, reports and the repeal reading rooms in Ireland. In addition, in every town in England, Scotland and America where Irish emigrants had settled, branches of the Association were formed. In Ireland Ray reported that in April 1845 there were at least 71 reading rooms in operation and that the number was expected to treble by the next quarter, reaching no less than two hundred. Later there were at least three hundred repeal reading rooms in existence and the Association resolved to increase them to three thousand, making them centres of organisation and education which under penal times had been a forbidden luxury censured by heavy penalties. This aim was not achieved as Hudson in the *History of Adult Education* states that 'from the want of books and magazines' they soon became mere gossipping rooms and were given up.

Parallel with the Repeal Movement there developed the Young Ireland Movement, which from its inception was essentially a literary movement. Its objective was 'to create and foster public opinion in Ireland and to make it racy of the soil'. Its founders, Thomas Davis, Charles Gavan Duffy and John Dillon were men of genius and together they produced a newspaper that was to have the most profound effect on the people of Ireland. The first number of *The Nation* was published on 15 October 1842. Its prospectus and list of contributors had excited considerable interest and its appearance was eagerly awaited. The prospectus, written by Davis stated:

> Nationality is our great object – a Nationality which will not only raise our people from their poverty by securing to them the blessings of a domestic legislation ... a Nationality which may embrace Protestant, Catholic and Dissenter, Milesian and Cromwellian, the Irishmen of a hundred generations and the stranger who is within our gates.

In shape and size and distribution of contents it differed from any other newspaper of the day and the new format was chosen to reflect the new spirit of the time. It was well edited and well printed. The first number, of which 12,000 copies were printed, sold out early on the day of publication. Davis stated that one of his office windows was broken owing to the impatience of the newsmen to get extra copies of the paper to sell, and he estimated that double the quantity printed could have been sold.

Whilst O'Connell had the material interests of the people at heart, the editors of *The Nation* sought to restore to the people their ancient culture and nationhood. From the first issue the writers began to inculcate the people with ideals of Irish nationality, writing of ancient heroes dimly remembered by the people, and of Irish history and antiquities. It was to change the reading habits of a nation. The Halls in their tour through Ireland in the late 1850s reported that while staying in a small inn in Dunmanway, West Cork, the little man was afraid 'we'd be dull in such a poor place and brought us an old volume of the *Hibernian Magazine* which like all the numbers of that periodical contained an abundance of everything that had no reference to Ireland'. *The Nation* changed all that.

So for the first time for hundreds of years the Celtic people of Ireland were presented with a newspaper which sought to raise their self-respect as a nation and in doing so to disinfect the political life of the country. It was imbued with high ideals of nationality which over the years attracted a brilliant band of writers and which inspired such confidence and enthusiasm over all classes of readers and after a time over every sector of the community.

*The Nation* was a great educational agency and brought a message of hope and encouragement to the people urging union between all sections of the country, Catholic and Protestant. Its teaching opened up to a large number of the people a new national vista whose outlook had been blurred or distorted through centuries of neglect. Many of its most advanced writers were members of the Loyal National Repeal Association and afterwards of the Irish Confederation, when the disagreement with O'Connell culminated in their secession from the Association. Amongst its earliest recruits were a group of antiquaries who delighted to see studies that they had pursued in the shade and without sympathy suddenly becoming popular, and from that time on few cultivated Irishmen who went to the Continent failed to return without some contribution about the exiles in Paris and Louvain, the Irish manuscripts in foreign libraries, and stories of the churches and colleges founded by Irishmen in Europe.

From the beginning *The Nation* outstripped all other Irish newspapers. It was read by the cultured classes and also by those to whom reading was not a necessity. Dillon, writing in 1843 from Ballaghaderin in County Mayo, was amazed to find 23 copies of *The Nation* coming in every Sunday, in a village which was probably among the poorest in the county, and which hardly had 23 houses in it.

The readership of *The Nation* was estimated to be in excess of a quarter of a million. At that time every copy of a newspaper bore a penny stamp which carried it through the post, and the returns of stamps issued show clearly the quantity of each paper printed. The stamps consumed by *The Nation* exceeded ten thousand, and as the price of the paper was 6d a copy people paid £250 a week for it. Of course, the actual numbers printed do not reflect the number of times a paper would be read, and it was known that three hundred copies at least went to newsrooms and teetotal societies, and each paper was read by at least fifty persons. 1100 copies went to the repeal wardens and were read aloud at weekly meetings, each copy thus reaching between 50 and 100 people. Nine thousand copies were sold by agents or went direct to subscribers, and as *The Nation* was preserved for binding it is certain that many of these copies must have reached a dozen readers each. As a paper, it was not just read, it was devoured, (see Figure 7.1). People waited in a fever to get the next issue, and this fever extended to the official classes through whose hands the paper passed for distribution. There were constant complaints about copies going missing and of parcels arriving at the agents with fewer copies than they set out with. Someone without due reverence for authority suggested that to remedy the situation an additional paper should be attached to each parcel clearly labelled 'Please to steal this copy'.

The stamp return for the quarter ended 31 December 1843 illustrates the undoubted popularity of the paper relative to the other Dublin press.

| | | | |
|---|---|---|---|
| The Nation | 10,730 | Evening Post | 2,932 |
| Weekly Freeman | 7,150 | Evening Packet | 1,948 |
| Weekly Warder | 7,230 | The Pilot | 1,923 |
| Weekly Register | 3,154 | Daily Saunders | 2,461 |
| The World | 2,038 | Daily Freeman | 1,410 |
| Evening Mail | 886 | | |

A move to crush the Repeal Movement led to O'Connell's arrest, together with other repealers, including Thomas Mathew Ray, O'Connell's son John, and the editors of the three repeal newspapers, Charles Gavan Duffy of *The Nation*, Dr John Gray of

**FIGURE 7.1**
**READING *THE NATION***

the *Freeman's Journal*, and Richard Barrett of *The Pilot*. All were charged with conspiracy to incite ill-will amongst the Queen's subjects, to weaken confidence in the administration of justice, and of trying to obtain a change of government and the constitution of the country by unlawful means. At the trial extracts from *The Nation* were read out in evidence against the repealers. A carefully manipulated jury list, a packed jury and a partisan court ensured a verdict for the Crown.

O'Connell was sent to prison along with the other defendants, but they were released on bail on appeal to the House of Lords in September 1844. O'Connell was worried by the drift of the Young Irelanders Movement. He had always preached constitutional agitation and with the Young Irelanders the hydra of rebellion was striking out its head again. On 13 July 1846 O'Connell declared war on the Young Irelanders, appealing for amelioration of the political situation by legal and peaceful means, and disconnecting the Repeal Association from any newspaper published in Britain and Ireland. This was of course aimed at *The Nation*. His son John O'Connell declared that all those not agreeing with the resolution ceased to be members of the Association. The Young Irelanders thus denounced left the Repeal Association, taking with them a great deal of its driving force. Within a year O'Connell, its leader, had died.

Every effort was made by the Loyal National Repeal Association to boycott *The Nation*. The Repeal Association had allowed districts that contributed £10 to the repeal rent to select a weekly newspaper to be sent to the reading room. Owing to its popularity this managed to secure over £1,000 per annum for *The Nation*. In an epistle sent by the secretary Ray to all the reading rooms it was indicated that *The Nation* would no longer be sent, and that instead the other major repeal paper *The Pilot* would be distributed. This news was received with wild objections and some of the reading rooms refused to expel *The Nation*. One reading room went on paying for the newspaper itself. But the Association decided that any repeal reading room receiving *The Nation* would receive no more assistance from the Association and would be disconnected from it. *The Nation* lost the money previously earned in this way as over 12,000 districts remained within the Association.

They need hardly have bothered. The famine was upon Ireland and within a very short time the population was decimated, either by death or by emigration, often only to a watery grave. The death of the Liberator in 1847 and the abortive insurrection of 1848, quarrels amongst the members gradually led the Repeal Movement to its decline, and the reading rooms fell into disuse. The famine greatly weakened political agitation.

*The Nation* however, although suppressed, continued for a few months in 1848. Its first and most brilliant period was from 1842 until its suppression in 1848, when it was edited by Davis from 1842 until his death in September 1845. It was revived by Gavan Duffy from 1849 until 1855 when he emigrated to Australia, and from 1855 by A.M. Sullivan when he became sole proprietor.

The library of the Loyal National Repeal Association was put up for sale by auction at their premises at the Corn Exchange, Burgh Quay on Wednesday 15 November 1848. A note on the catalogue states that persons unable to inspect the books should note that each work has the library stamp attached to it. The catalogue lists some 457 items or sets of items, and some extensive pamphlet collections, as well as four large mahogany bookcases for sale. Some of the books listed were extremely rare, including works published in the seventeenth century, including long runs of the *Gentleman's Magazine*, Watson's Dublin Almanacs and Directories, journals of the Irish House of Commons, Journals of the Irish House of Lords, and Walker's *Hibernian Magazine*. Many of the books dealt with government and constitution matters, but there was a fair proportion devoted to Irish history and topography. Additionally there were some books dealing with the French Revolution, and some New World travel books.

As well as the newspaper, three other important enterprises of the founders of *The Nation* were the *Spirit of the Nation*, the *Library of Ireland* and the *Voice of the Nation*. Of these, the *Spirit of the Nation* contained the songs and ballads of Ireland and was first published in two parts in 1843, price 6d. These were popular amongst Irish people all over the world, and were a revelation to thousands of Irish people who had been reared in an un-Irish atmosphere.

The *Library of Ireland* was started by Charles Gavan Duffy and its success was immediate. The reception of the *Spirit of the Nation* indicated that the reading public was ready to support a more ambitious venture. The proposal was to publish a series of shilling volumes of biography, poetry and criticism on a monthly basis calculated to feed the national spirit. Each volume sold for a shilling in ornamental wrappers and two shillings for green boards. Each author was paid a fee of £40. The volumes appeared for nearly two years until the conflict with O'Connell and the famine directed the energies of the contributors elsewhere. Titles that appeared in this series included:

*Ballad poetry of Ireland*, by Gavan Duffy
*Life of Aodh O'Neill*, by John Mitchel
*The History of the Volunteers of 1782*, by Thomas MacNevin
*The History of the American Revolution*, by Michael Doheny

*The Confederation of Kilkenny*, by Father C.P. Meehan
*Irish writers of the 17th century*, by Thomas D'Arcy McGee
*A Memoir of the life and conquests of Art McMurrough*, by Thomas
D'Arcy McGee

The original idea had been to write a history of Ireland plugging
the gaps in the national literature and filling the void with an
adequate history of the country. It was to be a mammoth task but in
the end the design was put on a more manageable footing with the
monthly production of the *Library of Ireland*. These little books had
immediate success and new editions appeared year after year, long
after their authors had died.

The extent of their wishing to educate the people is evident in
papers written to Davis by William Smith O'Brien in 1845:

> I wish you could get something done by the Repeal Association
> towards providing good prints, very cheap for the poor. I
> observe in almost every cottage where absolute destitution does
> not exist a disposition to hang up prints on the walls. Generally
> they ware wretched productions, having neither grace nor
> truth. Could we not induce some competent artist to give us
> lithograph sketches which could be circulated through
> hawkers and pedlers at a low price?

Religious, military and temperance prints were popular at this time.
O'Brien further desired that the Reformed Corporations would
found picture galleries in the town halls of several towns, and if each
Corporation in the kingdom (of Ireland) would order from some
Irish artist one picture each year 'what great and immediate
encouragement would be given to Irish art'. This design never took
effect but it illustrates the fertile minds of these men whose
educational ideas were ahead of their time.

The third notable project was the publication of the *Voice of the
Nation*, published as a companion volume to the *Spirit of the Nation*
in 1844 at the price of 1s.6d. It consisted of articles and essays on
nationality which the editors felt it desirable to keep before the
public. The *Voice of the Nation* went through several editions but did
not attain the same popularity as the *Spirit of the Nation*.

Charles Gavan Duffy, by then Sir Charles, revived the
publications in 1893 as the *New Irish Library*, a series which
comprised thirteen volumes and had amongst its authors such
eminent persons as Douglas Hyde, who wrote the *Story of Early
Gaelic Literature*, Richard Ashe King, who wrote *Swift in Ireland*,
and Standish O'Grady, who contributed *The Bog of Stars and
Sketches of Elizabethan Ireland*.

James Duffy was the publisher of the Young Ireland Movement. Born in 1809, he had begun his working life as a pedlar in the counties of Cavan and Meath, but when he was 30 he set up a small bookshop at 25 Angelsea Street, Dublin. Here he published a number of highly successful religious books at popular prices. In the notice of his death which appeared in *The Nation* in 1871 it was stated that Duffy was the most extensive publisher that Ireland had produced, that he had done more for the literature of Ireland, sacred and profane, than all the other publishers who had preceded him, and that he was the first Irish publisher to issue works of a high-class character and of great value at prices that brought them within the reach of the people.

Whilst the repeal reading rooms were essentially for the great mass of the working people in Ireland and as such provided a kind of education and self-instruction for them, they were also libraries established with a political means in view – that of repealing the Act of Union. They were not however the only working class library movement in the country at the time. The idea of Samuel Smiles' Self Help also took root in Ireland, culminating in the Irish Mechanics' Institute movement which although active never received the same support that it had in England.

# 8 Adult education and the Mechanics' Institute libraries

The Irish working class always had a deep desire to educate their children. This was evident from their support for the hedge schools. Education for adults had received little support, lacking as it did the impetus of the industrial revolution with its need for an educated work force. The workers in Ireland were mainly rural and agricultural. There was no real history of education for adults, except for the adult schools established with the aid of the London Hibernian Society, which in 1816 had 347 schools in Ireland. These were attended by 27,776 pupils with upwards of one thousand adults. By 1817-18 the number of adults had reached 1,250. Hardly a large number, but to use a simple but significant observation of an old man at the time 'they kept the boys away from bad work', or put another way, they kept their minds off political dissatisfaction. This was no idle remark, with the 1798 rebellion fresh in everyone's memory, the Napoleonic Wars in full swing and Ireland, the back door to England, with envoys at Buonaparte's court. By 1823 the number of adults under instruction had risen to 9,160 and in the following year it was 10,117.

In addition to the London Hibernian Society schools, during the late eighteenth and early nineteenth centuries efforts were made by the upper and middle classes throughout Ireland for the intellectual and moral improvement of the lower classes. These efforts took the form of Athenaeums, literary societies and Mechanics' Institutes, none of which really gained any lasting success. Mechanics' Institutes were formed in the following centres: Ardee, Armagh, Athy, Belfast, Birr, Carlow, Carrick on Suir, Cashel, Celbridge, Clonmel, Coleraine, Cork, Downpatrick, Drogheda, Dublin, Dundalk, Ennis, Galway, Limerick, Newry, Tipperary, Waterford and Wexford – although very little of the original records has survived (see Figure 8.1). These Mechanics' Institutes never prospered for any length of time for a variety of causes, not least of which were the strong political and sectarian differences which crippled the managing committees. Hudson stated in his *History of Adult Education* that if earnestness and enthusiasm alone could have secured the well-being of these Institutes then the middle class would have completed the work. But in Ireland other factors were at work which prevented these institutions from achieving the same success they had in England.

# FIGURE 8.1
# MECHANICS' AND LITERARY INSTITUTES IN IRELAND

| Place. | Title of Institute. | Subscription | Members | Vols. in Library | Annual Issues. | Pupils in Classes. | Newsrm Lectures &c. | Secretary. |
|---|---|---|---|---|---|---|---|---|
| *Ireland* | | | | | | | | |
| Ardee | M I | .. | 150 | 600 | 500 | .. | 20 | J.O'Rourke |
| Ballymoney | Y M S A | .. | 35 | 500 | 200 | .. | 25 | W. Orr |
| Belfast | M I | 10/, 5/ | Susp | .. | .. | .. | .. | Grimshaw |
| " " | S prom. K | 21/, e 21/ | 200 | 10000 | 1000 | .. | N | J. Ridley |
| " " | Work C Ass | 2/6, 1/6 q | 960 | 750 | 1000 | .. | N | Montgomery |
| CastleBelling | .. | .. | 30 | .. | .. | .. | 6 | |
| Clonmel | M I | 2/6, q | 50 | .. | .. | .. | 10 | J. Cuddihy |
| Cork | Royal I | 21/. | 270 | 12000 | 4000 | .. | N 6 | W.O'Logan |
| " " | M I | 2/6, q | 90 | 800 | 1000 | .. | N 12 | W. Kelcher |
| Downpatrick | M I | 1/6, q | 130 | 300 | 700 | .. | N 12 | Montgomery |
| Drogheda | M I | 2/6, 1/6, | 150 | 250 | 500 | 30 | N 20 | W. Leonard |
| Dublin | Lib. S | 21/. | 500 | 20100 | 2000 | .. | N | J. Raper |
| " " | M I | 2/6, q | 250 | 4000 | 1000 | . | N | C R.Mahoney |
| Dundalk | M I | 10/, 6/, 3/ | 204 | 1800 | 3750 | 22 | 27 | J. Brown |
| Dungannon | L S | 10/ | 60 | 300 | 100 | .. | N 16 | W. Nevill |
| Ennis | M I | .. | 50 | .. | .. | .. | .. | M.McNamare |
| Galway | M I | 2/6, q | 160 | 50 | 36 | 30 | N 6 | R. M. Gill |
| Garvagh | Y M I | .. | 20 | 100 | .. | .. | 10 | R Robinson |
| Kilrea | Y M I | .. | 20 | 100 | .. | .. | 10 | G. Becknell |
| Limerick | I | 40/. | 160 | 4200 | 9000 | .. | N 6 | R. Anglim |
| Newry | I | 3/6, q | 120 | 400 | 600 | .. | N 10 | C. Jennings |
| Portaferry | M I | 1/6 q | 16 | 550 | 5000 | .. | .. | J. Wallace |
| Tuam | M I | .. | 30 | .. | .. | .. | .. | |
| Waterford | M I | 2/6, 1/6 q | 300 | 1000 | 4000 | 100 | NM 20 | J. G. Davis |

From *The History of Adult Education* by J.W. Hudson, London, 1851, Longman Brown, Green and Longman

Many of the Irish Mechanics' Institutes had comparatively short lives despite the enthusiasm of the founders and their philanthropic intentions. Usually the Institutes were concerned with the instruction of operatives in the practical sciences, and to this end lectures were organised and libraries provided. The aim was to create and foster a desire for learning in scientific and literary fields leading to increased invention and improvement for the operative classes. In theory the Institutes would achieve this by placing within the reach of all the means of improvement enabling the operative 'to raise himself to that position in the social scale to which his genius and industry naturally entitle him', (Thom's *Irish Almanac and Official Directory*, 1846). In practice the Irish Institutes, for a variety of reasons, became the domain of the middle classes and those who could afford the fees charged.

In a flurry of enthusiasm the first meeting to convene the Mechanics' Institute in Dublin was held in September 1824 when an overwhelming 600 subscribers were received. It was proposed that the Institute should be financed from a ten shillings subscription from its members, the money to be used mainly to provide lectures and to procure books. At a preliminary meeting on 15 December 1824 to adopt rules and regulations Mr George Hume offered to the Institute an office rent free, and also rent free accommodation in his rooms at the Theatre of Arts. It was decided that at least nine of the eighteen committee members had to be operatives or mechanics, thus ensuring that the class for whom the Institute was formed played an important part in its management.

One of the earliest actions of the committee was to agree that a library should be founded and it was resolved that to extend the full benefit of the Institute to the mechanics of Dublin a collection of standard works be procured in the various departments of the sciences and the arts. These were to form the nucleus of the library which was to be sustained in the future by the current subscriptions of the Institute's members. Early efforts to establish a library had been made by encouraging members to present books from their own collections, but some books were purchased, including scientific journals. Gifts of money were used to buy the required volumes, and the committee was also successful in acquiring gifts of books. The reference library opened in April 1825 with a librarian who was paid £1 a week.

The committee wished however to form a lending library, as they felt the operative's taste for useful knowledge would only be gratified if he was allowed to take books home to imbibe information in the hope of improving his moral condition. The need for this library was considered to be so urgent that in July 1825 the member mechanics, frustrated by the apparent inaction, resolved to donate a volume each toward the lending library, which was in fact opened towards the end of that year. These early moves to establish an Institute failed, but the whole conception was revived again in November 1837.

By 1839 the annual report for the previous year was showing a huge growth in the use of the Dublin Mechanics' Institute library. At the beginning of the year the library had contained only 110 volumes, but by the end of the year this figure had increased to 500. Over 300 donations of books and maps had been received but nearly £40 had been spent on the purchase of books as well. Despite this growth the board of directors had constantly regretted their inability to buy more books as there was an increasing demand for them. The year had started with 120 members in the Institute and it ended with 700. The board tried to provide works that were likely to prove useful as well as popular, and had to face the problem of buying numerous books of comparitively little educational value cheaply, or of purchasing stock of a more educational character. They chose the educational books as they felt it their duty to guard against misdirecting the reading habits of those for whom the lasting benefits of the Institute had been formed. The board was convinced that the reading of one really sound and useful book was better than that of twenty idle or indifferent ones. The reading room of the Institute was extremely well-used especially in the evenings, and the board felt that the good arising from the provision of a reading room alone was well worth maintaining the Institute. In the reading room newspapers and all works of a political nature were vigorously excluded.

The library was open for loans on Monday and Thursday evenings from 8 to 9 p.m. for returns, and from 9 to 10 p.m. for the issue of books. Each member of the institution could use the library on production of his admission ticket and could borrow one book at a time on payment of a deposit or by providing the signatures of two respectable persons as sureties for the safe return of the book. There was apparently no attempt to place a proper value on individual books as 2s.6d. had to be deposited for an octavo and smaller, and 5s. for larger works. The loan period again differed according to the size of the book! The issue periods were two weeks for octavos or smaller, three weeks for quartos, and four weeks for folio volumes. Fines were incurred if a book was kept overdue at the rate of one penny a day for the first week, and fourpence a day for the second week. These charges must have been prohibitive. If the overdue book was not returned within fourteen days the member was charged the value of the book. The names of defaulters were posted up and they ceased to be members of the library. Any damaged book was charged for at the full replacement price.

A stock check was done once a year, the library closing for one week for that purpose. An issue book was kept to record all loans and a book was also provided for the members to enter any remarks or suggestions concerning the management of the reading room. All books belonging to the Institution were stamped on the title-page with the Institution stamp and this was put on the plates as well.

Rules appearing in the annual report for 1838 indicate that no disputes or discussions were allowed in the reading room, nor were readers allowed to partake of refreshments there.

By 1842 the board of directors' annual report showed that the Institute was firmly established and was growing slowly but steadily. The membership in the previous year totalled 1,594 which included eight lady members, and the library was recording an average daily issue of 87 books. The board lamented the trend of the readers to request novels and yet more novels, and they wanted their borrowers to pursue more useful courses of reading. What are novels, it was asked?

> Novels are in general very unprofitable reading. When read exclusively they enfeeble the mind and unfit it for serious exertion: just as a continual round of amusement destroys the virtuous energies of our nature, novels therefore should only be resorted to occasionally, as a recreation or relaxation from profitable and severer study.

The board emphatically requested that the members endeavour to cease the great demand for novels and to read the books relating to the respective professions of the members and which related to their duties as citizens and as children of the Eternal Father. The reading room of the Institute continued to be attended by numerous readers who behaved in a creditable way. No dispute, no indercorum. This was probably due to the fact that all partisan and sectarian publications continued to be excluded from the newsroom.

In Thom's *Irish Almanac and Official Directory* for 1846 the following information about the Institution is recorded. There were eighteen members of the committee, including a carpenter, a teacher, a clerk, a silk mercer, a brassfounder, a merchant tailor, an engineer, a coachmaker, a factor, a civil engineer, a brazier, a cabinet-maker, a basket manufacturer, a surgeon's artists and a printer. By this time the Institute had the reading room, well-supplied with all the literary and scientific periodicals of the day, and a library containing over 3,000 well-selected volumes. The newsroom was fully operational by the end of 1847, with members paying one penny for admission. Newspapers were also sold at half-price. Courses of lectures were delivered periodically, to which members were admitted free with the added privilege of introducing a lady. All this was within the reach of the mechanics for a mere ten shillings a year payable yearly, half-yearly or quarterly.

In addition, and this was something which probably boosted the membership figures, members could get tickets to the Northumberland and Irishtown Baths at reduced rates. They could also get into the Portobello Gardens at reduced prices, and could use Monsieur Maccaud's Gymnasium in Grafton Street at the low subscription of four shillings a quarter. Presumably the ladies were excluded from that particular privilege. In addition, members could join classes at very low premiums – mathematics classes for 2s.6d. a quarter, drawing 2s.6d. a quarter, French, Latin, elocution and dancing were each five shillings a quarter, and instruction in vocal music cost a mere one shilling a month. A chess club was also opened in 1847.

By 1849 the Institute had moved to new premises in Lower Abbey Street and had opened a new lecture theatre. The membership continued to increase with 162 additional members, making 2,862 in all. Of all the facilities it was the library that was the most extensively used, the issue of books having risen to 93,000 in 1850. In the honorary secretary's report for the year he records that the library must be the means of enabling many thoughtful readers to enjoy at once domestic life and intellectual gratification with members of their families participating in the advantages of the library. He concluded that the beneficial effect upon the community of the library was great indeed and should be fostered and promoted, whether its effect was just to keep the family circle together, or elevating it through literary instruction and reading, or winning men 'from other, and in many cases injurious habits'. He was here presumably referring to the effects of drink.

Books had been purchased for the library, some of them from funds arising from the sales of tickets to concerts and the theatre. The total number of volumes added to the library in 1850 amounted to 2,152. A catalogue of the library had also been printed at a cost of £20 and these were on sale at twopence per copy. The use of the library was such that an assistant to the librarian had to be appointed in that year, enabling the library to be kept open from 9 a.m. to 10 p.m. for the issue and return of books. The Dublin Mechanics' Institute seemed to be going from strength to strength, but over the next few years events occurred which promised to destroy the existence of the Institute itself.

One of the fundamental problems was the addition to the stock of two volumes likely to offend the decency of some of the members. These two volumes were *The History of Prostitution* and *Natural History of Monks and Monkeys*. Many of the members were Catholics and took offence at the distribution of tracts in which their religion and the Pope were brought into disregard. Members of the board were charged with sectarianism. There were accusations of proselytising and partisan and private meetings. James Haughton, one of the trustees of the Building Fund and also treasurer of the Institute was resented because a donation of his of £25 had brought about an eventual part-ownership of premises valued at £2,000. Much of the trouble led to internal arguments, bickering and petty squabbling. The secretary was dismissed for alleged misappropriation of funds and books, while some members were arrested for taking part in brawls and public fighting.

The library did not escape the atmosphere of strife, and by the mid-1850s the library which had been so full of promise in the preceding decade was in a state of complete chaos with many of the carefully collected books missing. The attitude of the librarian left something to be desired as the annual stocktaking normally undertaken within one week stretched into five weeks with no sign of the library reopening. The members of the Institute had reason to feel aggrieved when having paid their subscriptions found they were deprived of access to the most popular facility offered by the Institute. Membership dropped radically as the reputation of the Institute plummetted to an all-time low. The Institution ran into debt, and lecturers offered their services free to help the Institute clear its liabilities. The board of directors continued to profess a keen desire to educate and elevate the working classes of Dublin. James Haughton the secretary delivered lectures on the elevation of the working classes, covering intellectual, moral and industrial knowledge as well as the losses sustained by the use of alcoholic liquors. The results of over indulgence and intemperance were castigated and the operatives urged to forgo the use of tobacco, alcohol and ardent spirits generally. The behaviour of the board of directors was hardly a suitable example when trying to encourage the lower classes to better themselves!

Happily the worst was over and by the end of the 1850s the Institute was once again firmly established with the rancour and bitterness of the previous years put behind them. A new catalogue was prepared for the library and new acquisitions began to be added to the decimated stock of the library. The recovery of the Institute was not achieved without the generosity of several newspapers, which reduced their bills, and the Alliance Gas Company did the same. The recovery was complete by 1860 when a Literary and Debating Society was formed, an Irish class offered to operatives who wished to study their native tongue, and the Institute had a balance of £50. It was entirely out of debt and clear of the troubles that had dogged it for the previous ten years or so. The library continued to be popular and during 1859 the book issue totalled 12,672 with the reading room attracting some 29,000 visitors. The effects of the Young Ireland Movement were also apparent in the Institute, with lectures being held on Ireland past and present, and on Irish novelists.

The Post Office Directory for Dublin 1860 lists a Library Society at 19 New Row South, late of Brown Street, and established in 1848. This Library Society was composed of young men of all Protestant denominations. Its object was the acquisition and diffusion of useful knowledge for the attainment of which a lending library containing a considerable number of valuable works was available. It also had a reading room supplied with the principal newspaper and periodical literature of the day. Educational classes were also formed.

In Belfast there had been some reading societies established in the late eighteenth century for the use of the working classes and the rising middle classes. Notably the tradesmen of Belfast had started a literary and book society in 1788. The Belfast Literary Society was formed in 1801 and in 1821 the Belfast Natural History and Philosophical Society was founded. The Belfast Mechanics' Institute thus opened in 1825 in a city that was already fertile with societies concerned with the elevation of the working man through education and reading. The Institute operated from a leased property in Queen Street rented for £17 per annum, and it started with a comparatively small membership of just over 400.

The aims of the Institute were admirable and like all Mechanics' Institutes wished to promote a knowledge of the arts and sciences through lectures, classes and the establishment of a library. As elsewhere the stock of the library was most definitely to exclude novels. The Institute was managed by a secretary, treasurer and 24 directors of whom at least 16 were to be tradesmen. The annual subscription of twelve shillings per annum entitled members to vote at meetings, attend all lectures, and to use the library. Five trustees were appointed for life who were to take the property of the Mechanics' Institute in charge.

However well-intentioned the aims were, the Institute was un-successful in attracting members and within twelve years the sole remaining trustee, Robert Grimshaw, found himself faced with an ejection order for the non-payment of rent for the premises. For a mere £30.7s.7d. the lease and contents of the building, including the library, were put up for auction. The premises were bought by one of the members who tried unsuccessfully to re-open the Institute for the use of subscribers, but by January 1839 the project had failed.

More successful was the establishment in 1845 of the Belfast Working Classes Association for the promotion of General Improvement. This organisation ran lectures and operated a working class library known as the People's Circulating Library. The premises were at 4 Castle Chambers, which housed both the library and a people's newsroom. Members paid 1s.6d. a quarter for the use of the library, but only one shilling if they already subscribed to the newsroom. The library opened in 1847 with 700 volumes in stock, but by 1856 this had risen to 3,000 volumes. The library opened every day for the issue of books from 2 to 4 p.m. and from 7 to 8 p.m. in the evening. The rules for the use of the library were fairly strict with only one volume being lent out at a time, except novels which could be lent out in sets. Books were issued for one week if they were octavo volumes, two weeks for novels, and three weeks for larger volumes. Fines were charged for overdue books at the rate of one penny per day, and strangely books had to remain in the library for a day before they could be taken out again. Books on loan could be renewed but only for a week if another reader had put in a request for them. Reference books did not circulate but bound volumes of periodicals were allowed out on loan.

A circulating library is recorded in Belfast in 1865-66, run by C. Aitchison at 12 Castle Place. He was a bookseller and stationer who stocked new and standard works in every department of literature. In addition he organised the Belfast Select Reading Club, for which he promised to stock every new work of interest immediately on publication, with extra copies purchased according to demand. Mention must also be made of the Athanaeum News Room company, which had set up a newsroom for the purpose of supplying better facilities for people to acquire information through the public press and telegram. Charges were described as moderate. In addition there was a circulating library run by M. Speer at 10 Upper Townsend Street.

By 1865 the Belfast Peoples' Reading Rooms, the object of which had been the promotion of literary and scientific knowledge among the working classes, merged with the remains of the Mechanics' Institute and became the Belfast People's Literary Institute. Its aims were similar to its predecessors: 'to promote increased literary and scientific knowledge amongst the working classes by the provision of newsrooms, circulating libraries and lectures'. This movement survived for fourteen years but, through lack of funds, was itself forced to combine with the Belfast Working Men's Institute in 1879. The Working Men's Institute and Temperance Hall provided a library and newspaper room for the working classes in Belfast. Under the terms of its establishment it could not be used for political purposes and its objectives were the social, moral and intellectual improvement of the working classes through the promotion of the temperance cause.

These Working Men's Clubs flourished in the north of Ireland which was more of an industrial area than was the rest of the country. In Lisburn, with a population of just over 11,000 in 1881 there flourished no less than three reading rooms. These are listed in a directory of 1888 as the Conservative Working Men's Club, the Working Men's Club, and the Lisburn News Room. In Carrickfergus the YMCA established in 1873 had 130 members by 1881 and possessed a library, a reading room and a cafe. The population had just topped 10,000. In Ballymoney which had a population of 3,049 in 1881 a library was founded by a local benefactor James Cramsie who bequeathed £20 a year to help towards the maintenance of a public library and newsroom. These were managed by a committee of which in 1888 the secretary and treasurer was David Leitch. By then the library had acquired over

1,500 standard works.

In Larne's McGarel Town Hall there was a newsroom and library containing 2,000 books half of which were for reference and the other half used as a circulating library. Use of the facilities was by subscription of five shillings for participating in the advantages of the reading room, and 7s.6d. for the library and reading room. At this time Larne had a population of 5,000. Engagingly, as well as providing the Town Hall, Charles McGarel also laid out the local cemetery. Ballyclare, population 1,475, had a reading society as early as 1840 and is described as a place where 'Societies for promoting the development of the mind and body flourish'. The Reading Society had some 800 volumes by the 1880s, and these were all available for home reading. A newsroom was also established for which the members had to pay ten shillings a year for admission.

Still in the North a Mechanics' Institute was established in Dundalk in June 1844 by local citizens desirous of improving the minds and conditions of all classes in the community. The library was central to the aims of the Institute, and the committee's specific aims were admirably commendable. Novels and works of immoral teaching, books likely to excite political or religious animosity were to be excluded as they were not felt to fit in with the main objective which was the diffusion of useful knowledge. The Institute began optimistically, absorbing biographical, historical and travel books from the defunct Dundalk Literary Society. A room in the market house was used as a library with the luxury of a librarian appointed at a salary of £10 per annum. The initial membership was not large but had increased sufficiently by 1845 to allow for the appointment of an assistant to the librarian, whose salary had been generously raised to £15. By 1848 the membership of the Institute had risen to 211, the majority being tradespeople. However, in famine-ravaged Ireland the initial interest in the venture could not be maintained and by the early 1850s the Institute was experiencing financial difficulties. In 1853 the Dundalk Mechanics' Institute changed its name to the Dundalk Literary and Scientific Institution, but it continued to decline rapidly until there were only 26 members by 1856. The library of 1,600 volumes belonging to the Institute was handed over to the Town Commissioners in 1857 to be added to the newly founded Dundalk Free Library.

The Drogheda Mechanics' Institute provided a series of lectures mostly on scientific subjects, though there was also one devoted to Irish literature. Here too a reading room formed the nucleus of the Society and it was intended to encourage the working man to forsake the places of vice which were his normal resort. Like many others this Institute did not last long. Drogheda also had a literary debating society and a circulating library attached to the Total Abstinence Society in West Street. A rather pious comment in 1844 from the historian of Drogheda stated: 'there are some respectable residents in the town but society is not much cultivated at present'.

More successful were the Mechanics' Institutes of Galway, Cork and Clonmel. As early as November 1791 an Amicable Literary Society had been formed in Galway by respectable persons of both persuasions for the purpose of acquiring and disseminating useful knowledge on agriculture, commerce and science. However, the working man did not gain entry for although the members were numerous the mode of election rendered them select and middleclass. The Society did possess a good library with English and Irish papers and periodicals. As in most of these kinds of societies in Ireland all religious and political discussions were prohibited. In 1838 this Society became the Royal Galway Institution. Reading rooms abounded and by 1820 there were two separate reading rooms in the Mercantile Coffee Room which had been opened by subscription of local gentlemen. These took the principal London and Dublin newspapers as well as the local ones – proof positive of the anxiety of the townspeople for information and improvement and since the mitigation of the penal laws the benefit of education was keenly felt. Literary taste became more general, notably amongst the numerous and respectable middle class.

Given such a background it is not surprising to note the establishment of a Mechanics' Institute in Galway for the labouring classes which was extremely well-supported by the citizens of Galway with gifts and financial encouragement, including a valuable collection of books, catalogues and maps from the Galway historian James Hardiman. The Institute got off to a flying start in November 1826 with Mr Martin of Ross putting rooms over the Corn Exchange at its disposal. The subscription to the Institute was ten shillings per annum which many felt the use of the library alone justified.

The Institute progressed very well initially with a splendid library of architectural, mechanical, scientific and historical works, with the reading room offering two Galway papers as well as the Dublin newspapers. Trouble was imminent however as the master mechanics became jealous of their skills and felt threatened by the operatives anxious to improve themselves. More particularly the Institute, whose membership was almost entirely made up of Roman Catholics, was rent apart by the religious and political problems which were rife in this period.

The Protestant Archbishop of Tuam who had ably supported the Mechanics' Institute at its inception declined to renew his subscription owing to anonymous threats that if he entered Galway again he might well have to fear for his life. The Mechanics' Institute sent a deputation to the Archbishop profusely apologising and affirming their own respect for him. This was well-received by the Archbishop but not by the local townspeople. The crux of the matter lay in the fact that the Archbishop was the President of the London Hibernian School Society which had been established in Galway, and while he professed himself against sectarianism his Society was busy proselytising. Secondly the newsroom was stocked with material which led to the accusation that the Institute fostered political discord.

Whatever the ultimate reason the landlord took action and when the next rent was due he called an auction and sold off the books and furniture for one-tenth of its real value. The Institute's support had come from the patronage of those in higher positions who viewed political controversy with alarm and by 1830 this support had totally collapsed.

The Institute was resurrected in 1840 with encouragement from the local Temperance Society and donations from the local gentry. One of the first rules of the Society was that no person would be admitted to the Society unless he was able to produce testimonials of his having taken the pledge. Any member seen contraverting the temperance pledge was reported. A library was re-established and stocked by some donations, and each member contributed three-pence a week to purchase books, hire the premises and help sick members. This time the Mechanics' Institute flourished, although political arguments almost brought the Institute to its knees in 1845 when *The Pilot* newspaper was banned from the reading room for carrying an article in favour of the Mullingar line and against the Irish Great Western Railway, which the mechanics wished to support. The Institute was accused of being pro-Tory and anti-repeal, and for some considerable time it had difficulty in defending its name as an educational rather than as a political establishment.

The 1850s saw a continuation of the Institute despite the terrible ravages of the famine period. The Institute remained active with lectures and debates. The abstinence from alcohol of its members and the importance given to social areas probably led to the survival of the Society and its role gradually transformed from one of education to one of recreation. The Society continues to this day although very much removed from its original aims under the title of Mechanics' Institute.

The rules for the use of the Galway library are interesting as they differ slightly from the norm. Members could borrow books for a fortnight and there is no mention of the loan period being related to the size of the book. A librarian was appointed from among the elected council of the Institute who in turn selected three members to assist in the management of the library. Loans were not free and it cost one penny to borrow a book for a fortnight, and only one volume could be borrowed at a time. No non-fiction works could be lent out at all.

The Wexford Mechanics' Institute was supported by the Temperance Movement and had use of the Temperance Hall in the 1840s. Due to a donation from Sir Francis Le Hunte the library received 1,000 volumes and £100 towards the building fund. A three-storeyed building was erected and opened in 1858. On the death of Sir Francis Le Hunte he bequeathed a further £600 and this enabled the Institute to equip itself with committee rooms, a billiards room and a reading room.

One of the more successful and active institutes was that at Clonmel in County Tipperary, which was not established until 1842. This Institute always had the support and help of the local gentry and affluent tradesmen, particularly the Society of Friends, who saw in the Institute a way of improving the commercial life of the city to their mutual advantage. In addition, the founders wished to create an atmosphere of cordial neutrality for men of all creeds and parties. The Clonmel Institute was well-supported by the local clergy of all denominations, and from the first a library was considered of the utmost importance in the furtherance of its work. As was now almost universal in Ireland newspapers and all works and discussions of a religious or political nature were to be excluded, and no books on these topics were accepted as donations. Smoking and other 'disorderly conduct' was prohibited in the library which was open from 11 a.m. to 3 p.m. and from 7.30 p.m. to 10.30 p.m. Although newspapers were excluded, periodicals were taken for the operatives to read.

The subscription was 2s.6d. per quarter, with life membership offered to those who donated £5 or books to the value of £8 for the library. The committee which consisted of an equal number of scientific or professional men, master employers and artisans met once a month. The committee laid great emphasis on the importance of the lectures and from the first managed to attract some of the best speakers, including a woman whose appearance caused much surprise and comment. The members enrolling in the Institute rose from just over 200 in 1842-43 to 369 in 1844, this latter figure including 35 women.

The library, initially just one of reference, contained about 500 books in 1843 but a lending library was very quickly set up under a special library committee. Although only one volume could be borrowed at a time the loan period depended on the size of the book.

Loans were only allowed if guaranteed by a solvent person. By 1845 the stock of the library had increased to 1,400 volumes. The library was obviously very well-used with loans in 1844 totalling 9,602, which was very good considering that the membership was only 369. The stock was wide-ranging, covering most branches of knowledge – biography, history, travel, geology, chemistry, mathematics, astronomy, natural philosophy, essays, letters, fiction, agriculture, French and Latin. Lighter literature was available in the form of magazines.

The committee was extremely active on the library front, making catalogues and withdrawing from stock works which they considered to be obsolete. At the same time they were busy acquiring new books, either by donation or by purchase. The number of periodicals was increased and the use of the library in 1847 amounted to over 10,000 loans. Care was taken to improve the issue system, including the imposition of fines and checks on the condition of the books.

During the famine years the use of the Institute fell off but it recovered in the early 1850s when members requested that newspapers should be taken by the library. It was felt inconsistent that political literature stocked in the book collection was deemed acceptable as it was retrospective, whereas newspapers containing news of advances in the arts and sciences were excluded. By the late 1860s newspapers were being taken in the Clonmel Mechanics' Institute and among these were many London and Dublin publications as well as the *Cork Examiner* and the local Tipperary papers.

Additions to the library continued and the stock had risen to 2,290 by 1854. A local Literary Society had been formed by members of the Mechanics' Institute and discussions were conducted on the many excellent texts in the library. By 1873 this Literary Society had absorbed its parent Mechanics' Institute, the new organisation being known as the Clonmel Literary Society. This move merely reflected what had happened to Mechanics' Institutes not only in Ireland but also in England and Scotland when the roles of the Institutes changed from being for scientific instruction to being more literary and social organisations. When the town adopted the Public Libraries Act in 1899 the Society handed over the buildings and books to the Corporation.

The Mechanics' Institute in Cork was founded to give the mechanics of Cork and its vicinity the opportunity to learn scientific principles behind the everyday practices of their respective trades. Its support was essentially middleclass. The secretary was Richard Dowden, a temperance campaigner, one of the best-known philanthropists in Cork during the early nineteenth century and librarian to the Royal Cork Institution.

While lectures were offered as one of the facilities of the Mechanics' Institute most of the resources went towards creating a library of scientific and art books. The Institute had the intention of establishing a lending library as soon as possible, and when it did one penny a week was charged in advance for the loan of each book. The library was run by a sub-committee which met twice or three times a month to select improving works. This sub-committee reported to the directors who always had the final word when it came to book selection. A library catalogue was produced and a Mr McCarthy was appointed to the post of librarian. The library was open every weekday from 10 a.m. to 3 p.m. and from 6 to 10 p.m. On Sundays it was open from 2 to 6 p.m. The use of the library rose and operatives were to be seen in the library during the evenings 'calling the mind into action'. Thirty library visitors were appointed by the directors to assist the librarian in promoting decorum by one of them each evening attending at the library in succession. There was also a study room where absolute silence had to be observed.

After such a promising start it is sad to relate that the Institute very quickly fell into debt and within a few years of its establishment in 1825 the directors were looking at ways of saving money. Membership fell off and it was proposed to close the library during the day in order to save on the librarian's salary. For modern librarians it is refreshing and encouraging to view the response of the directors to this proposal. Richard Dowden particularly believing that the Institute could not function without an efficient library insisted that the library stay open and that savings be found elsewhere. The obvious solution of reducing the librarian's salary was firmly rejected as the directors believed that to attract a librarian of the right qualities the salary would have to reflect the duties expected of that person. In the event it was the library servants or menials whose jobs and hours were altered, resulting in a saving for the library of just over £26 per annum. At this time – 1827 – the library expenditure was reaching £186.3s.0d. while the income was only £142, made up of grants, subscriptions and library receipts. Although set up for the working classes the Mechanics' Institute in Cork was in competition with the Royal Cork Institution, the Cork Scientific and Literary Society, and the Cuverian Society, all of which derived their support from the middle classes. The Cork Mechanics' Institute continued for sometime but without ever becoming an important factor in the life of the city.

Limerick Mechanics' Institute was originally founded in 1825 but only survived for one year as it was bereft of proper funding. It did however have a reading room and a small library. It was re-instituted in 1827, being managed entirely by operatives. The rooms were in Charlotte's Quay and contained a library and newsroom stocked with newspapers from London, Dublin, Cork and Limerick itself. The Temperance Hall in Limerick, which at its peak had 11,000 members, had declined to a membership of about 300 by the turn of the 1850s. This Hall had a library and took newspapers. It refused, however, to admit any discussion or disputation on politics. It also had a benefit society.

Apart from the Clonmel and Dublin Institutes not one really flourished. Government influence and funds were extended to the failing institutions but this was coldly received. William Smith O'Brien, MP when giving evidence to the Select Committee on Education in 1836 had put forward the idea of a mobile corps of lecturers, funded by government aid and given under the sponsorship of the Royal Dublin Society or Board of Education. He suggested that these lectures should be available to the Mechanics' Institutes or Literary Societies in order to foster a spirit of intellectual development. The incentive of governmental financial aid was forthcoming for the Royal Dublin Society was directed to embark upon a provincial lecture scheme. This was of considerable help to the financially hard-pressed Mechanics' Institutes who thus found themselves supported by government funds for providing lecturers. This support underpinned the revival of the Institutes which had previously been struggling under financial constraints.

Notwithstanding the attractions of the talented lecturers and the subsequent relief to the funds the effects were evanescent. The Mechanics' Institutes continued to flounder although their libraries were always the backbone of the facilities offered.

A perusal of the books in the libraries of these Institutes will give some indication of the importance with which libraries were imbued by those responsible for the Institutes. Ireland was nearly always the poor relation of England but statistics taken from Hudson's *History of Adult Education* quoting returns from the Literary and Mechanics' Institutes for 1851 indicate bookstocks which were comparitively healthy.

|  | No. of Institutes | Members | Volumes | Newsrooms |
|---|---|---|---|---|
| England | 610 | 102,050 | 691,500 | 372 |
| Wales | 12 | 1,472 | 6,855 | 8 |
| Scotland | 55 | 12,554 | 59,661 | 15 |
| Ireland | 25 | 4,005 | 57,500 | 13 |

The following grid shows the use of the Institutes by the members.

| | Issues of books in 1850 | Nos. attending evening classes | No. of lectures given in 1850 |
|---|---|---|---|
| England | 1,820,748 | 1,620 | 5,234 |
| Wales | 16,800 | 280 | 115 |
| Scotland | 154,747 | 1,638 | 481 |
| Ireland | 33,800 | 182 | 210 |

Why then did the Institutes fail in Ireland? By 1851 the majority of the Mechanics' Institutes were on the decline, offering fewer lectures to fewer members. The chief impediment being the difficulty of procuring competent lecturers able to communicate their knowledge in a form their audience would understand. The funding of the Institutes was often unsatisfactory and many of the operatives could not afford the entrance fee or subscription. There was a universal complaint that the Mechanics' Institutes and similar bodies were used by those of a higher rank than those for whom they were designed. In effect the Institutes were mainly used by those who could afford them. One more cause for the gradual decline of the Institutes was the start of the movement to establish free public libraries in Ireland in the 1850s.

Mr G.A. Hamilton, MP, giving evidence to the Select Committee of the House of Commons on Public Libraries in 1849, stated that in Ireland a large proportion of the population could read yet the supply of libraries was very limited. The population did not read

**FIGURE 8.2**
**PHILOSOPHICAL INSTITUTIONS IN IRELAND**

| | PHILOSOPHICAL INSTITUTIONS. | | | | 237 |
|---|---|---|---|---|---|
| Place. | Title of Institute. | Rate of Subscript. | Members. | Departments. | Secretary. |
| Belfast | N His & P S | 10/ | 250 | M | J. M'Adam |
| Cork | L & S I | .. | 60 | .. | W. Whitelegg |
| ,, | Cuverian S | 10/ | 40 | M | F Jennings |
| ,, | Archælog S | .. | 50 | .. | J Wyndell |
| Dublin | UnivrstyPS | 10/ | 80 | 10 | D. C. Heron |
| ,, | Geolog. S | 20/e 20/ | 160 | M 8 | R. Ball |
| ,, | N His S | 20/ | 120 | 6 | W. Andrews |
| ,, | L & S I | .. | 50 | .. | Dr. Todd |
| Killyleagh | L & S I | .. | 30 | 10 | Dr. Kincks |
| Londonderry | N H S | 10/ | 50 | M | |
| Waterford | L & S I | | 100 | M 20 | W. Maclean |

*Learned and Royal Institutions, and Societies for the promotion of the Fine Arts, as well as the London Scientific Institutions, are omitted from this return.*

From *The History of Adult Education* by J.W. Hudson, London, 1851 because they had no access to books and not because they were unable to read. As proof of the penury of books in Ireland amidst a population becoming daily more capable of using them, it was stated that there were in Ireland 73 towns, containing an average population of 2,300, in which a bookseller's shop was not to be found! The report of the Select Committee went on to say that the future character of the agricultural population may depend on the formation of village libraries, through which information on material and moral welfare could be transmitted and a taste for something 'better than animal enjoyment'. It was also thought that the village library could furnish information on a subject of vital importance to the Irish population, that of emigration,

> in as much as a large proportion of our people annually withdraw from the mother country to seek, under another hemisphere, the support which their parent land denies them, it is necessary that they should be previously supplied with the most exact and ample information, in town as well as in country libraries, on a subject so closely connected with their future fortunes.

Cliffe Leslie[1] located a total of 35 Mechanics' and Literary Institutes in Ireland in 1852 of which five were in Belfast and three were in Dublin. Of the 35, 27 replied to his request for information. Of these:–

> 23 had periodical lectures; 20 had libraries; 8 had newsrooms; 5 had regular classes; 3 opened for some hours on Sundays; 4 admitted to providing what may be called amusement; 7 were in the process or already possessed separate buildings.

Cliffe Leslie formed the following impressions regarding the membership:

| | |
|---|---|
| Shopkeepers, shop assistants and clerks | 50% of the total membership |
| Tradesmen, workmen, mechanics carpenters, masons, etc. | 25% |
| Professional men and merchants | 20% |
| Members of the higher classes | 5% |

Complaints were made of the lack of efficient secretaries and of the high cost of books for the libraries. The absence of support from the wealthier classes and the deficiency of the education of the lower classes to warrant their appreciation of the advantages of the institutions were factors that prevented the Mechanics' Institutes developing further. Some employers feared that an educated workforce would demand higher wages while others saw the literate mechanic as a radical and a revolutionary. Lastly the secretaries reported that Sunday closure of the reading rooms when people were free to use them was an impediment and that the obstacles to peaceful association were created by religious and political feelings. It eventually transpired that what the mechanics really wanted was a news and reading room of light, amusing and ephemeral publications rather than enforced study. However, the libraries, newsrooms and lectures of the Mechanics' Institutes were the main source from which the largest portion of the population got all its literature.

The Mechanics' Institutes were not total failures as the circulation of books from their libraries and the provision of information from their newsrooms did cultivate the taste for reading among the lower classes.

Cliffe Leslie suggested a union of all the Mechanics' Institutes led by the Dublin Statistical Society might be appropriate to overcome the problems they were all encountering. In advance of his time he suggested the reciprocal advantages of the interchange of books, manuscripts, newspapers, lectures, privileges and information.

The growth of the public library movement in England was reflected in Ireland but with separate legislation to cope with the specific local situation. The 1850s were a decade when Ireland was dealing with the after-effects of the famine and the break-up of the old traditional ways. Ireland was poor and agricultural unlike England which epitomised industrial strength and wealth. The Young Ireland Movement had supported the idea of public libraries as a way of educating the people towards Irish nationalism and radicalism. But Ireland also had active middle classes who read books in English and who listened to music and discussed it at great length.

The first public library act followed the findings of the Select Committee of the Commons on public libraries which sat in 1849. Those giving evidence from Ireland were Mr G.P.R. Colles of the Royal Dublin Society who also gave evidence as regards the King's Inn Library, Marsh's Library and Trinity College Library. Mr Eugene O'Currey gave evidence on Irish libraries and the manuscripts they contained, and Mr G.A. Hamilton gave evidence on the state of education in Ireland.

The resultant Public Libraries and Museums Act of 1850 allowed town councils in England and Wales to levy a rate of one halfpenny in the pound for the purposes of establishing public libraries in their areas. This Act of 1850 was extended to Ireland in 1853 but had no immediate effects since it allowed municipal authorities with populations of 10,000 and upwards to establish libraries, but there were hardly any such authorities in Ireland.

By 1855 Ireland had a new public library law known as the Public Libraries Act (Ireland) 1855, and it remains today the principal Act for Ireland. It is an adoptive Act which applied to any borough council or Board of Municipal Commissioners of towns of 5,000 population or over. The decision to adopt the Act could be taken at a public meeting of householders provided that a two-thirds majority was in favour of the establishment of a public library.

The first Irish city to adopt the Act was Cork in 1855 but unfortunately despite the initial enthusiasm it was not until 1892 that the rate was actually applied to support a library in Cork. The percentage of the population recorded in the census of 1861 and that of 1871 for both the city and county of Cork presents an interesting

Francis Guy's County and City of Cork Directory 1875/76
*Extracts of the Census Returns for the City and County of Cork*

*Number and percentage of illiterate persons of 5 years of age and upwards*

| | Roman Catholic | Episcopalian Protestant | Presbyterian | Methodist | Other Sects | Total |
|---|---|---|---|---|---|---|
| County 1861 | 202,296(54%) | 342(11.9%) | 67(7%) | 98(6.4%) | 43(10.8%) | 205,933(50.7%) |
| County 1871 | 160,001(45.9%) | 2,468(9%) | 48(4.6%) | 120(6%) | 477(16.3%) | 163,114(42.7%) |
| City 1861 | 21,686(36.8%) | 875(9.1%) | 34(4.5%) | 34(4.4%) | 34(4.6%) | 22,662(32.1%) |
| City 1871 | 19,830(33.7%) | 502(6%) | 38(4.3%) | 23(3.6%) | 55(6%) | 20,448(29.4%) |

*Number of persons and percentage of persons belonging to each religious profession*

| | Roman Catholic | Episcopalian Protestant | Presbyterian | Methodist | Other Sects | Total |
|---|---|---|---|---|---|---|
| County 1861 | 426,894 (91.8%) | 32,822(7.1%) | 1,118(0.2%) | 1,760(0.4%) | 2,103(0.5%) | 464,697(100%) |
| County 1871 | 400,905 (91.5%) | 31,297(7.1%) | 1,216(0.3%) | 2,228(0.5%) | 2,788(0.6%) | 438,434(100%) |
| City 1861 | 67,148 (83.8%) | 10,632(13.3%) | 881(1.1%) | 893(1.1%) | 567(0.7%) | 80,121(100%) |
| City 1871 | 66,716 (84.8%) | 9,196(11.7%) | 1,028(1.3%) | 718(0.9%) | 984(1.3%) | 78,642(100%) |

*Extract from the Census 1871 in Francis Guy's County and City of Cork Directory 1875/76*

Degrees of elementary education in the municipal borough of Cork. 1871

| Religious professions | Read and write | Read only | Illiterate |
|---|---|---|---|
| Roman Catholics | 31,258 | 7,742 | 27,716 |
| Protestant Episcopalians | 7,422 | 418 | 1,356 |
| Presbyterians | 789 | 55 | 184 |
| Methodists | 612 | 12 | 94 |
| Other Sects | 830 | 30 | 124 |
| Total | 40,911 | 8,257 | 29,474 |

Total population 78,642 persons.

A perusal of some of the country areas in the county of Cork indicates an even worse picture of illiteracy. All details are from the 1871 Census.

FERMOY
Read and Write 4220
Read only        587
Illiterate      2530
Total Population 7337 (of these 1587 were under 12 years and 1669 were 40 years and over).

MALLOW
Read and write  2076
Read only        448
Illiterate      1641
Total population 4165

QUEENSTOWN
Read and write  5889
Read only        903
Illiterate      3542
Total population 10,334

A breakdown of these figures reveals that 2371 persons were under 12 yrs old, 1557 persons were between 12 – 20 yrs, 3782 persons were between 20 – 40 yrs, and 2624 persons were 40 yrs and over. There is no breakdown available by age and illiteracy.

YOUGHAL
Read and Write  2855
Read only        600
Illiterate      2584
Total population 6039

SKIBBEREEN
Read and write  1712
Read only        274
Illiterate      1709
Total population 3695

At this time the town of Queenstown had four booksellers and stationers listed in the directory but as this was a busy harbour it must be presumed that the bulk of their trade was not with the local population.

# Levels of rate levied for libraries in Ireland 1865

**Rate not exceeding 1d.**

| | | |
|---|---|---|
| Dublin | Donabate | 1d |
| Dublin | Glencullen | ½d |
| Kerry | Listowel & R.D. | 1d |
| Kerry | Cahirciveen | 1d |
| Kerry | Kenmare Dist. | 1d |
| Kerry | Castleisland | ½d |
| Kildare | Naas | 1d |
| Limerick | Rathkeale | 1d |
| Limerick | Newcastle West | 1d |
| Louth | Dundalk | 1d |

**Rate not exceeding 1d to 1½d**

| | | |
|---|---|---|
| Cork | Youghal | 1½d |
| Dublin | Balbriggan | 1½d |
| Dublin | Malahide | 1½d |
| Dublin | Garriston | 1½d |
| Dublin | Lusk | 1½d |
| Dublin | Skerries | 1½d |
| Dublin | Swords | 1½d |
| Waterford | Lismore | 1½d |

**Rate not exceeding 1½d to 2d**

| | | |
|---|---|---|
| Antrim | Larne | 2d |
| Armagh | Lurgan | 2d |
| Down | Newry | 2d |
| Louth | Drogheda | 2d |

**Rate not exceeding 2d to 2½d**

| | | |
|---|---|---|
| Limerick | Limerick | 2½d |

**Rate not exceeding 2½d to 3d**

| | | |
|---|---|---|
| Antrim | Belfast | 3d |
| Down | Bangor | 3d |
| Dublin | Rathmines and Rathgar | 3d |
| Kilkenny | Kilkenny | 3d |

**Rate exceeding 3d**

| | | |
|---|---|---|
| Dublin | Dublin | 6d (but supporting an Art Gallery) |

backdrop to the illiteracy in Ireland. There is no reason to believe that the figures are other than average for the whole of the country, underlining as they do yet another excuse for the slow adoption of the Public Libraries Act.

The first public library to open under the Act was in Dundalk in 1858. Dundalk had adopted the Act in 1856 and applied the rate for the maintenance of a reading room and library two years later. Ennis in Co. Clare adopted the Act in 1860 but the sum of money raised was so small as to make the establishment of the library unrealistic and for many years there was no public library in Ennis. Apart from these three, no other Irish town attempted to adopt the Act until nearly the end of the nineteenth century. Poverty was the main reason for the Act remaining ineffective for so long. There was little encouragement for towns to adopt the Act, and even when towns of 5,000 population and over were interested in setting up a public library, the penny rate failed to raise enough to support the enterprise.

Despite this, the Act was important for it laid down the principle of the free public library by saying: 'Admission to all libraries and museums established under this Act shall be open to the public free of all charge'. This, it was hoped, would eventually resolve the problems encountered by those too poor to pay the subscriptions for the reading rooms and libraries of the Mechanics' Institutes. The Act further provided for the purchase of land and buildings, the setting up of a library committee, the appointment of salaried officers and servants, and the right to make rules and regulations for the safety and use of the library.

The next Act affecting libraries in Ireland was the Public Libraries (Ireland) Amendment Act 1877 which allowed for the library committee to have members who were not necessarily members of the council or commissioners. The Act also conferred the power to borrow money. This year too saw the movement to establish a public library in Dublin and at a public meeting it was decided almost unanimously to vote for a resolution impressing on the town council the need to set up a free public library service. The corporation did not act but the year nevertheless remains important for libraries in Ireland as the state took over the direct administration of most of the library of the Royal Dublin Society and by an Act of Parliament re-named it as the National Library of Ireland. No doubt the corporation felt that with the National Library on its doorstep there was no real need to proceed with the establishment of a public library service.

However, a few years later in 1883 the Corporation of Dublin appointed a library committee and on 1 October 1884 two municipal libraries were opened in Dublin at a ceremony attended by members of the Library Association of Great Britain. Belfast adopted the Public Libraries Act in 1882 and levied the rate in 1883, opening its first library in 1888, four years later than Dublin. The rate at this time in Belfast was producing more than £4,000 per year. Kingstown adopted the law in 1884, Rathmines in 1887, and Limerick in 1889, the latter opening its library in 1893. Waterford adopted the Act in 1894 and opened its library two years later.

On the whole the penny rate produced pitiful sums in the small Irish towns and it was usually not enough even to consider a library service. The impetus needed to extend the number of libraries came with the Public Libraries (Ireland) Act 1894 which was promoted by the Young Ireland League. This Act extended the provision of the Acts to all urban districts and enabled local authorities to adopt the Acts by resolution. It further allowed two or more neighbouring districts to combine together to have a joint committee and to share the cost of the purchase, erection, repair and maintenance of the library building, as well as those of stocking the library. Under that provision as extended by Section 65 of the Local Government Act 1925 Longford-Westmeath, and Tipperary North and South Riding formed the joint library committees.

But the Act that had the most effect was the Public Libraries (Ireland) Act 1902 which gave the right to adopt the principal Act of 1855 to any rural district and allowed any library authority to enter into agreements with the managers of schools for the use of the school as a library. The Council of Cumann na Leabharlann (The Library Association) however tried to urge rural district councils that the public library movement could best be served by the establishment of libraries separate from schools. The council felt that a school could not be used in the same sense as a public library and that a newsroom in a school would not be workable. They also feared the denominational character of schools in Ireland would prevent some sectors of the community from making use of the library, and the council thus advocated separate and independent buildings.

At the same time the council recommended that books should be lent to the schools through the public libraries so that school libraries should be supplemental to but should not supersede the regular public libraries in the district. As an illustration they referred to the Public Libraries Committee of the City of Dublin which in 1904 supplied sixty schools in the city with 70 volumes each on loan from the local public libraries in their districts.

The 1902 Act also allowed county councils, out of funds available for technical education, to make grants to library authorities in their areas for the purchase of books or towards the maintenance of public libraries. This Act led to a flurry of libraries being established in rural areas, and by 1905 public libraries had been established in:

Co. Cork     – Rural District Councils of Kinsale, Mallow, Youghal.

Co. Dublin    – Rural District Councils of Balrothery, North Dublin, South Dublin, Rathdown, no.1.

Co. Kerry     – Rural District Councils of Cahirciveen, Dingle, Killarney

Co. Limerick – Rural District Councils of Limerick no. 1, Rathkeale

Co. Wicklow – Rural District Council of Rathdown no. 2

Regrettably, despite the limited value to be gained from the penny rate, some of the district councils actually limited the rate to one halfpenny, and one to as low as one farthing.

Boroughs and municipal towns that adopted the Public Libraries Act, although not all had erected libraries by 1905, were as follows:

Co. Armagh     – Lurgan, Portadown
Co. Antrim      – Belfast, Larne, Lisburn
Co. Cork        – Cork, Youghal
Co. Derry       – Coleraine, Derry
Co. Down       – Banbridge, Newry, Newtownards
Co. Dublin      – Blackrock, Clontarf, Drumcondra (both by then part of Dublin), Dublin, Kingstown, Rathmines
Co. Kildare     – Naas
Co. Kilkenny   – Kilkenny
Co. Limerick    – Limerick
Co. Louth       – Drogheda, Dundalk
Co. Sligo        – Sligo
Co. Tipperary   – Clonmel, Nenagh
Co. Waterford   – Waterford
Co. Wicklow     – Bray

This activity in establishing libraries was reflected by the people working in the libraries. The Cumann na Leabharlann was founded on 2 June 1904 at a general meeting held in the Public Library at Lower Kevin Street, Dublin. Among the founding members of the Library Association were Douglas Hyde and Sean T. O'Kelly, both subsequently Presidents of Ireland, as well as Padraig Pearse, the leader of the 1916 uprising. It was desired that in name, objects and essence the association should be of Ireland and for Ireland. T.W. Lyster proposed the following motion when it was agreed that an association to be called Cumann na Leabharlann be formed. It had as its objectives

1 The promotion of public libraries and reading rooms
2 To influence those engaged in library work to recognise the opportunities for good which their positions afford and the importance of the duties and obligations attached to such positions.
3 To promote the study of bibliography, limited in special relation to Ireland
4 Improvement of library administration and method.

An incidental objective was that with the creation of a reading public, the printing and publishing trades which were so extensive at the close of the eighteenth century would be re-kindled into greater life than they had then, also that this new life would be reflected in the Irish bookbinders' art which would flourish as in the past. The association was to be governed by a committee consisting of a president, four vice-presidents, two honorary treasurers, two honorary secretaries and twenty ordinary members all of whom were to be elected by the members by ballot.

The first president was Thomas Kelly, with vice-presidents John Kells Ingram, Thomas W. Lyster, Seumas Macmanus and Edward Martyn. Among the committee was listed Arthur Griffith. Those attending the inaugural meeting came from all over the country and included E.R.M'C. Dix, the Irish bibliographer. The association consisted of members and associates. Members were entitled to the journal free and to vote at all meetings of the association. Associates could attend all meetings other than the business meetings of the association, but they were not entitled to vote or to receive the journal. Members' subscription was ten shillings a year, while associates paid 2s.6d. annually.

Monthly meetings were to be held in the winter and spring, together with an annual congress. The association which was not long lived, produced a quarterly journal, the first issue of which was published in January 1905 entitled *An Leabharlann*. Five numbers and a supplementary volume were issued between 1905 and 1909.

The wider aims of the association are written up in the first issue of the journal. These aims were to place Ireland in the position she ought to occupy by providing opportunities for study and general reading, by creating a thinking people able to serve their country, and also better able to advance themselves. The leading article lamented the lack of suitable reading material to occupy the intellects of the youth of Ireland. Culture, such as it was, ceased upon the termination of school life, leaving the street corner or the public house as the only remaining attractions. The Cumann attempted to counteract this condition by unceasingly urging the local authorities to provide opportunities for reading and study by establishing newsrooms and libraries, these to be maintained out of the public rate and without class distinction or subscription preventing entrance. They also hoped for the establishment of reference libraries in the cities and towns of Dublin, Belfast, Cork and Limerick. The promoters of Cumann na Leabharlann felt the need for an organisation exclusively devoted to library propaganda as essential if libraries were to be generally provided in the immediate future. Staff working in public libraries were urged to understand the opportunities for good which their positions afforded. Librarians were encouraged to make the readers feel at home, to entice non-readers into the library and to help and guide others in its use. These ideas, so pressing in 1905 for the founders of Cumann were in reality far in advance of their time.

Arthur Griffith's involvement with the Cumann na Leabharlann was not out of character. He was in any case a member of the Dublin Public Library Committee. As a very young man he became a profound reader and developed a great love of music. At the early age of seventeen he ran the Eblana Literary and Debating Society and contributed to the journal *Eblana*. This society soon merged with the Leinster Literary Society which indulged in discussions, debates and readings of papers and poems as well as holding musical evenings. The Leinster Literary Society was eventually abandoned by most of its members who under the leadership of William Rooney formed themselves into the Celtic Literary Society. At this time many young men belonged to Fireside Clubs which had been established thanks to the enthusiasm of the poet Rose Kavanagh. At these gatherings, held by candlelight in rented rooms the talk was about books they had read, or about Ireland.

In effect the Irish literary revival was another reason for the slow start to public libraries in Ireland, for the public library system represented the English culture. In addition, at the same time that the library movement was endeavouring to found a reading society in English the Gaelic League was founded in 1893 to revive the fast disappearing Irish language. The League was formed by three scholars, Douglas Hyde, Eoin MacNeill and Father Eugene O'Growny. A year earlier in 1892 W.B. Yeats and T.W. Rolleston had founded the National Literary Society. These two organisations symbolised the rebirth of feeling for the traditional Irish civilisations and culture while at the same time kindling a fervent nationalistic spirit.

But there were other movements which recognised the need to

# FIGURE 9.1 LIST OF ONE HUNDRED BOOKS TOWARDS THE FORMATION OF A VILLAGE LIBRARY

**THE IRISH HOMESTEAD.** JANUARY 20, 1900

LIST OF ONE HUNDRED BOOKS TOWARDS THE FORMATION OF A VILLAGE LIBRARY.

| | Name of Book. | Author. | Publisher. | Paper Edition. | Cloth Edition. |
|---|---|---|---|---|---|
| 1 | "A Short History of Ireland" | Dr. Joyce | Longmans | None | 10s. 6d. |
| 2 | "A Literary History of Ireland" | Dr. Douglas Hyde | Fisher Unwin | None | 16s. |
| 3 | "The Story of Early Gaelic Literature" | Do. | Do. | 1s. | 2s. |
| 4 | "Ireland's Ancient Schools and Scholars" | Dr. Healy | Gill and Son | None | 7s. 6d. |
| 5 | "Hibernian Nights' Entertainments" (3 vols.) | Ferguson | Sealy, Bryers, and Walker | 1s. per vol | 2s. per vol. |
| 6 | A local book on Antiquities and Topography, such as "Kilmacduagh" | Dr. Fahey | —— | 7s. 6d. | Gill & Son |
| 7 | "Life of Owen Roe O'Neill" | J. F. Taylor | Fisher Unwin | 1s. | 2s. |
| 8 | "Rise and Fall of the Irish Nation" | Barrington | Duffy and Co. | 1s. | 2s. |
| 9 | "Irish Names of Places" (2 vols.) | Dr. Joyce | Gill and Son | None | 10s. |
| 10 | "Life of Sarsfield" | Todhunter | Fisher Unwin | 1s. | 2s. |
| 11 | Writings | Finton Lalor | O'Donoghue | 1s. | 2s. |
| 12 | "All Ireland" | O'Grady | Sealy, Bryers, and Walker | 1s. | None |
| 13 | "Jail Journal" | John Mitchell | Cameron | 1s. | 2s. |
| 14 | "Finn and his Companions" | O'Grady | Fisher Unwin | None | 2s. 6d. |
| 15 | "The Celtic Twilight" | W. B. Yeats | Lawrence & Bullen | None | 3s. 6d. |
| 16 | "Ancient Legends of Ireland" | Wilde | Chatto | None | 3s. 6d. |
| 17 | "General Sketch of European History" | Freeman | MacMillan | None | 1s. 6d. |
| 18 | "A Short History of the English People" | Green | MacMillan | None | 8s. 6d. |
| 19 | "Decisive Battles of the World" | Creasy | MacMillan | 1s. 4d. | 3s. 6d. |
| 20 | "The Conquest of Mexico" | Prescott | Routledge | None | 3s. 6d. |
| 21 | Plutarch's "Lives" | | Do. | None | 3s. 6d. |
| 22 | "Old Celtic Romances" | Dr. Joyce | D. Nutt | None | 2s. 6d. |
| 23 | "The Life of Johnson" | Boswell | Sands and Co. | None | 3s. 6d. |
| 24 | "The Laughter of Peterkin" | Fiona MacLeod | | None | 5s. |
| 25 | Prose Writings | Thomas Davis | W. Scott | None | 1s. 6d. |
| 26 | "Tour in Ireland" | Young | G. Bell and Son | 6d. (abgd) | 7s. 2 vols. complete |
| 27 | "Natural History of Selborne" | White | W. Scott | None | 1s. 6d. |
| 28 | "Self-Help" | Smiles | J. Murray | None | 3s. 6d. |
| 29 | Report of the Recess Committee | | —— | 1s. 6d. | None. |
| 30 | "Psychology for Teachers" | Sully | Longmans | None | 6s. 6d. |
| 31 | "Handbook to Ireland" | Cooke | J. Murray | None | 9s. |
| 32 | "Irish Literary Ideals" | | "Daily Express" | 1s. nett | |
| 33 | "Simple Lessons in Irish" (4 parts) | O'Growney | Gill and Son | 1s. 6d. nett | — |
| 34 | "Legends of St. Patrick" | De Vere | MacMillan | 3d. | 6d and 3s |
| 35 | Poems | Thomas Moore | Warne | 6d. | — |
| 36 | Poems | J. C. Mangan | Haverty (New York) | None | 8s. |
| 37 | "Collected Poems" | W. B. Yeats | Fisher Unwin | None | 7s. 6d. |
| 38 | "Lays of the Western Gael" | Ferguson | Sealy, Bryers, and Walker | 1s. | 2s. |
| 39 | "Lyra Celtica" | Sharpe (Editor) | Geddes | None | 6s. nett. |
| 40 | "Love Songs of Connacht" | Dr. Douglas Hyde | Gill and Son | 2s. 6d. nett | — |
| 41 | "Religious Songs of Connacht" | Do. | Not yet out | | — |
| 42 | "The Spirit of the Nation" | | Duffy | 6d. | 1s. |
| 43 | "Lays of Ancient Rome" | Macaulay | Cassell | 3d. | 6d. |
| 44 | Homer's "Iliad" | Chapman (Translator) | Warne | None | 2s. |
| 45 | { Complete Works or { Works | Goldsmith; Goldsmith | MacMillan; Warne | None; None | Ch'ndo's; 3s. 6d. |
| 46 | "Short History of Art" | Turner | Sonnenschein | None | 4s. 6d. nt |
| 47 | "The Heather Field" and "Maeve" | Martyn | Duckworth | None | 5s. |
| 48 | "Reliques of Ancient English Poetry" | Percy | Warne | None | 2s. |
| 49 | "The Golden Treasury" | Palgrave | MacMillan | None | 2s. 6d. nt; edit. 2s. |
| 50 | "Grania" | Lawless | Smith, Elder & Co | None | 6s. |
| 51 | "Irish Idylls" | Jane Barlow | Hodder | None | 6s. |
| 52 | "A Queen of Men" | O'Brien | Fisher Unwin | 1s. | 3s. 6d. net |
| 53 | "Moral Tales" | Edgeworth | MacMillan | 1s. (Blackie's Edition) | 3s. 6d. |
| 54 | "House by the Churchyard" | LeFanu | Do | None | 2s. |
| 55 | "The Poor Scholar" | Carleton | Duffy and Co. | 6d. | 1s. |
| 56 | "The Collegians" | Gerald Griffin | Do. | 1s. | 2s. |
| 57 | "The Boyne Water" | Banim | Do. | 2s. | 2s. 6d. |
| 58 | "Knocknagow" | Kickham | Do. | None | 3s. |
| 59 | Mystery of Killard" | Dowling | Downey and Co. | 2s. | |
| 60 | "Treasure Island" | Stevenson | Cassell | 6d. | 3s. 6d. |
| 61 | "Beside the Bonnie Briar Bush" | MacLaren | Hodder | 6d. | 6s. |
| 62 | "Lorna Doone" | Blackmore | S. Low and Co. | None | 2s. 6d. |
| 63 | "The Newcomes" | Thackeray | Nisbet | None | 2s. 6d. |
| 64 | "Waverley" | Scott | Black | 6d. | 1s. and 2s |
| 65 | "The Last Days of Pompeii" | Lytton | Routledge | 6d. | 2s. |
| 66 | "Tales of Mystery and Imagination" | Poe | Ward, Lock | 6d. | 2s. |
| 67 | "Uncle Tom's Cabin" | H. B. Stowe | Warne | 6d. | 2s. |
| 68 | "That Lass of Lowrie's" | Burnett | Warne | 1s. | 1s. 6d. |
| 69 | "Mr. Isaacs" | Crawford | MacMillan | 1s. | 3s. 6d. |
| 70 | "Little Lord Fauntleroy" | Burnett | Warne | None | 3s. 6d. |
| 71 | "Misunderstood" | Montgomery | MacMillan | 6d. | 6s. |
| 72 | "Helen's Babies" | Habberton | Richards | 6d. | 6s. Illus. |
| 73 | "Lost on Du Corrig" | O'Grady | Cassell | None | 2s. 6d. |
| 74 | "Alice in Wonderland" | Carroll | MacMillan | 6d | 2s. 6d. net |
| 75 | "Animal Stories" | Weir | Routledge | None | 3s. 6d. |
| 76 | "Robinson Crusoe" | Defoe | Warne | 6d. | 2s. |
| 77 | Liverpool School of Cookery, Bury Cookery Book (one dozen) | | —— | 1d. | |
| 78 | "Capt. Cook's Voyages" | Cook | Routledge | 6d. | 2s. 6d. |
| 79 | "Handicraft for Handy People" | Joyce | Gill and Son | None | 2s. |
| 80 | "First Year of Scientific Knowledge" | Paul Bert | Relfe | None | 2s. |
| 81 | "Astronomy" | Ball | Longmans | | 1s. 6d. |
| 82 | "The Book of the Dairy" | | Bradbury | None | 2s. 6d. |
| 83 | "Elements of Agriculture" | Fream | Murray | None | 3s. 6d. |
| 84 | "Live Stock of the Farm" | | Bradbury | None | 2s. 6d. |
| 85 | "Crops of the Farm" | | Do. | None | 2s. 6d. |
| 86 | "Soil of the Farm" | | Do. | None | 2s. 6d. |
| 87 | "Equipment of the Farm" | | Do. | None | 2s. 6d. |
| 88 | "Lessons with Plants" | Bailey | MacMillan | | |
| 89 | "Practical Poultry-keeping" | Wright | Cassell | None | 3s. 6d. |
| 90 | A set of the Publications of the Royal Agricultural Society of England" | | | | |
| 91 | "British Beekeeper's Guide Book" | Cowan | Houlston | 1s. 6d. | None |
| 92 | "Manures and Manuring" | Scott | | None | |
| 93 | "Agricultural Note Book" | M'Connell | Lockwood | None | L'ther 6s. |
| 94 | "Hygiene for Beginners" | Reynolds | MacMillan | None | 2s. 6d. |
| 95 | "Lessons in Domestic Science" (two parts) | Lush | MacMillan | 6d. each | |
| 96 | "Practical Dressmaking" | Broughton | Do. | | |
| 97 | "Primer of Geology" | Geikie | Do. | 1s. | |
| 98 | "Some Irish Industries" | | HOMESTEAD Office | 4d. | — |
| 99 | "Field and Hedgerow" | Jefferies | Longmans | None | 3s. 6d. |
| 100 | "Political Economy" | Devas | Do. | None | 6s. 6d. |

From *The Irish Homestead*, 20 January 1900

establish suitable libraries in the rural areas of Ireland. Father J. O'Donovan published an article on village libraries in the *Irish Homestead* on 20 January 1900. This journal had held a competition to find the best list of books suitable for a parish or village library and it subsequently published the list which was an amalgamation of the first and second prize-winning lists, (see Figure 9.1). Father O'Donovan advocated the extension of the cooperative movement to establishing small circulating libraries in association with the Cooperative Societies. His idea was to improve the quality of reading matter available to the vast majority of the people 'who for the most part read nothing but wretched trash', usually 'low London productions which are neither good literature nor good morals, papers that often pander to the lowest impulses of man's depraved nature'. This theme was to be echoed in Ireland for a long time to come. Father O'Donovan went on:

> There is much talk of national rehabilitation, but let those whose hearts are devoted to the cause have a care lest when it comes, Cockneys are not found seated in every cabin throughout the land. It will be owing to no lack of effort on the part of *Ally Sloper*, *Comic Cuts*, *Chips*, *The Budget* and other similar London abominations.

Strong words indeed, but one knows what he meant, and he was no doubt sowing the seeds for the later Censorship Board. He hoped for the establishment of libraries in parishes to give life to the dying national spirit. He urged libraries to stock books in Irish, thus helping the work of revival already started by the Gaelic League, as well as classes to study the language. He was not a romantic however, because he also stressed the need for books of a technical nature in the village library, especially on the two problems then concerning Ireland – agriculture and industrial development. He felt that every Cooperative Society in Ireland should devote £10 towards such an enterprise, and he drew up a list of twelve rules for the setting-up of the parish libraries which he advocated should have interdenominational committees. A small entrance fee was to be charged of threepence plus one penny per month for every book taken out. All persons in the parish were deemed eligible for membership.

Father O'Donovan's ideas were reflected in a scheme devised by Canon Gately of Strokestown, Co. Roscommon, known as 'Canon Gately's Automatic Library'. The essential features of the scheme involved the creation of a circle of twelve persons or households and the selection of twelve books as varied as possible in their contents but not differing greatly in price. Each subscriber contributed one twelfth of the total amount of the money spent on the purchase of the books. When received, the books were distributed to members of the circle, each of whom kept his volume for a month before passing it on to the next member according to a regular scheme of rotation drawn up and pasted into each book. At the end of the year the books were all returned to the manager of the scheme with members then drawing lots for first, second and third choice of them, and so on until each member had become the possessor of one book out of the twelve. At the same time the books for next year's scheme were given out and started their round. It was felt that the advantage of this scheme was that each member became the owner of one book a year besides having read the twelve, and the chances of the ballot added a certain 'sporting interest' which was perhaps not without its attraction to the gambling instinct of the participants!

The legislation, in the shape of the Public Libraries (Ireland) Act of 1902, had a side-effect of calling into existence the Irish Rural Libraries Association, whose president was none other than the persuasive Father O'Donovan and on whose committee sat such eminent people as Douglas Hyde, F.J. Bigger, T.W. Lyster, Lord Mounteagle, the historian Revd E. A. D'Alton, and Stephen Gwynn.

The Irish Rural Libraries Association was founded on 22 April 1904 at a public meeting held in the Mansion House, Dublin. Its aims were to circulate extensively among rural district councils and the public generally a clear and concise statement of the legal powers in force for the establishment of libraries in rural districts, and to draw up a scheme for the exercise of those powers to enable rural districts to take advantage of the Act in a simple and effective manner. The association further produced and circulated a priced list of books suitable as the nucleus of a rural library. This list contained recommended titles in the following categories: mythology, folklore (Irish and English), history (Irish), English and Continental history, classical history and literature, prose fiction, Irish poetry and drama, other poetry and drama, essays, biography and belles lettres, art and agriculture. With over 600 titles, the list was an enlargement of a previous list of 100 books for a village library published by *The Irish Homestead*, but it also included titles in Irish. Membership of the association was not less than five shillings per annum and the association, as always, aimed to be non-political and non-sectarian.

The skeleton scheme for the rate-aided rural district library under the 1902 Act worked out by the association was first put into practice with great success by the Rathkeale Rural District Council. In its task the Council was aided by a grant of £2,800 for building purposes from Andrew Carnegie, and a grant of £15 from the Department of Agriculture and Technical Instruction for books on industrial and scientific subjects. The skeleton scheme was comprehensive and covered the incorporation of existing voluntary libraries, in which case the rural district council became responsible for them to constitute themselves free public libraries under the Act. The scheme covered the appointment of staff, and the six-monthly circulation of books, usually a quarter or one half of the stock, from library to library. Advice was given on the setting up of a committee made up partly of members of the RDC, members of the clergy, and other residents in the neighbourhood. The actual purchase of the books was entrusted to a books sub-committee chosen by the library committee from its members who were qualified by education and experience for the purpose. The librarian merely acted as secretary to the committee. This last provision was to cause problems of censorship and restriction for many years and was the bane of many a librarian's life. Other duties of the librarian involved the preparation of a complete alphabetical catalogue in slip or card form. The association recommended that two sets of cards should be kept, one at the centre and the other at headquarters, so that books could be sent on to the next centre with a complete set of cards. These instructions were admirable and played a considerable part in stimulating the growth of the rural libraries. The Rural Libraries Association was not against the formation of voluntary libraries and it gave advice on this. Further, they pointed out how the general public could requisition a rural district council to adopt the Acts and how to ballot the voters. If the majority of voters favoured adoption, the Acts were deemed to be adopted forthwith. If after six months the Acts were not being effected, the Local Government Board could appoint commissioners for the purpose. In effect the association wished to promote the extension and utilisation of public libraries in Ireland in all ways which were desirable and practicable.

The Public Libraries (Art Galleries in County Boroughs) (Ireland) Act 1911 raised the maximum rate limitation by one halfpenny to 3d in the £ where county boroughs provided art galleries. This provision however did not greatly aid the development of the public library system in Ireland, and indeed during the 1914-1918 War the plight of the libraries worsened as the value of money depreciated. This eventually led to representations being made to the government, and these resulted in the passing of the Public Libraries (Ireland) Act 1920. Under this Act the rate levy was raised to 3d in the £ with the proviso that the said limit of 3d in the £ might with the consent of the Local Government Board be exceeded to an extent not exceeding an additional 3d in the £.

In reality the growth of public libraries had been slow in Ireland compared to England, Scotland and Wales during the same period. This is demonstrated by the following tables taken from the *Report on Library Provision and Policy* presented by Professor W.G.S. Adams to the Carnegie United Kingdom Trust in 1915.

|         | England | Wales | Scotland | Ireland |
|---------|---------|-------|----------|---------|
| 1840-49 | 1       | –     | –        | –       |
| 1850-59 | 18      | –     | 1        | 1       |
| 1860-69 | 12      | 1     | 1        | –       |
| 1870-79 | 38      | 5     | 5        | –       |
| 1880-89 | 51      | 5     | 9        | 5       |
| 1890-99 | 121     | 17    | 15       | 8       |
| 1900-09 | 125     | 29    | 42       | 12      |

The above indicates the number of rate-supported libraries established in each successive decade. Further there was a marked contrast between public library coverage in different parts of the United Kingdom as may be seen from the following tabulation.

|          | Total Population 1911 | Population in Library Districts | Percentage of Total Population |
|----------|-----------------------|--------------------------------|--------------------------------|
| England  | 34,194,205            | 21,103,317                     | 62                             |
| Wales    | 2,025,202             | 938,303                        | 46                             |
| Scotland | 4,760,904             | 2,403,283                      | 50                             |
| Ireland  | 4,309,219             | 1,245,766                      | 28                             |
|          | 45,370,530            | 25,690,669                     |                                |

Here it can be seen that just over a quarter of the population in Ireland had access to a public library and that this figure compared very unfavourably with the rest of the United Kingdom. In addition there was the thorny problem of the annual income raised for the rate-supported libraries, and the following table, based on the information furnished by the Parliamentary Returns on the Public Libraries Acts in 1884, 1889-90 and 1910-11, clearly illustrates this.

|                   | 1884 £   | 1889-90 £ | 1910-11 £ |
|-------------------|----------|-----------|-----------|
| England and Wales | 115,911  | 193,827   | 726,247   |
| Scotland          | 5,361    | 7,746     | 68,466    |
| Ireland           | 2,394    | 4,481     | 18,005    |
|                   | £123,666 | £206,054  | £812,718  |

This shows a steady and sizeable increase in public library expenditure, but not in Ireland. The following table represents a fairly complete analysis of library income in the year ending 31 March 1911. It will be noted that most of the rate-supported Irish libraries had less than £200 per annum to manage the service.

Number of libraries and their income 1910-11

| | Under £100 | £100–£200 | £200–£350 | £350–£500 | £500–£750 | £750–£1000 | £1000–£1500 | £1500–£3000 | £3000–£5000 | Over £5000 | |
|---|---|---|---|---|---|---|---|---|---|---|---|
| England | 55 | 50 | 59 | 38 | 35 | 25 | 29 | 45 | 26 | 29 | 391 |
| Wales | 21 | 13 | 6 | 4 | 1 | 2 | 1 | 3 | 1 | 0 | 52 |
| Scotland | 23 | 15 | 12 | 9 | 5 | 5 | 4 | 2 | 2 | 3 | 80 |
| Ireland | 9 | 14 | 4 | 2 | 0 | 2 | 0 | 1 | 1 | 1 | 34 |
| Total | 108 | 92 | 81 | 53 | 41 | 34 | 34 | 51 | 30 | 33 | 557 |

In general the rate remained still at one penny in the pound and was limited to that except where special authority had been obtained by a Local Act of Parliament. In consequence the expenditure on books, periodicals and salaries appears very low.

One of the most important factors in library development was the extension of the Carnegie grants to Ireland. As a rule they were made between 1897 and 1913 to support local effort and to encourage local authorities which had adopted the Acts and had imposed the penny rate. In 1913 Andrew Carnegie created the Carnegie United Kingdom Trust whereby the future administration of the grants was placed under the control of a permanent body of trustees. The grants were nearly always for buildings including, but not always, the furnishing, the practice being for the local authority to provide a site free of cost. There were rarely any endowments for the maintenance of the book stock. Normally the grants were of a definite amount and the liability of Mr Carnegie ceased with each individual grant. Despite limitations, the Carnegie grants had a far-reaching influence on the library movement and brought home the idea of the public library as an important local institution. It is apparent that the majority of the Carnegie grants had been made without sufficient knowledge of the local conditions. In fact one of the main features of the library movement from 1902 to 1914 was the erection, in rural district council areas, of library buildings which rapidly fell into disuse. The chief criticism was overbuilding, and in some cases library buildings had been provided involving great upkeep expenditure which left insufficient means to carry out the library's main purpose, that of providing books for the local population.

The reasonable assumption that the local authorities, relieved of having to meet capital, expenditure on buildings, would be willing to supply adequate stocks of books, attributed to local authorities and their ratepayers a greater appreciation of public libraries than was sometimes justified. In many areas the Carnegie building was used for everything except library purposes. Village bands practised there, temperance meetings were held in them, and they were vandalised. In one library the enterprising caretaker had resorted to burning the books to save himself from being bothered by persistent would-be readers! In another, the first use of the restored library was for the organisation of a Sinn Fein meeting with over 150 members being enrolled to the accompaniment of the singing of rebel songs. Jack Yeats the artist, in response to the general feelings of the intelligentsia, painted a picture of an Irish village hiding behind the hills in the hope that it might escape the offer of a Carnegie library!

The buildings absorbed the greater part of the income raised by the penny rate, leaving a mere pittance for the purchase of books, and often there was not enough money available to provide a librarian worthy of the building or competent to create a true library. In consequence, the Adams Report recommended that statutory enlargement of the library districts should be secured and that county councils should become library authorities. Adams suggested not waiting for legislation but to select five areas in the United Kingdom with an existing library centre, an energetic librarian and a sympathetic authority to be set up as model schemes. One of these was to be County Antrim. He also recommended that care of the local library be vested in an educated person like the schoolmaster so that library and school should merge to become the centre of educational activity.

Another important recommendation was the establishment of a central lending library for the adult school movement and the Workers' Educational Association. Adams saw the importance of having professionally trained librarians and recommended higher training associated with university institutions. London, he said, was the best centre, but he also wanted the trustees to consider whether higher courses for librarians could be arranged in other cities such as Manchester, Liverpool, Glasgow, Edinburgh, Cardiff and Dublin.

The table on p.188 illustrates the exact effect on the Irish library situation generated by the Carnegie grants. The statistics apply to the year 1913.

| Name of Place | Pop. in 1911 | No. of libs. | Carnegie libs. | Grant in £ | Rate in £ | Yield of rate £ | Amount on books and binding £ |
|---|---|---|---|---|---|---|---|
| *1 Places with yield of rate of £50 per annum and under* | | | | | | | |
| Downpatrick | 3,199 | 1 | 1 | 2,065 | 1d | 18 | – |
| Naas | 3,842 | 1 | 1 | 600 | 1d | 25 | 10 |
| Rathdown (Wicklow) | 5,450 | 1 | 1 | 1,400 | 1d | 36 | 8 |
| Lusk | 1,426 | 1 | 1 | 400 | 1d | 38 | – |
| *2 Places with yield of rate between £50 and £100 per annum* | | | | | | | |
| Swords | 1,937 | 1 | 1 | 1,000 | 1d | 54 | – |
| Skerries | 3,032 | 1 | 1 | 1,000 | 1d | 55 | 10 |
| Banbridge | 5,101 | 1 | 1 | 1,000 | 1d | 56 | 13 |
| Malahide | 2,501 | 1 | 1 | 1,000 | 1d | 65 | 20 |
| Dublin South R.D. | 13,676 | 3 | 1 | 1,600 | ¼d | 92 | 15 |
| Balbriggan | 4,244 | 1 | 1 | 2,000 | 1d | 95 | 7 |
| Larne | 8,036 | 1 | 1 | 2,500 | 1d | 97 | 12 |
| Drogheda | 12,501 | 1 | 1 | 2,500 | 1d | 100 | 20 |
| *3 Places with yield of rate between £100 and £200 per annum* | | | | | | | |
| Portadown | 11,727 | 2 | 1 | 1,000 | 1d | 114 | 5 |
| Cahirciveen | 20,785 | 1 | 1 | 2,000 | 1d | 115 | – |
| Kilkenny | 10,514 | 1 | 1 | 2,100 | 1d | 120 | 30 |
| Bray | 7,691 | 1 | 1 | 2,200 | 1d | 130 | – |
| Rathgale | 13,863 | 1 | 1 | 2,880 | ½d | 145 | 50 |
| Bangor (Co. Down) | 7,776 | 1 | 1 | 1,500 | 1d | 155 | 13 |
| Waterford | 27,430 | 1 | 1 | 5,200 | 1d | 150 | 25 |
| Blackrock | 9,081 | 1 | 1 | 3,000 | 1d | 190 | 12 |
| Killarney | 35,986 | 1 | 1 | 2,100 | 1d | 195 | 525* |
| *4 Places with yield of rate between £200 and £350 per annum* | | | | | | | |
| Lismore | 12,000 | 1 | 1 | 3,000 | 1d | 210 | 40 |
| Limerick | 38,403 | 1 | 1 | 7,000 | 1d | 298 | 60 |
| Kingstown | 17,277 | 1 | 1 | 3,784 | 1d | 300 | 50 |
| Rathdown (Dublin) | 9,754 | 6 | 3 | 3,700 | 1d | 320 | – |
| *5 Places with yield of rate between £750 and £1,000 per annum* | | | | | | | |
| Cork | 76,673 | 1 | 1 | 11,000 | 1d | 756 | 165 |
| Rathmines | 38,190 | 1 | 1 | 8,500 | 1d | 776 | 150 |
| *6 Places with yield of rate between £5,000 and £10,000 per annum* | | | | | | | |
| Dublin | 309,272 | 6 | 1 | 16,300 | 1½d | 5,900 | 903 |
| Belfast | 385,492 | 5 | 3 | 15,000 | 1½d | 5,900 | 2,564 |

*Includes initial outlay on books

At this time the following places had received building grants from Andrew Carnegie but no information had been obtained relating to their upkeep or expenditure.

|            | £     |
|------------|-------|
| Ballyboden | 1,250 |
| Cabinteenly | 1,000 |
| Lurgan     | 2,000 |
| Mill Street | 2,000 |

One result of the Adams Report was that in 1915 the CUKT appointed Lennox Robinson to act as organising librarian for Ireland at a salary of £150 a year. Lennox Robinson was not a qualified or experienced librarian. He was a literary man, a writer, and a former manager and producer at the Abbey Theatre where he worked with W.B. Yeats and Lady Gregory. He mixed freely with the best-known figures of the Irish Literary Movement including Maud Gonne and George Russell (A.E.) The CUKT representative in Ireland was Sir Horace Plunkett who knew Robinson well.

Robinson's initial duty however was to reorganise the libraries in Rathkeale, Co. Limerick and to supervise the spending of the library grant to Newcastle West, and while doing so he stayed at Sir Horace's home Kilkeragh. Robinson also had to assist in formulating policy for the development of the Irish library service, encouraging the local Boards of Guardians to adopt the Acts, while ensuring that the Trust's money was well spent. On the whole Robinson was reasonably successful, using libraries to improve local cultural life. Not unexpectedly, given his theatrical background, he encouraged the holding of concerts in libraries, and in one he helped to found a dramatic society. However, many parts of the country had little or no library provision. As another palliative, the CUKT gave £10,000 for the Dublin Book Repository which was instituted as a temporary measure to help existing rural and small town libraries, pending the establishment of the country libraries. Christina Keogh ran the Book Repository. In 1914 another £10,000 was given towards a Cooperative Reference Library in Dublin which was to supply agricultural literature to the farming population. The last grant was mainly due to Sir Horace Plunkett's deep interest in Irish agricultural affairs.

By 1920 the troubles in Ireland made the future of libraries uncertain. In what was described in a newspaper report as 'temporary political conditions' in Ireland, the Cork Public Library, had been destroyed by fire on the night of Saturday 11 December 1920 and lost some 14,000 volumes, many of them of rare historical interest. The destruction of the city was such that the 'Cork

Examiner' for 13 December 1920 could only afford a few lines to describe the loss.

> Cork City Hall and the Carnegie Library fired during the night
> – Approaching 6 a.m. on Sunday morning it was found that the
> work of destruction continued. At this time the City Hall and
> the Carnegie Library became ablaze. Both of these buildings
> were completely gutted and only the walls were left standing.

A new library was opened in 1930 at a cost of £24,000, the amount of £30,000 having been received as compensation for the earlier loss.

Other library losses during the troubles were at Listowel, Co. Kerry, where the library was burned down on the night of 7 March 1921, the burning of the library at Cahirciveen, and the library at Kenmare burned in 1921. Rathkeale reported that no books had been bought since the burning of the Union, the library at Newcastle West was burnt down, Drogheda reported that it intended to re-stock the library when conditions became more normal, the Sligo library was occupied by Free State troops, Castleisland library was burned down in the autumn of 1920, the Tralee library had been closed since 1920 and was to remain closed until 1924. Many libraries sent in no reports at all to the CUKT because the political situation was so bad. Robinson himself gave refuge to men on the run.

However bad the disruption and destruction of the public libraries, the worst loss to the country was the burning in June 1922 of the Public Record Office in Dublin. This housed legal records and documents from the year 1170. Attached to the Four Courts, the Public Record Office was used as a bomb and mine factory by the republican Rory O'Connor. In a bombardment from the Free State troops on 30 June the fire spread rapidly and reached the main explosive dumps in the cellars. In one of the most massive explosions of the Civil War the Public Record Office was blown apart and priceless and irreplaceable documents were destroyed to the chagrin of all Irish scholars ever since.

In 1921 the CUKT, following a suggestion of Professor Adams, set up an Irish Advisory Committee in Dublin which it was hoped would best understand the local conditions. Members of the IA Committee were:

Dr J.H. Bernard, Provost of Trinity College
Revd T.A. Finlay
Thomas Lyster, Librarian of the National Library (who died in 1922)
James Wilkinson, Librarian, Carnegie Library, Cork
Lady Gregory

Dermod O'Brien
Thomas O'Donnell
George Russell (A.E.)
Lionel Smith Gordon
Miss Christina Keogh

Lennox Robinson was appointed as secretary and Thomas McGreevy was the assistant secretary. In July of that year Col Mitchell, the secretary of the CUKT, and two trustees visited Ireland to investigate the situation for themselves, staying at Sir Horace Plunkett's home, Kilkeragh. The IA committee met on July 18, 1921, and the meeting was attended by the Scottish visitors. Lady Gregory received instruction to charm the visitors and to get as much money as she could for Irish libraries. She reported that Sir Horace felt that the Carnegie Trustees were ignorant of the Irish situation and also prejudied against Ireland.

The Anglo-Irish Treaty setting up the Irish Free State was signed on 6 December 1921. The result of this treaty was a political split in the country with 26 counties constituting the Free State, later the Republic of Ireland, and six counties in the North remaining true to the union with Great Britain. As far as the CUKT was concerned the original deed had applied to the whole of the United Kingdom and the foundation of the Irish Free State did not affect the operation of the Trust. However in the circumstances the experiment of the Irish Advisory Committee was a failure as it was a grave error to treat Ireland as a whole operating through a committee in Dublin, especially as many on the committee were not unsympathetic to the new order in the Free State.

More fundamentally, religious and other difficulties began to hinder the work of the IAC. Robinson left the CUKT in 1924 under a cloud of moral condemnation after the publication of his short story 'The Madonna of Slieve Dun' described as a 'very dirty story'. This had appeared in a journal called *Tomorrow*, noted for its criticism of the Catholic Church. 'The Madonna of Slieve Dun' was accused of being anti-Catholic. Father Finlay, S.J. resigned immediately from the IAC and he was supported by the Provost of Trinity College. Since the secretary of the Irish Advisory Committee had written such 'filth' it raised the moral dilemma of whether the CUKT was to be trusted with book selection for Catholic Ireland. Book selection had always been a moot point in Ireland and the Trust had already received complaints about the book-stock in some rural libraries, the critics actually believing that the trustees themselves selected the books. However, here was the man, responsible for making appointments to the library system, for choosing Irish librarians and hand-picking men to work in the

191

Carnegie libraries, who had himself published a 'blasphemous story'.

This incident, treated as a farce by all right-minded people, nearly caused the whole of the Irish public library movement to founder. It became obvious to the trustees that in order to avoid further ideological conflicts the Irish Committee would have to be dissolved. Henceforth all Irish business was handled from the Trust's headquarters at Dunfermline and the Irish Advisory Committee was deemed a failure.

Frank O'Connor has described the trials and tribulations of attempting to set up a library service in Co. Wicklow after the fuss over Lennox Robinson's publication. Even before the library committee met there was fierce opposition from the local parish priest, who intended at the first meeting to propose that the committee adjourn permanently. This was out-manoeuvred by Seamus Keely, a nationalist ex-gaolbird masquerading as a representative of the CUKT. The presence of the exemplary Catholic, fresh from an internment camp, assured the committee that no one's faith was in danger, but according to Frank O'Connor, the Wicklow County Libraries owed their beginnings to a complete masquerade. Local sanction was also needed to establish local deposit collections which after the Lennox Robinson affair was not easily forthcoming.

At the start of the 1920s it had been Lennox Robinson who had interviewed Michael O'Donovan (Frank O'Connor) for a post as librarian and started him on his career by sending him to work in Sligo. O'Donovan, recently released from internment, was earning a few shillings a week teaching Irish in Cork, came into libraries not became he wished to be a librarian but because he never had enough books to read. The starting salary for the position was 30s. a week, not enough to live on away from home, but his mother gallantly subsidised him by 2s.6d. or 5s. a week.

The Carnegie United Kingdom Trustees' next report was prepared by its secretary, Col. J.M. Mitchell, who was later to become President of the (British) Library Association. It was on the Public Library System of Great Britain and Ireland, 1921 to 1923, and was a sequel to the Adams Report of 1915, since which time the penny rate limitation had virtually disappeared. One of the greatest barriers to the development of public libraries even in the larger centres such as Dublin, Belfast and Cork was the limitation of the library rate. Indeed, from 1902 onwards the Dublin Public Libraries Committee had pursued a rigorous campaign for the development of libraries and had made a sustained and intensive effort to secure the removal of the penny rate limitation.

In England and Wales this had happened under the Public Libraries Act 1919 which removed all rate limitations whatsoever. This legislation was followed with more grudging concessions in the cases of Scotland and Ireland where the rate limit was raised to 3d. in the £ and to 6d in the £ in the case of Irish county boroughs. The effects of this were not immediately evident mainly because of the 1914-18 War during which people's energies had been directed elsewhere, and there had been very little replenishment of library stocks, and both rebinding and replacement programmes had fallen seriously into arrears.

The following table shows the state of staff salaries in libraries at this time in the United Kingdom. The position in Ireland is seen to be not particularly encouraging.

### Staff Salaries

|  | England | Wales | Scotland | Ireland | Total |
|---|---|---|---|---|---|
| Under £100 | 33 | 11 | 25 | 19 | 88 |
| £100-£200 | 37 | 9 | 5 | 4 | 55 |
| £200-£300 | 33 | 2 | 7 | 1 | 43 |
| £300-£400 | 25 | 4 | 4 | – | 33 |
| £400-£500 | 16 | 2 | 2 | – | 20 |
| £500-£600 | 31 | 1 | 3 | 1 | 36 |
| £600-£700 | 10 | – | 3 | – | 13 |
| £700-£800 | 9 | – | 1 | – | 10 |
| £800-£900 | 13 | – | – | – | 13 |
| £900-£1000 | 8 | 1 | 2 | – | 11 |
| £1000-£1500 | 27 | 2 | 4 | 1 | 34 |
| £1500-£2000 | 23 | 1 | 1 | – | 25 |
| £2000-£3000 | 16 | – | – | – | 16 |
| Over £3000 | 41 | 1 | 4 | 2 | 48 |
| Total no. of libraries | 322 | 34 | 61 | 28 | 445 |

An analysis of the money spent on the provision of newspapers and periodicals is interesting for it shows just how the book funds were used. The report argued that it was probably not wise to spend so much on 'the casual reader of the daily press who spends an hour or so studying the sporting or athletic columns' as they 'cost a great deal more (and on average contribute a great deal less) than the steady reader who borrows three or four books a week'. Thus was raised the old argument re-echoed from earlier times. At this time of

## FIGURE 9.2
## ANNOUNCEMENT OF LIBRARY RATE

' PUBLIC LIBRARIES' ACT,' (IRELAND) 1855'

## NOTICE.

IS hereby given that a rate of 1d in the £ has been duly made on all property situate within the Borough of Ennis, under the paovisions of tne abovementioned act, and will be payable on the 4th day of September, next.

The Rate Book is in my custody, and may be inspected by any person affected thereby at the Town Commissioners' office Town Hall, any day except Sunday between the hours of 1 0 o'clock in the forenoon and 4o'Clock in the afternoon.

Signed this 7th day of August, 1865.

DANIEL TUOHY, Town Clerk.

From *The Clare Freeman and Ennis Gazette*, 26 August 1865

the 29 Irish libraries submitting returns to the CUKT 16 of them spent more on newspapers and periodicals than on books, and 21 spent more than half as much on newspapers and periodicals as on books (this figure includes the previous 16). In the report the following counties did not possess legislative powers to run public libraries: Antrim, Donegal, Fermanagh, Kilkenny, Londonderry, Sligo and Wexford.

Following the Adams recommendation County Antrim was made an experimental county system in 1922 with the CUKT bearing the bulk of the expenses, closely followed by Donegal and Wexford, but due to the intense fighting all over the country, although the public library idea was taken up as early as 1920 no librarian was appointed to Donegal until January 1922 and the Wexford scheme did not start until January 1923.

County book selection sub-committees were established consisting of five members who could co-opt up to three additional members. It was suggested that one or two of the members of the books sub-committee should have special knowledge of the industries of the county, that there should be one specialist in children's books, that one should know the Irish language and that at least one member should be a woman.

Early in 1920 the Dublin Secretariat of the Trust issued a standard list called 'Three thousand best books', and many sub-committees ordered this list *en bloc*. Usually after two years of the Trust's administration the county council took over the library scheme but in the early stages the County Councils were not library authorities. The CUKT continued to meet the capital and running costs of the rural library schemes until the end of 1924 in Northern Ireland and to the end of 1925 in the Free State. After that until 1930 grants continued for the initial capital costs of the new schemes with the County Councils being required to meet other costs out of the rates.

The CUKT commissioned R.N.D. Wilson, the county librarian of Sligo, to produce a pamphlet on the county library service in Ireland. Although published in 1927 the pamphlet was aimed at the whole of Ireland without distinguishing between the North or the Free State. It was prepared to give students and general readers throughout Ireland an account of the library facilities at their disposal, and to act as a guide to public bodies which were unaware of their powers and responsibilities with regard to the public library service. These powers had devolved on them since the passing of the Public Libraries Act (Northern Ireland) 1924, and the 1925 Local Government Act in the Free State. Both these Acts gave the power to county councils to adopt the previously existing Public Libraries Acts, thereby constituting each council as the public library authority for its area.

Formerly, as has been seen, the provision and control of public libraries had been restricted to urban and rural district councils. This alteration in the law was to a large extent inaugurated by the trustees who were responsible for the remarkable growth of the county library systems. Under the Irish Free State Local Government Act 1925 the rural district councils were abolished and the powers transferred to the county councils. Until 1922 the rural districts had been almost entirely without a library service of any kind although the cities had built up fairly efficient systems. In Dublin, for example, two libraries had been opened in 1884, one at Thomas Street and the other at Capel Street. Another branch opened in 1899 at Charleville Mall, another at Kevin Street in 1904, followed in 1912 by yet another at Pearse Street.

The pamphlet gave advice on how to start a county system and it listed the counties where schemes had been inaugurated since 1922. In all there were fifteen in the Free State: Tirconnaill (Donegal), Monaghan, Sligo, Mayo, Galway, Dublin, Kildare, Laoighis (Laois), Offaly, Wicklow, Wexford, Kilkenny, Tipperary, Cork and Kerry; and four in Northern Ireland, these being Antrim, Londonderry, Fermanagh and Tyrone.

The objective of the county library was to bring books within the reach of the readers scattered over the country. No expensive building was required but a room in the county town acted as a central book store usually termed the County Book Repository from whence boxes of books were sent out periodically to small towns and villages. In these places a small committee was formed, usually of the clergyman, school teacher and other interested persons who were responsible for the care of the books and who nominated an honorary librarian. In Ireland the majority of these branches were housed in the local schools, but also in the country post offices, shops and sometimes at the Cooperative Society, the latter probably due to Father O'Donovan's influence. Sometimes the collections were at village halls or institutes.

The book collections were usually changed at intervals of from three to four months. Transport of the books could be primitive with pickups arranged on carts and lorries travelling from the outlying districts into the county towns. Rail transport was used where it existed. In Co. Dublin and Co. Cork special motor vans had been fitted up with book shelves but this ideal was normally beyond the pocket of the average county. The annual cost of running a county system along these lines was £550 per annum upwards depending on the size of the county. In most cases the county was able to run a reasonable library service because money was spent on books not on the upkeep of an expensive building.

The recommended stock was 4000 volumes for a small county but for larger counties 12,000 volumes was the aim, and the CUKT made grants to defray the heavy initial outlay in establishing the library system. In return the trustees attached conditions, as follows.

1  That there should be a genuine intention to institute the library service as a permanent one and with a view to this the county was to adopt the Public Libraries Acts for its area and from the outset to declare a rate adequate to maintain the service.
2  That the county librarian appointed to administer the scheme should be a trained competent librarian and should be paid a salary of not less than £250 per annum. (Significantly by 1935 many librarians were still earning only £250 per annum with a few rising to just over £300 per annum.)
3  That statistics showing the development of the library be sent annually to the trustees.

The librarian usually acted as secretary to the library committee, the personnel of which was fixed by statute in Northern Ireland. In the Irish Free State however no definite schedule existed, though it was considered necessary that the committee should contain one member of the county council for each electoral area and that the clergy and teaching profession be well-represented. It was also thought advisable to invite the cooperation of the Inspectors of National Education and the County Committee of Agriculture and Technical Instruction. In addition representatives from the Gaelic League could be nominated. The committee could co-opt additional members with the CUKT having the right to nominate not more than five.

The main function of the county and small town library was to provide for the general reader. The cost of purchasing specialist books for the serious reader or student was usually outside its resources and the Trust felt that the service would suffer unless provision were made to tap resources outside the county areas. For this reason the CUKT recommended and financed the establishment of a Central Library for Students to supplement the resources of the urban, borough and county libraries. From this students could borrow by post any book of a serious nature not available at the local library, providing that the book cost not less than six shillings and not more than two guineas. The headquarters was in London and a branch was established in Dublin. The book repository in Harcourt Street and the reference library were re-constituted as the Irish Central Library for Students in April 1923. Applications for loans had to be made through the local library and books were loaned for a six week period. Postage both ways had to be defrayed by the reader of the local library. Through the Irish Central Library for Students books could be borrowed from the Royal Irish Academy, the Society of Antiquaries, the London School of Economics and other libraries in the United Kingdom and Ireland.

The CUKT financed the Irish Central Library for Students to the tune of £15,000 and bore the entire cost for the next 25 years. In its early days the Central Library acted as a reserve for county libraries only, but by the end of 1924 its service was extended to cover all libraries whether town or county.

# Public libraries in Northern Ireland since 1922

The first public library in Ulster to be established out of the public rate was the Belfast Public Library in 1888. Belfast opened branches with the aid of the CUKT at Ballymacarret in 1903, Oldpark in 1907, Falls in 1908 and Donegall Road in 1909. As we have already seen, urban districts that had adopted the Acts were Lurgan in 1895, Newtownards in 1896, Newry in 1897, Banbridge 1902, Portadown 1904, Downpatrick 1905, Larne 1905 and Bangor in 1910. Londonderry City established a library service in 1924 and Holywood in 1947. The earlier libraries had all been assisted by Carnegie library building grants.

The experimental county system set up with the aid of the CUKT was in Co. Antrim in 1922. Under the scheme the CUKT maintained the county library system for two years. The start of the Antrim scheme led to the setting up of a committee to administer the library, and all public, educational and denominational bodies in the county were represented on this. When schemes were implemented in Londonderry and Fermanagh similar committees were also established. The objectives of these committees were threefold. First, to organise the book supply in the county; secondly, to make the public aware of the scheme so that when the two years had elapsed they could be taken over by the respective county councils; and thirdly, to press for legislation enabling county councils to become library authorities. The Antrim committee was energetic and tried to ensure that the Education Act then before Parliament had a clause inserted to allow county councils to establish libraries. It was not successful but the government did promise to give the matter sympathetic consideration. Eventually a bill to enable county councils to become library authorities was introduced into Parliament and passing through all its stages became law as the Public Libraries Act (Northern Ireland) 1924. Under the provisions of the Act urban areas could relinquish some or all of their powers to the county council.

As soon as the Antrim scheme reached the end of its experimental period the county council immediately adopted the Act and undertook the maintenance of the library service, receiving from the CUKT the existing book stock, fittings and organisation. This also happened in County Londonderry and County Fermanagh. County Tyrone initiated a scheme in 1927, Armagh in 1928 and Down in

1940. By 1927 in Antrim, Londonderry and Fermanagh alone there were 260 library centres.

In each of the library centres there was a local committee which selected the books with one or more members acting as librarian. Attempts were made to provide library services to urban areas and in Ballymena a centre had been set up and was administered by a local committee. In Portrush the urban council had formed a centre during the experimental period. When the Public Libraries Acts were adopted by the county councils it was decided that there should be some cooperation between the urban and the county council, and accordingly both in Ballymena and Portrush, which had adopted the Acts and had levied a rate for public library purposes, part of that rate was paid to the county council for the maintenance of the county library. In return the county library agreed to augment the urban library with a supply of books from the county's stock, these to be exchanged every six months. Through this cooperation the urban council which could not really have raised much money for additional materials was able to have a wider variety of books, frequently exchanged.

School provision, even in those early days, was considered essential and in Co. Fermanagh the Regional Education Committee entered into an agreement with the County Library Committee for the supply of books to the elementary schools.

After the passing of the Public Libraries (Northern Ireland) Act 1924 there were several reports on libraries in the Province starting in 1929 with the Report of the Departmental Committee on Public Libraries in Northern Ireland which was appointed by the Northern Ireland Government to examine library provision. There was also a report in 1944 of the Committee on Adult Education in Northern Ireland, and the Report of the Library Association (Northern Ireland Branch) 1947. In addition the Northern Ireland Library Advisory Council made recommendations to the Ministry of Health and Local Government in 1961. In essence all these reports said the same thing, urging the extension of the public library service to those areas not already covered, and the relinquishing of library powers by smaller authorities which were not able to provide adequate services. More particularly it was urged that a central reference service and bibliographical service be established. With more cooperation leading to an improved library service for the Province, training of staff was recognised as of the utmost importance, but it was not until 1965 that a school of library studies opened at Queens University Belfast with a diploma in library studies being awarded to successful students. The director of the library school at its inception was Peter Havard-Williams. Up to this period poor salary gradings and a shortage of qualified staff had led to a consistent loss of staff to more lucrative posts outside Ulster.

The Northern Ireland Library Advisory Council was set up in September 1949 to consider ways in which the public library service in Northern Ireland could develop and expand. Membership consisted of the librarian and authority member from each of the main library authorities in the Province. It was a prime mover in the establishment of the library school and in its report of 1961 urged the appointment of a committee to investigate the public library service in Northern Ireland and to make recommendations for its development.

The result was the appointment in 1964 of an advisory committee to consider the public library service under the chairmanship of Dr J.S. Hawnt. At this time there were sixteen public library authorities in Northern Ireland of which six were county councils, two were county borough councils, five were borough councils and three were urban district councils. Northern Ireland was conscious of the developments in England and Wales following the Roberts Report on the Public Library Service in England and Wales which had led to the passing of the Public Libraries and Museums Act 1964. The advisory committee was aware that Northern Ireland had to develop and maintain a library and information service no less advanced than that on the mainland, although the Province being small faced differing problems with comparatively poor local authorities and scattered rural communities. The members of the committee visited all the sixteen public libraries and generally found inadequacies in book provision with standards of service varying widely. Although the committee had no brief to look at school libraries, they found that there was one authority, Londonderry, which was providing permanent collections of books to schools. The interlinking responsibilities of the public library and school provision were unavoidable and the committee felt that good library services should be provided for children during school life and through into adult life. In the event the committee recommended that each library authority should provide a schools librarian to advise teachers on library matters and that all schools, whether county or voluntary, should be provided with books out of public funds, with a separate library room being provided in secondary schools and in the larger primary schools. Public libraries were to act as agents of education committees in providing library services to schools, ensuring closer cooperation between libraries and schools.

When the Hawnt Committee reported in September 1964 it recommended the amalgamation of some of the library authorities to effect an improved service, although they felt the best structure was to retain the county or county borough system, but they suggested linking Tyrone and Fermanagh, Armagh and Down, and Londonderry City with Londonderry County. Library authorities were made responsible to the Minister of Education who in turn was to be advised by a statutory Library Advisory Council. The Ministry of Education was to require library authorities to submit development schemes. The Library Advisory Council was to consist of practising professional librarians representing local and central interests.

One of the recommendations was the formation of a provincial library based on the book stock and services provided by the Belfast Central Library. This proposed provincial library was to provide a central collection of reference and lending books, a bibliographical service, centralised ordering and cataloguing of non-fiction stock for local libraries, and in addition it was to act as an interlending bureau. The provincial library was to supervise the subject specialisation scheme, to purchase books costing more than £15, foreign and specialised materials as well as government and international publications. The proposed provincial library would also store books removed from circulation on account of lack of current demand. In order to achieve all this it was suggested that a working party be formed to deal with the problems arising from the creation of the provincial library from the Belfast Central Library. The branch libraries in the city were to be left under the control of the Belfast Corporation. This provision however did not meet with the approval of all members of the Hawnt Committee and a reservation to this suggestion was made by Ivor Crawley, May Haughton, Peter Havard-Williams, W.S. Henderson, R. Lillie and A. McGonigal, all of whom objected to the dismantling of the Belfast public library system. In the event the objectors won the day. Other members of the committee apart from the chairman were Professor M.J. Boyd, J.J. Campbell, W.H. Fenning, H.J. Heaney, J. Malone and L. Mitchell.

The Hawnt Report also recommended that a library adviser responsible to the Minister of Education should be appointed to advise on the development and the running of the services in the Province. It further suggested a system of grants to be made to the local authorities for approved library expenditure from the Ministry of Education, and in addition that the Linenhall Library and the Armagh Public Library established by Archbishop Robinson be supported by annual grants from public funds.

Summarised, the Hawnt Report's recommendations were as follows:

1 The establishment of a statutory advisory council
2 The establishment of a provincial library
3 To provide for the submission of schemes by authorities for the constitution, powers and duties of library committees
4 To enable the Ministry to grant-aid library services
5 To ensure the attainment and maintenance of standards and to ensure the duty of every library authoritiy to provide an efficient and comprehensive library system
6 To require urban and borough authorities to relinquish library powers to the county and to enable the drawing-up of agreements with other library authorities for the extension of library facilities and to enable the provision of special services to institutions such as prisons
7 Other legislation was thought to be necessary to cover the holding of meetings and lectures with the right to make a charge, fines to be levied for the non-compliance with the regulations and, unlike England and Wales, to separate libraries and museums for the purposes of legislation.

The Hawnt Report was very comprehensive, covering all aspects of the library service in the Northern counties. It not only reviewed the public library situation but investigated as well the provision of library services to hospitals, prisons and borstals, recommending an integrated and coordinated service to all sections of the community. Staffing salaries and conditions of work were given consideration so that Northern Ireland might keep pace with other parts of the United Kingdom in the matter of career prospects. The provision of adequate and suitable premises was also considered. Altogether the Hawnt Report had far reaching and forward looking ideas, creating a forum for providing more up-to-date and efficient library services in the future.

In addition there was a report in 1970 of the review body on local government in Nothern Ireland, known as the Macrory Report. This contained a recommendation that a system of not more than five area boards should be established having regional functions covering education and libraries. This led to an Education and Libraries Bill being presented to the Northern Ireland Parliament on 17 February 1972, its aim being to set up education and library services in five areas with a board having statutory responsibility for the administration of the library service. Before the Bill could become law however, direct rule from Westminster was introduced and the Northern Ireland Parliament prorogued. The proposals for the Bill were later put forward in the Education and Libraries (Northern Ireland) Order 1972 which took effect from 1 October 1973. The area boards ignored the county boundaries and did not implement the Hawnt Report's suggestion of amalgamating the counties. The Order provided that the primary duty of the boards was to "provide a comprehensive and efficient library service".

The boards are directly responsible to the Minister of Education and each board serves a community of a minimum population of a quarter of a million people. The proposed provincial library was not introduced. The Library Advisory Council (Northern Ireland) agreed to a new constitution and was re-structured in 1977 with another new constitution being ratified in 1981. The objectives of the council are:

1 to seek to achieve the highest standards in library services for all people of Northern Ireland and to coordinate the efforts of all library authorities towards this end
2 to promote and encourage the interchange of ideas on questions relating to the library services and to provide a forum for debate on such matters
3 to supply information and advice on library matters
4 to exercise vigilance in relation to all proposed legislation, regulations and administrative arrangements affecting library services and to take action where deemed necessary for the safeguarding or improvement of standards in the services affected
5 to provide a collective voice for library services

Membership of the council has been streamlined from almost 30 members to an Executive Committee of 17. The director of the Library Council of Ireland (An Chomhairle Leabharlanna) is a coopted member. Panels sit regularly to discuss topics relevant to Irish librarianship. The panels are the audio-visual panel, the educational and research panel, the government libraries panel, a special libraries panel, and an HMSO consultative committee.

The Library Advisory Council meets with other Library Advisory Councils of the United Kingdom to consider library issues and problems which are better pursued on a UK basis, and to review recent proposals for the coordination of library and information policy and development. Joint ventures between the Republic of Ireland and Northern Ireland take place, one good example being the *Computerised List of Serials Holdings in Irish Libraries*. The list was mainly funded by the National Board for Science and Technology with a financial input from libraries of £1000, this sum being shared evenly at £500 each by An Chomhairle Leabharlanna and the ten major libraries in Northern Ireland. The Northern Ireland Library Advisory Council having no finance could not pay the Northern Ireland share.

The five Education and Library Boards are as follows:

1 Belfast Education and Library Board based in Belfast and having responsibility for the library service to the city
2 North Eastern Education and Library Board based in Ballymena, Co. Antrim and serving among other places the towns of Greystone, Ballymoney, Coleraine, Portrush, Portstewart, Carrickfergus, Glengormly, Larne and Rathcoole
3 South Eastern Education and Library Board which has its headquarters in Ballynahinch, Co. Down. Under the local government re-organisation in 1973 the twelve Co. Down libraries and two mobile libraries based at Ballynahinch amalgamated with Holywood, Newtownards, Lisburn and Dunmurry branches and the Lisburn Mobile Library to form the new South Eastern Education and Library Service
4 Southern Education and Library Board based in Armagh. It consists of the eastern half of Tyrone, the southern tip of Londonderry, the whole of Armagh and the southern and western parts of Down. This meant welding together four different county library areas together with the four independent authorities of Portadown, Lurgan, Newry and Banbridge
5 Western Education and Library Board which is based in Omagh, Co. Tyrone and covers the western halves of Co. Londonderry and Co. Tyrone and all of Co. Fermanagh including such centres as Limavady, Londonderry, Strabane, Omagh and Enniskillen.

Despite the enormous setbacks affecting the Province as a result of continued terrorist campaigns and ensuing political unrest, the library services have actually been developed and many innovations introduced. It is to the credit of so many that so much has been achieved in such a short time.

The Belfast Education and Library Board inherited five Carnegie libraries built between 1888 and 1909. These had been followed by the building of libraries in the Shankill Road in 1928, Holywood Road in 1942 and the Ligoniel Branch Library in 1946. There had also been a fairly substantial building programme from 1954 with the building of Euston Street library in 1954 and culminating in the opening of a temporary branch in Whiterock Road as part of the Belfast Areas of Need programme. A more permanent branch for Whiterock in West Belfast is planned with building starting in 1983. In 1973 the Belfast Education and Library Board acquired two buildings from the North Eastern Education and Library Board. These were the Andersonstown and Finaghy branches formerly operated by Co. Antrim.

A new central library had been planned on Peter's Hill which would have resolved all the storage problems at the existing Central Library, but the idea that Peter's Hill would become one of the new cultural centres of the revitalised Province had to be abandoned as the civil unrest in the North made it obvious that instead of becoming a cultural complex the Peter's Hill library would become a fortress to be fought over by the warring factions. The project was therefore reluctantly abandoned in 1976. This left the city library with enormous storage problems with reference materials housed in as many as thirteen different sites. Pressure on the Central reference library had altered but not entirely ceased with the troubles but its pattern of use had changed from being busiest in the evenings to being busiest in the afternoons. There was also a marked rise in postal and telephone enquiries, indicating that readers were generally not inclined to venture out unless it was absolutely necessary.

A new book store of 58,000 sq. ft. (c. 5,500 sq. metres) on seven floors was therefore planned at the rear of the Central Library to locate on one site the unique collections of the reference library. These cover the humanities and general reference, arts and literature, music, Irish and local history, science and technology and a business information library. The bookstack now houses over half a million items and the service to readers requesting items has been reduced from in some cases a wait of one week to one day or less. Information is available on Teletext (Ceefax and Oracle). A computer terminal was ordered for the Central Reference Library and the library subscribes to Dialog, a computerised information retrieval system with access to over 100 databases. In addition the Central Library staff have been involved with the Prestel Input Experiment based at the Queen's University Belfast School of Library and Information Studies.

The economic recession is evident as the development of the branch library system continues to be limited due to lack of capital funding, but recently new or renovated library buildings have been opened in Ardoyne and Chichester Road. The school library system is the responsibility of the board and the Youth Services Section serves primary and secondary schools as well as four technical colleges. There is also a service to prisons, hospitals and housebound readers. The East Belfast Talking Newspaper for the Blind is received by over 100 blind or partially sighted readers and is being made available to housebound and bedridden people. With *Model Times*, a talking newspaper for North Belfast these newspapers are now reaching nearly 300 people. The Belfast Public Library also has a free music lending service to blind residents in the city with the library bearing the cost of posting the tapes. In addition Belfast operates two mobile libraries. The service now comprises twenty branch libraries as well as the Central Library, most of the branches using the Plessey light pen computerised system. The catalogue of the library is on microfilm.

The North-Eastern Education and Library Board has increased its branch libraries from 24 in 1973 to 33 in 1982. The building programme is currently affected by the economic cuts but a small branch library was included in the 1981-82 capital programme and opened in 1982 with two similar projects under way. The service also has mobile libraries with eleven serving the county, one for the housebound and four serving the schools. The service has the fourth largest bookstock in the UK for school provision. Each school has a per capita allowance of 62 pence in the primary schools with a minimum of £46, and secondary schools with children up to 16 having a per capita allowance of £1.25 and 16 plus having £2.25. In addition all have 5 per cent to compensate for out-of-print books, plus loan exchange two or three times a year supplemented by project collections. A separate teachers' collection is maintained.

The hospital library service started in 1974 with a specially purchased stock. Handicapped readers are served with a range of reading aids. The North Eastern Education and Library Board was the first authority in Northern Ireland to become involved with talking newspapers and there are four separate groups in the area. In the whole system there is a policy of mobility of book stock and each small branch and mobile library receives enough books for a complete change of stock at least once a year. The larger branches have a complete change of stock every two or four years, thus greatly increasing the range of material available to the readership. The board edits the joint *Northern Ireland Local Studies* list of book and many non-book items relating to the Province. Like the other boards contributions are made to the joint *Public Service Information Bulletin* which is edited by the staff of the Western Education and Library Board.

The South Eastern Education and Library Board inherited the Co. Down library system which was the last county to adopt the Acts. The board operates the Library Order 1972 by providing library centres through the branch and mobile service points. Services are also provided to people who normally have no access to such facilities. This includes those resident in hospitals, old peoples' homes, sheltered dwellings and prisons, as well as housebound readers. Prior to the reorganisation the hospital service in the Province had been provided on a voluntary basis. The board serves the Maze prison with a book stock which now amounts to some 10,000 volumes in both the compounds and the H blocks.

The board now has 23 service points and five mobile libraries. It covers 13 hospitals as well as residential homes, penal institutions and lighthouses. Over 250 schools receive a library service via two mobiles as well as three teachers and five outdoor pursuits centres. The board also provides an audio-visual library service, lending cassettes for public use and slides for work being done with children in local libraries.

The board ventured into video when it participated in the cooperative scheme administered by the five boards to lend video cassettes on art acquired by the Arts Council of Northern Ireland. Following discussions with the Educational Psychology section of the board a pilot scheme was initiated in 1978 to make toys for pre-school children available in libraries in addition to board games. The scheme proved successful and has now been introduced in all libraries.

The Southern Education and Library Board is currently planning a new divisional library headquarters and branch library in Newry, a new branch for Keady and one as part of a combined project for Crossmaglen. In addition an extension is planned for Lurgan and a new central reference library and divisional library headquarters and branch library for Portadown.

The service was lucky to start out with a new library building at Market Street, Armagh in August 1973, replacing previous inadequate premises, and a new library at Tandragee opened also in 1973. Three libraries however suffered from bomb damage which disrupted the service at Cookstown, Newry and the new premises at Armagh. A rather daunting beginning to a new library service in any guise. The old Armagh county library headquarters which had adequately served the county population of 80,000 suddenly in 1973 became the nerve centre for the new board which was attempting to serve 280,000 people. A temporary headquarters was found in August 1974 in a new branch library at Brownlow, Craigavon. The reserve stock and the mobiles remained at Armagh. The development programme included the local government information service, the audio visual service, the Local History collection, and the Hospitals and Associated Services, all achieved with the headquarters at one time operating from five separate buildings spread over a fifteen mile radius. Fortunately a new library became available for use in January 1981.

As with the other boards, a service is provided to hospitals and to housebound readers. The board has a new mobile for handicapped readers brought into service in April 1980. This has a hydraulic lift at the rear to allow readers in wheelchairs to enter the vehicle and select their own material. The board also administers the distribution of three talking newspapers to Craigavon, Dungannon and Armagh. The 'housebound' mobile visits 449 stops and a service is provided to 14 hospitals. The five mobiles have a total of 335 stops. There are 19 branches in the board area with one local government library and 55 library centres. Primary, secondary and grammar schools are served as well as 8 technical schools and 53 playgroups. An active building programme involved the opening of a new library at Kilkeel in 1978, a new divisional library headquarters at Dungannon in 1979, while Fivemiletown had a new library in the same year, (see Figure 10.1). Unfortunately the latter was damaged by a bomb blast in May 1981 which seriously affected the service. Another new library was opened at Banbridge in 1979, and there has also been an active programme of refurbishing older premises.

The Western Education and Library Board was the first service under the guise of the Tyrone County Library to introduce a system wide audio lending service in Ireland, though this lent records only. Records and cassettes are now available at every service point including mobile libraries. There is also a self-financing video loan service running systemwide in the board's area. The board is also the only system in Ireland to run an integrated container size mobile and trailer library service to its rural areas, and it is planning an up-dated and improved transportable library to rural areas. The population of 240,000 is scattered over an area measuring 90 miles by about 30 miles with towns of 10,000 population and above accounting for about 47 per cent of the total. There has been a determined attempt to develop a modern multi-media library service spreading the benefits to as many people as possible. In the last eight years ten branch libraries have been opened and two large projects are planned, notably a new Central Library for Londonderry and an area headquarters and divisional headquarters for Tyrone, plus a branch library for Omagh and a teachers' centre at an estimated cost of £2.5 million and having an area of 50,000 sq. ft. (c. 4,500 sq. metres).

There is a highly developed Special Services section to care for the library needs of the blind, the partially sighted, the handicapped and the housebound, delivering materials to homes, hospitals, centres and clubs. An information service is provided to business and industry in the area. There is also a fine collection of Irish and local history materials and these are actively exploited locally.

The service to schools and youth is responsible for covering the needs of all the educational establishments in the board area. Books, periodicals and audio-visual materials are purchased through the

FIGURE 10.1 FIVEMILETOWN BRANCH LIBRARY AND MUSEUM, OPENED AUGUST 1979

board for schools and colleges. A collection of some 24,000 items in three centres is available for loan to teachers.

The need to establish the Library Association of Ireland was raised at a Conference of Library Officials held in 1923 at University College Dublin. Two resolutions had been passed at the conference which were to have important consequences for libraries in Ireland. The first was:

> That this conference of Irish librarians and persons interested in the education of Ireland urges on the Government of Ireland the necessity of amending the law; and giving powers to the county authorities to levy a rate in support of public libraries, and to extend the powers of existing library authorities to cover free lectures and other educational work.

Two years later this resolution was successful with the passing of the Irish Free State Local Government Act 1925.

The second resolution reflected the need for a forum to discuss policy and professional problems from an Irish point of view, and was as follows:

> That an Association of Irish Library Workers be inaugurated having the following as its objectives:
>
> To promote the better administration of libraries
>
> To promote whatever may tend to the improvement and qualifications of librarians
>
> To promote the adoptions of the Public Libraries Acts
>
> To promote the establishment and development of reference and lending libraries
>
> To watch legislation affecting libraries and to assist in the promotion of such further legislation as may be necessary for the development of libraries, and to hold examinations in librarianship and to issue certificates of proficiency, and to hold conferences and meetings for the discussion of matters relating to libraries.

This second aspiration was not realised until 1928 when the Cumann Leabharlann na hEireann was founded. The fledgling Association received support from the CUKT who provided free accommodation and financed the publication of reports.

Its first official journal appeared quarterly and was edited by James Barry. Called *An Leabharlann*, it urged the adoption of legislative and other measures for the development of the library services and aimed to foster an awareness of the importance of the public library in Irish society. Among the reforms that the Association was able to achieve were the abolition of the library rate limitation, the formation of a Library Council, the granting of state aid to public libraries, the establishment of the hospital aid to public libraries and the setting-up of the Hospital Library Service.

The Library Association of Ireland undertook to speak on matters of library policy affecting the whole of Ireland, and the existence of the Northern Ireland Branch of the (UK) Library Association as a separate unit seemed likely to limit its scope. To rectify this a Liaison Committee was formed with the members approved both by the Executive Committee of the LAI and the Northern Ireland Branch of the LA.

One of its first acts was to better conditions for library staffs with a view to improving the service to the public. The growth of the county library service had led to an increased demand for staff but it was usually only the municipal services that attracted those with professional qualifications. The Association welcomed the news that a School of Library Training at University College, Dublin was to be established for graduates, those who were not graduates taking a course of study leading to a Diploma in Library Training. However, the Executive Board of the LAI was not happy with the syllabus as it omitted some professional subjects and the Diploma could be awarded to persons who had had no practical experience of library work.

Another important issue for the Executive Board was the condition of libraries throughout Ireland and the establishment of a national library service. Ideas for the national service included voluntary cooperation between neighbouring libraries, the grouping of libraries around regional centres, a federation of special libraries pooling their resources for research purposes, and the setting up of a Central Library.

Following its first meeting in May 1929 the Association passed a resolution emphasising the ultimate aim of Cumann Leabharlann na hEireann as the creation of a national library service and requesting the appropriate government department to appoint a Commission of Enquiry to explore the possibilities of instituting such a service. As a first measure the Executive Board sent a questionnaire to all public and other libraries in the country asking for particulars such as the nature of the service. The response was so discouraging that it was felt the time was not ripe to set up the Commission of Enquiry. At this time only fifteen counties in the Irish Free State had established county library systems with the help of the CUKT, and the offer of financial assistance to do so was due to be withdrawn at the end of December 1930. The most immediate problem was to persuade those authorities without libraries to adopt the Public Libraries Act while the grants were still available. The Association's encouragement was such that by the time the grants were withdrawn seven more county authorities had adopted the Acts and secured the financial aid. These were Cavan, Clare, Carlow, Roscommon, Meath, Leitrim and Waterford. This was a good indication that the Association was determined to meet its objectives.

By 1933 the LAI felt more confident and at the conference held in Galway at University College, a resolution was again passed that the government of Saorstat Eireann (the Irish Free State) be requested to appoint a commission to enquire into the present position, resources and requirements of public libraries and to make recommendations for the improvement of the service. The Executive Board renewed its efforts to conduct a survey of public library conditions before asking for a Government Commission. Since the results of the earlier survey had not been encouraging the CUKT was approached for assistance and this, coupled with a sympathetic interest from the local government department led to the survey 'Report on Public Library Provision in the Irish Free State, 1935' which was submitted by Christina A. Keogh in April 1936.

With the exception of Westmeath and Longford every county in the Irish Free State had a library system, (see Figure 11.1 List of library centres in Wicklow in 1933), the two county councils of Tipperary, the South Riding and the North Riding, forming a County Tipperary Joint Library Committee in 1925. Almost without exception they were running on very inadequate funds, representing a framework of public library provision but with no connecting link between them. Christina Keogh found that though the public library service was much extended it was frequently being run on totally inadequate staffing levels. In Donegal for example one librarian and an assistant had to service 208 centres with a book stock of only 12,350 books, which meant that each centre must have had only 50 to 60 books each, and that at least four centres had to be visited each week if they were to have even one visit a year! This illustrates that the success of the county library system was dependent on the unpaid and voluntary help given by the national teachers and others who manned the local centres. Insufficient funding meant the stock was limited and to some extent the shortcomings of the public library system had a prejudicial effect, linking public libraries with the provision of light fiction only. Miss Keogh urged that library provision should be extended to cover the cultural and educational life of the people, and noting that the provision of a first-rate library

# FIGURE 11.1   LIST OF LIBRARY CENTRES
# IN WICKLOW IN 1933

## LIST OF CENTRES.

**LIBRARY BUILDINGS**

| Town | Address | Hours of opening | No. of vols. in stock. |
|---|---|---|---|
| Bray | Florence Rd. | Daily | 200 |
| Enniskerry | | Sun., Mon. Wed. 12 to 2 p.m. Fri., 8 to 9 p.m. | 160 |
| Greystones | | Daily 10 a.m. to 5 p.m. | 1,225 |

**ROOMS SHELVED**

| | | | |
|---|---|---|---|
| Arklow | Courthouse | Mon., Sat 8 to 10 : Wed, 3-5 | 875 |
| Baltinglass | Tech. School | Fri. 4-5 ? Sun., 12 to 1 | 345 |
| Kilmacanogue | Annex to R.C. Church | Sunday 12.15, to 1.30. | 120 |
| Rathdrum | A.O.H Hall | Friday 4 to 5 p.m. | 350 |
| Wicklow | Bellevue House | Mon., Thurs 3 to 5 p.m. Wed., 4 to 5 ; Sat. 11 to 12 | 1,042 |

**CENTRES FOR ADULTS AND CHILDREN**

| | | | |
|---|---|---|---|
| Annacurra | Parochial Hall | Sunday, 12.15. to 1 | 65 |
| Ashford | Schoolhouse | Friday, 3.30, to 4.30 | 72 |
| Askinagap | ,, | Friday, 3.30, to 4.30. | 65 |
| Avoca | ,, | Sunday. 1 to 3 p.m. | 130 |
| Aughrim | ,, | Friday 3.30, to 4.30. | 125 |
| Ballinacarrig | ,, | Friday, 3.30, to 4.30. | 50 |
| Balyduff | ,, | Friday, 3 to 4 p.m. | 52 |
| Barndarrig | ,, | Friday, 3 to 4 p.m, | 50 |
| B'essington | Annexe to Shop of Mr. Moore, M.C.C. | Daily | 165 |
| Carnew | Schoolhouse | Tues., Fri. 3.30, to 5 | 240 |
| Clara Vale | ,, | Friday, 3 30, to 4.30. | 50 |
| Coolfancy | ,, | Friday, 3.30, to 4.30. | 50 |
| Crossbridge | ,, | Friday, 3.30. to 4.30. | 65 |
| Curtlestown | ,, | Friday, 3 30, to 4.30. | 54 |
| Delgany | ,, | Friday, 3 to 4 | 65 |
| Donard Cross | Miss Phillips' House | Daily | 75 |
| Dunlavin | Imaal Hall | Tues & Fri, 3 to 5 | 450 |
| Glenealy | Schoolhouse | Fri., 3 30, to 4.30. | 65 |
| Glendalough | ,, | Fri., 3.30, to 4.30. | 85 |
| Granabeg | ,, | Fri., 3.30. to 4.30, | 50 |
| Grangecon | Hall | Fri., 4 to 5 | 230 |
| Hollywood | Schoolhouse | Fri., 3.30. to 4.30. | 50 |
| Johnstown | ,, | Fri., 3.30. to 4.30. | 65 |
| Kilcandra | Miss Bolton's House | Sunday, 12 15. to 1 p.m. | 100 |
| Kilcool | Co-Operative Store | Daily | 55 |
| Kilpipe | Schoolhouse | Fri, 3 to 4 | 75 |
| Ki'quiggan | ,, | Fri., 3 to 4 | 100 |
| Kiltegan | ,, | Fri., 3.30, to 4.30. | 70 |
| Knockananna | ,, | Fri., 3 30, to 4, 20 | 80 |
| Moneystown | ,, | Sun., 12.15. to 1.30. | 52 |
| Newcastle | ,, | Fri., 3.30, to 4 p m. | 52 |
| Newtown-Mt-K. | ,, | Fri., 3.30. to 4.30. | 140 |
| Rathdangan | O'Toole Hall | Sun., 12.15. to 1 | 50 |
| Redcross | Brookside | Daily | 100 |
| Roundwood | Schoolhouse | Friday, 3.30, to 4.30, | 85 |
| Shillelagh | ,, | Tues. & Fri. 3 to 4.30. | 120 |
| Stratford | ,, | Fri., 3.30. to 4.30. | 65 |
| Tinahely | Courthouse | Sun., 3 to 5 | 130 |
| Valleymount | Schoolhouse | Fri., 3.30. to 4 | 52 |

**SMALL READING GROUPS** — No. of Vols,

| | |
|---|---|
| Glanmore Castle | 25 |
| " Petrol " Lightship | 40 |
| Rathdrum Co. Home Staff | 35 |
| Wicklow Girls' Secondary School Staff | 25 |

**VOCATIONAL CLASSES**

| | |
|---|---|
| Aughrim | 42 |
| Barndarrig | 20 |

**SCHOOL CENTRES FOR CHILDREN ONLY**

| | |
|---|---|
| Arklow Boys' School | 60 |
| ,, Girls' ,, | 60 |
| ,, Secondary Girls' School | 25 |
| ,, Vocational School | 65 |
| Greystones Girls' School | 45 |
| Rathdrum Boys' School | 50 |
| Redcross School | 40 |
| Wicklow Girls' Secondary School | 35 |

**STUDY GROUPS**

| | |
|---|---|
| Arklow—Social Study | 15 |
| Rathdrum—Irish History | 25 |
| Wicklow—Social Study | 36 |

Total No. of Issues for year ending March 31st. 1933—85, 404
Total Number of Borrowers for year ending March, 31st 1933—5,134

system was a national necessity.

To improve matters she recommended that steps be taken to form a national library service as suggested by the Executive Board of the LAI. She went on to suggest that library authorities be asked to contribute a small amount of their annual book funds to the Irish Central Library for Students to advance the cultural and educational aspects of the public library service. In addition she urged that efforts be made to acquire a state subsidy for the Irish Central Library. Throughout the report stress was laid on the need for more financial support since most of the shortcomings of the public library service sprang from lack of adequate funding.

Apart from what was said in the report there were other things to plague Irish librarians besides lack of adequate funds and censorship was not the least of their troubles. Libraries and librarians in Ireland in the 1930s and 1940s enjoyed neither status nor authority. Libraries were regarded as 'seed beds of filth' which needed to be kept firmly under control by all right-minded citizens. The new Irish state had taken over the whole body of British statute law with only a few exceptions and consequently the main statutes dealing with obscene publications were the Obscene Publications Act 1857 and the Customs Consolidation Act 1876 Section 42, known as Lord Campbell's Act for more effectual powers preventing the sale of obscene books, pictures, prints and other articles.

Prior to 1922 there had been many individuals and groups who displayed active dissatisfaction with the type of periodicals and newspapers being read. The most important of these groups was known as the Irish Vigilance Association founded in 1911 and organised by members of the Dominican order. Local vigilance committees were established to get newsagents to sign pledges against stocking or selling objectionable newspapers. Moves were also afoot to combat what was termed objectionable literature and public opinion began to be stirred up by articles appearing which advocated the need for new legislation to revise the definition of the indecent and obscene to include birth control and race suicide, the drawing up of an official blacklist of obscene publications, and the prohibition of newspapers carrying birth control advertisements. At the same time the Catholic Truth Society set up a special sub-committee on evil literature which met for the first time on 1 May 1925, the aims of which were to revise the legislation.

These pressures eventually led to the Minister for Justice of the Irish Free State setting up a Committee of Enquiry on Evil Literature in 1926. This Committee received evidence from the Catholic Truth Society and from the Irish Vigilance Association which had the distinction of objecting to the works of James Joyce,

D.H. Lawrence, Warwick Deeping and many other writers. The only Protestant organisation to submit evidence, the Dublin Christian Citizenship Council, appealed for the freedom of the press and for positive action to improve education, libraries and reading clubs.

The report of the committee resulted in the Censorship of Publications Act 1929 which had new and wider definitions for the terms 'indecent' and 'obscene' to include anything likely to excite sexual passion. The Act contained provision for the establishment of a Censorship of Publications Board of five members including the chairman. Members were appointed for three years by the Minister of Justice with their work unpaid and part-time.

The board was directed to have regard to:

the literary, artistic, scientific or historic merit or importance of the book and its general tenor;
the language in which it was written;
the nature and extent of the circulation the books was intended to have;
the class of reader which was reasonably expected to read the book;
and any other matter relating to the book which appeared to the Board to be relevant.

The Act worked through the form of an official complaint with the complainant forwarding the books or periodicals to the Censorship Board for their examination. The Board could also examine books on their own initiative and could recommend the Minister of Justice to prohibit the sale and distribution of any publication which the Board felt to be 'in its general tendency indecent or obscene'. A register of prohibited publications was kept by the Minister and made available to the public and customs officials. The Minister for the Post and Telegraphs could prevent the importation of prohibited publications. The fervour with which these restrictions were put into operation reflected the mood of the more vocal do-gooders. Even before the passing of the Act there had been cases of armed men holding up trains carrying Sunday papers and burning newspapers which they considered to be 'filth' imported from England, filth which would sully the sanctity and purity of the Irish home.

The Irish censorship was tailor-made for a state that was predominantly Roman Catholic, and nationalistically it was aimed against the literature published in England – an England from which Ireland had so recently yanked herself free. In Ireland at this time the people looked inwards not outwards and foreign books, art and theatre all floundered under the full force of nationalistic prejudice.

216

Although Irish authors had the distinction of being banned, these writings were always in English, no books written in Irish were banned at all. An eminent example of this strange phenomenon was Brian Merriman's 'Midnight Court', a gloriously sensual poem written in the late 1700s and recited with glee generation after generation in the Irish tongue. When Frank O'Connor's translation appeared in English it was immediately banned!

Still most of the unsuitable books came from England and Irish customs officials felt themselves morally obliged to hold up parcels of books on suspicion that they might be suitable banning material especially if the author or publisher was already enrolled on the list of honours. At one time the customs officials became the Board's greatest customers.

In a period of fifteen years the Board banned about 1,700 books usually by reading marked passages, since as the Board worked part-time and were unpaid there was very little time to spend in reading the whole book. One tired censor read at the rate of fifty books a week, and arrived at the meeting having never read the books his colleagues wished to ban. Such pressure meant that no real consideration was given to the literary, artistic or historical merit of the books, a provision which was explicit in the Act. There was no appeal at this time against a decision to ban a book. The prevailing method of publishing lists of banned books was in the Iris Oifigiuil (Official Gazette), in the Register of Prohibited Publications, and in the *Irish Times*. In due course the Register of Prohibited Publications became known by the Irish wags as 'Everyman's Guide to the Modern Classics'.

The Act caused innumerable problems for librarians. It was also two-edged as those people who purchased a book prior to its banning kept it and read it. Libraries, if they had already bought the book were forced to remove it from their shelves. Many librarians became adept at judging in advance material likely to be banned, and therefore did not purchase it at all. A golden opportunity was missed here for when the ban was revoked on prohibitions of twelve years or more many of the 5,000 banned titles were out-of-print and unobtainable.

Pressures were put on librarians from several sources. The first three issues of *An Leabharlann* had a series of articles on book selection by Father Stephen Brown, S.J.,[1] the first of which dealt with censorship and the selection of books according to their moral value. Although Father Brown dealt with the positive aspects of book selection, his ideas were in tune with the prevailing mood of the censors – 'it is clear', he wrote, 'that a collection of books may be an arsenal of explosive ideas, social and intellectual dynamite, or a laboratory of corrosive and corrupting suggestions, a hot bed of disease germs'.

The pressure on the librarians came also from the self-appointed guardians of public morals who managed to capture practically anything worthwhile that might have slipped through without the notice of the board. Sean O'Faolain went into print on the seven different forms of national leprosy, these being – censorship by the board, the booksellers who feared notoriety, librarians who were afraid of their own shadow, library readers, committees, public representatives, and priests from platform and pulpit.

The range of books banned was impressive. In 1935 the Ballsbridge librarian Michael O'Donovan, alias Frank O'Connor, wrote to complain about the banning of the book by Sean O'Faolain called *Bird alone*, with not an indecent line in it. Books by H.E. Bates, Colette, Daphne Du Maurier, Robert Graves, Ernest Hemingway, Aldous Huxley, Georgette Heyer, Richard Llewellyn and Somerset Maugham appeared on the banned list. Practising librarians found to their cost that people regarding themselves as defenders of public morals could come into the library and accuse the librarian of having obscene publications in the library.

Dermot Foley has admirably described the hazards of librarianship in Ireland in the early 1930s when he took over the job of county librarian in Co. Clare. The first hazard he had to face were two .45 bullets delivered to him in an Oxo tin containing the short but peremptory message: 'Get out of the county! – you have a Clareman's job'. This however was nothing to the difficulties of dealing with the committee which appointed itself *en bloc* as a book selection sub-committee, and proceeded to sift with a fine toothcomb the list of suggested books for the library. Later, reflecting the mood of public scrutiny caused by the Censorship Act, the committee set up a panel of readers, 'a rag-bag of fifty-two upright citizens capable of spotting dirt at a hundred yards' and whose job it was to 'help the librarian in his very difficult task of getting good books'.

Sermons were preached from the local pulpits on the filth available in the public libraries and the books which eventually found their way to the shelves of the Clare libraries had little to do with the librarian's selection process but were the resultant concoction of the fifty-two vigilantes who had succeeded in 'serving up an Irish stew of imported Westerns, sloppy romances, blood and murders'.

The climate of changing public opinion however led to a new amended Act being placed on the Statute Book in 1946. This made two fundamental changes. First, a Board of Appeal was established and the banning orders were made by the Board instead of by the Minister for Justice. This represented a great step forward and the appointment of a High Court judge seemed reassuring. But no lawyer or witness could appear before either, and any author or publisher wishing to appeal had to submit five copies of the book and a deposit of five pounds. In addition, five members of the Oireachteas could jointly institute an appeal. About 85 per cent of the appeals in the first two years were successful, but during the first seven years of its existence the Board only received 208 separate applications.

It was not until well after the Second World War that ideas began to change. The war itself had changed moral attitudes, but another factor was that in the 1950s BBC television programmes could be received all along the east coast and along the border with Northern Ireland. This beamed into Irish homes much which the censor and moral protectors had hoped to prevent Ireland ever seeing or hearing.

The Library Council had been established by the Public Libraries Act 1947 for the purposes of accepting from the CUKT the gift of the Irish Central Library for Students, of operating a Central Library, and of assisting local authorities to improve their library services, and to advise the government on library development. After this the Irish Central Library was financed partly out of government funds and partly from contributions levied from local library authorities in proportion to their rateable values. The Carnegie Trustees made a final gesture of goodwill by authorising a tapering grant for the Library's maintenance until 1953. Under the terms of its foundation the ICL for Students provides free of charge to all public libraries in Northern Ireland a central lending service based on cooperation between libraries throughout Ireland.

The Library Council or An Chomhairle Leabharlanna consists of a chairman appointed by the Minister for Local Government after consultation with the Minister of Education, and twelve other members. Five of these are nominated by the universities, five by local authorities, one on the nomination of the trustees of the National Library, and one from an approved association which has been the Library Association of Ireland. Thus there is a fair spread of interests represented on the Council.

For the purpose of its functions the Library Council can purchase or take lease on land, build and equip premises, and also sell or lease any land. The expenses of the Council are defrayed out of moneys provided by the Oireachtas (Legislature) and grants could and were made to enable the Council to provide financial aid to the local authorities for the improvement of their services. The adoption of the principle of state aid for libraries represented a new lease of life for a sick and ailing service.

One of the first acts of the Library Council was to survey the existing public library services to ascertain their present condition. The survey, which was begun in June 1951 and finished by May 1953, was carried out by Dermot Foley and J.T. Dowling of the Dublin Public Libraries.

In the Republic of Ireland there was a noticeable deterioration of the library services after the discontinuance of the Carnegie grants in the late 1940s. The relatively poor state of the libraries in the country up to the 1960s would seem extraordinary given the fact that the Public Libraries Act had been adopted and that there was a long tradition of respect for books and libraries. One should not, however, look at the library situation in isolation, but instead put it into context with the political and economic realities of the country. Following hard on the heels of the famine of the late 1840s was the rise of the Fenian Movement, agrarian unrest, and the Land Leagues agitation. The First World War, interrupted by the Easter uprising in 1916, led to the guerilla war lasting until 1921, and this was followed by the Civil War which disrupted the whole country. During the Second World War, despite Ireland's neutrality, funds were very restricted and books difficult to obtain.

By 1945 all the county councils had adopted the Acts and with three exceptions all the urban district councils had handed over their library powers to the county councils. Thus in every part of the country there was an authority empowered to provide library facilities and except for the three urban districts the public library system was based on the administrative county or on combined counties, including county boroughs.

The survey which was published in 1955 came out under the title of 'The Improvement of Public Library Services – First series: County Libraries' (see Figure 11.2). The Library Council's main recommendations for improvement were first, that financial assistance be given; secondly, that the appointment of local committees where they did not already exist, would greatly strengthen the local machinery of administration; and thirdly, closer cooperation was urged between local and central authorities for the development of libraries. Most of the county systems were only providing a nucleus of a service with many not recognising the true function of a library for intellectual improvement and recreation, and the Council wished to see definite schemes of development to be implemented over a period of years.

Under the County Management Act 1940 the powers exercised by the library committees since 1925 were transformed to the County Managers. This Act had allocated the functions of the county council between the Councils and the Managers, those exercised by the former being known as reserve functions, and those exercised by the

## FIGURE 11.2  COUNTY LIBRARY EXPENDITURE (1952-53)

| AREA | EXPENDITURE | | LEVIED IN THE YEAR BY RATES | |
| | Amount | Per head of population | Amount | Equivalent rate in the pound |
| 1. | 2. | 3. | 4. | 5. |
| | £ | d. | £ | d. |
| Waterford  .. .. .. | 6,631 | 34 | 6,520 | 5·6 |
| Limerick  .. .. .. | *11,513 | 30 | 9,114 | 4·5 |
| Meath  .. .. .. | 6,479 | 23 | 7,006 | 2·9 |
| Dublin  .. .. | 9,035 | 23 | 10,000 | 5 |
| Longford-Westmeath  .. | 7,176 | 20 | 7,360 | 3·6 |
| Kilkenny  .. .. | 5,386 | 19 | 4,813 | 3·8 |
| Offaly  .. .. .. | 4,252 | 19 | 4,250 | 4·4 |
| Wicklow  .. .. .. | 4,048 | 19 | 3,982 | 3·8 |
| Monaghan  .. .. .. | 4,167 | 18 | 3,937 | 3·4 |
| Sligo  .. .. .. | 4,420 | 18 | 4,450 | 4·5 |
| Carlow  .. .. .. | 2,327 | 16 | 2,425 | 3·6 |
| Kildare  .. .. .. | 4,375 | 15 | 4,158 | 3 |
| Cork  .. .. .. | 16,932 | 15 | 17,786 | 3·5 |
| Louth  .. .. .. | 4,265 | 14 | 4,000 | 3·3 |
| Clare  .. .. .. | 4,970 | 14 | 5,059 | 3·5 |
| Galway  .. .. .. | 9,483 | 14 | 9,483 | 3·1 |
| Tipperary N.R. & S.R.  .. | 7,142 | 14 | 6,842 | 2·4 |
| Roscommon  .. .. | 3,368 | 13 | 3,708 | 2·9 |
| Cavan  .. .. .. | 3,764 | 13 | 3,850 | 3 |
| Laoighis  .. .. .. | 2,523 | 12 | 2,746 | 2·6 |
| Leitrim  .. .. .. | 1,848 | 10 | 1,875 | 3 |
| Kerry  .. .. .. | 5,380 | 10 | 5,528 | 3·8 |
| Wexford  .. .. .. | 3,579 | 9 | 3,700 | 2·2 |
| Donegal  .. .. .. | 4,745 | 9 | 4,810 | 3·5 |
| Mayo  .. .. .. | 3,243 | 5 | 3,237 | 2 |
| TOTAL  .. .. | 141,351 | 15 | 140,639 | 3·4 |

*Includes £2,638 expenditure on erection of buildings.

*From*  The Library Council: The Improvement of Public Library Services – First Series: County Libraries, 1955 latter as executive functions. The reserve functions were the right to strike the rate, to borrow money, and to make, amend or revoke bye-laws. Further the making or revoking of an order by virtue of which an optional enactment is brought into operation within the county or city, planning schemes under the Town Planning Acts, clearing and improving areas under the Housing Acts, were also reserved functions as were Parliamentary and local elections. The executive functions were every power, function or duty of a council which was not amongst the reserved functions, these being exercised solely by the county manager.

This refers in particular to the control, supervision, remuneration, privileges and superannuation of local officers. The County Management Act of 1940 did not preclude the delegation to the executive functions of the county manager to a committee, and the Library Council recommended that as far as library services were concerned the executive functions should be delegated to library committees on an advisory or consultative basis. Major items would be proposals for new buildings, the selection and purchasing of books, the withdrawal of obsolete stock, the provision of books for young people, school libraries, mobile libraries, local interest collections, preparation of an annual draft of estimates to submit to the county manager before he prepares his estimates, the popularising of the library, and preparation in collaboration with the county manager of the county library development scheme.

These schemes for library development were to include the siting of libraries and service points, the development of the book stock, its renewal and proportion to the population, the library service in the schools, the development of special services such as reference and information, children's libraries, local collections, propaganda on behalf of the libraries, staffing, and the time scale needed to implement the proposed work. Library authorities submitting development schemes were to be eligible for grants to put the schemes into operation. The report urged the development of the school library system through the public libraries with separate grants for the school collections.

At the time of the survey half the stock in the county libraries consisted of fiction, one-third was non-fiction, and the remaining sixth was for junior readers. Fiction accounted for almost two-thirds of the books issued. Book stocks, apart from being unsuitable and old, were also very sparse and in three counties there were only 25 books or less per 100 of the population. The report suggested subscriptions to basic bibliographical journals containing book reviews to allow for better book selection. Unsuitable buildings also came in for criticism as did the practice of circulating books in boxes to library centres, thus giving readers a very limited choice. County Antrim had a newly innovated mobile library service and the report suggested that the use of a mobile library be given a trial in the South. At this time four counties had vans which were used to display books for the convenience of the local custodians though not for the public.

The report also endeavoured to improve the status of library staff and recommended that library assistants should be expected to possess at least a school leaving certificate or to have matriculated from university, and that staff selection should be by means of a preliminary examination and interview. The office of the county librarian was to be filled by the Local Appointment Commissioners from candidates possessing a library qualification. Recommendations to make this an essential qualification together with a University degree at an opportune time ensured that eventually the right calibre of professional staff would be available.

The final recommendation of the report was the appointment of the Library Adviser to keep the Council informed of the development of the scheme and to assist the local communities in devising and implementing them.

Other provisions relating to the management and maintenance of libraries appear in a variety of other Acts. The Local Government (Officers) Act 1943 covers the appointment, promotion, remuneration, travelling expenses and other matters relating to public rate-supported staff. The Public Bodies Order 1943 covers the keeping of accounts and records, while the combined Purchasing Act 1939 orders that goods, other than books for library authorities, must be ordered from official contractors. The health of staff at work is covered by the Office Premises Act 1958 which provides for the protection of the health, welfare and safety of persons employed in offices and libraries. The Public Hospitals Act 1933 authorised the making of grants out of hospital trust funds for the purpose of defraying the cost of libraries in hospitals.[2] The Local Government Act 1946 abolished the rate limitation. Thus it can be seen that in the spirit of the law the movement towards an efficient library service was being encouraged by legislation.

Hot on the heels of the first report from the Library Council came in 1958 a second publication entitled 'The Improvement of the Public Library Service: Recommendations: Second Series – County Borough, Borough and Urban District Libraries'. At the time of the report there were four county borough libraries at Dublin, Cork, Limerick and Waterford; two borough libraries at Dun Laoghaire and Clonmel; and one urban district library at Bray.

The report found that the most extensive library service was that of the Dublin county borough with a joint stock of about 500,000 volumes which included the Gilbert Collection and just over 22,000 books in Irish. About 14 per cent of the population were registered borrowers and the children's libraries had a full-time officer responsible for the service and for organising talks and exhibitions for the children. In Dublin no library rate had been struck until 1909 as the library was supported by income surplus to the borough fund. The penny rate yielded an inadequate income and consequently the library suffered from a totally insufficient book fund.

By the passing of the Local Government Act 1930, Greater Dublin came into being absorbing the two adjoining townships of Rathmines and Pembroke, both of which had municipal libraries. A further extension in 1944 brought in the library at Howth which had been established a short time before by the Dublin County Council. Additional libraries were added from 1930 to 1955 at Ringsend, Phibsborough, Drumcondra, Inchicore, Marino and Terenure, and a further branch taken over at Baldoyle from the Dublin County Council.

The growth of the city and the increasing population created demands for libraries which clashed with more urgent problems of slum clearance, housing and roadmaking. By the time of the Public Libraries Act 1947 Dublin was seriously behind with library planning and provision. Even in 1955 with an expenditure somewhat higher than other public library authorities at 34s.6d. per head of the population, the amount spent on books and binding was rather low. Special comments about the Dublin service suggested that more separate children's departments should be formed, and that specialist staff be appointed and trained for that area of the work. The importance of the reference library was not overlooked either, and it was suggested that the libraries should have separate reference rooms. The need for a new Central Library was noted.

In Cork a new purpose-built library had been erected in 1930. The building had four sections, reference, magazine and newspaper section, children's section and an adult lending library with over 36,000 volumes. The number of readers registered in 1954-55 was 7,391. Cork local history was also collected. Two groups were not catered for at this time, children domiciled on the outskirts of the city, and adults residing just outside the city boundary, and it was thought that a cooperative scheme with the county council might resolve this problem. Extended accommodation was needed for the growing adult department, and storage problems over newspapers were to be resolved by the microfilming of materials. The library expenditure in Cork was 32s.6d. per head of population.

Limerick had a public library from 1906 but little progress had been made over the years and the library had been almost completely given over to newspapers and a reference department, scant attention being given to the lending library. In 1939 the first trained librarian was appointed and the service revitalised according to the needs of the day. Shades of the censorship of publications were very evident even in 1955 as there was a committee of nine people nominated by the corporation to deal with objections lodged by readers as to the unsuitability of some of the books included in the stock. Library expenditure amounted to 22s.7d. per head of population. Most of the book fund was spent on non-fiction but the annual amount spent on books as a whole was low, as was the number of registered readers.

It was found in the report that the readers in the municipal areas tended to use their libraries more than those in the county areas, but this was explained as reflecting a longer library tradition in the towns, which generally had more financial backing, better trained staff and more centralised areas of service. With the exception of Cork the most striking feature was the inadequacy of the reference services and the report recommended that reference departments should be further developed and that if possible a separate reference room should be provided with the appropriate qualified staff. The report supported the proposal to establish a central reference library for Dublin, notwithstanding that the National Library already met the needs of the research worker but it was felt that the library should provide for the needs of the business and industrial communities by supplying technical, commercial and scientific information. The report recommended proper provision for children within the public library, saying that only Dublin, Bray and Limerick had reasonable provision. Cork was the only library of those surveyed in the report to produce an annual report and it was urged that the others should follow suit by publishing annually news of progress and developments.

The recruitment and grading of staff was also dealt with as in the First Series of the Council's recommendations, but in addition a new grade of Library Clerk was to be added to those already in existence to undertake the routine clerical work.

These two Library Council reports had highlighted the problems of library development in Ireland and they made three main recommendations, as follows:

1 that financial assistance should be forthcoming from the Government;
2 that local control should be strengthened by the appointment of committees where these did not exist as a result of the County Management Act;

3   that closer links should be created between local and central
    authorities

One unqualified recommendation was that a library adviser should
be appointed. This was agreed in 1959 and in July 1960 Dermot
Foley, the first Director of An Chomhairle Leabharlanna, was
appointed.

A further two years were to elapse before it was announced that
the Council under the Public Libraries Act 1947 (Grants)
Regulations 1961, could put the financial aid promised in that law
into operation. This assistance was to take form of a fifty per cent
subsidy by way of loan contributions on capital investments towards
schemes of library development approved by the Council.

Exactly fourteen years had elapsed between the passing of the Act
and the announcement in 1961 as to the kind of financial aid that
would be available. The Library Advisory Council ranks as a public
body or local authority, and like any local authority its actions are
subject to the approval of the appropriate government minister. It is
therefore more than just an advisory body as it can take its own
decisions. Libraries hoping for the fifty per cent subsidy submit
their plans to the Advisory Council which if it feels the plans are not
suitable can reject the grant application. Libraries can be built by
library authorities without recourse to the Advisory Council but if
the grant is required the Council has the right to either approve or
reject the proposal. Once the project is approved by An Chomhairle
Leabharlanna then it is put forward with a recommendation to the
Minister. Loans may be raised for a 35 year period for buildings, ten
years for vehicles and five years for books, providing the books are
not fiction and providing also that they are used for subsidising
major acquisitions of books to stock new branch libraries or for the
substantial re-stocking of the existing library service.

The reports of the Library Advisory Council in the 1950s had
highlighted the serious under-stocking in both terms of quality and
quantity. Most of the county councils and other library authorities
were poor and there was what amounted to a book famine in most of
the public library systems. At the beginning of the 1960s it was
estimated that the public library system in Ireland spent only 8d. per
head of population compared with the recommended figure of 2s.6d.
per head.

The profession in the Republic began to feel a new breath of life
pulsating through an almost mortified corpse. The aim of the
Council's scheme was to encourage local authorities to undertake an
enterprising reorganisation of their library services. In this the
scheme was more than successful and new projects began to flood

into the headquarters of An Chomhairle Leabharlanna. Advice on the Public Libraries Grant Scheme 1961 was sent out to all libraries from the Council in March 1962 (GS 3) in which encouragement and advice on how to submit proposals that would be acceptable was given. The guidance covered the siting of buildings, hours of opening, stock which was to include reference material, children's literature (which could include fiction) and mobile libraries. From the submissions coming into An Chomhairle Leabharlanna it was possible to discern a pattern of long-term public library planning for the whole country. A further circular 'Planning for new library buildings in counties' was issued in January 1964 (GS 7) which gave information and guidance for submitting proposals on new town libraries and county library headquarters. In this circular the new Antrim County Library headquarters at Ballymena in Northern Ireland was quoted as one possible example of how a county library headquarters should be arranged.

Because some of the submissions to the Council were inclined to be speculative and lacking in pre-determined objectives the Council had set up a sub-committee to investigate the progress of the public library service since 1961. This led to the issue by the Council in March 1971 of 'Library development: a brief guide and some recommendations' (GS 9). From the interim report of the sub-committee it was apparent that no library authority in Ireland was at this time providing a full range of services and most of the towns were still without purpose-built libraries.

By January 1975 An Chomhairle Leabharlanna had adopted for Ireland the *Standards for Public Libraries* which had been issued in 1973 by the International Federation of Library Associations. An Chomhairle Leabharlanna sent a copy of the *Standards* to every library authority in the country indicating that any future projects to be submitted for approval should be prepared in conformity with the IFLA Standards.

Perhaps the problems can be illustrated by the Wicklow County Library service, although to be truthful any number of counties would admit to having experienced the same slow and small beginning. Carnegie libraries had been built in Greystones and Enniskerry in 1910 which under the 1925 Act became the responsibility of the County Council. In 1930 the county library headquarters was one small room with a stock of 2,000 books. Small grants from the CUKT plus the increase in the library rate permitted the gradual built-up of the stock and the setting up of branches in Greystones, Wicklow and Arklow, and the establishment of rural and school centres, (see Figure 11.1). In 1946 the headquarters moved from its small rented room to the Carnegie Library in

Greystones which allowed more spacious accommodation for books and equipment. The County Library Advisory Committee approved a plan for the development of the library service which included an extension to the headquarters, the establishment of libraries in villages and the employment of extra staff. At this time no addition had been made to the staff since 1930, but in 1951 an office boy and one assistant librarian were appointed.

In 1935 only £903 was spent on the Co. Wicklow library service. It had a book stock of 12,226 volumes. By 1975 however the stock had risen to 111,296. Readership had risen from 2,400 in 1935 to 20,131 in 1979. This is out of a county population which, excluding Bray whose library is financed by the Bray Urban District Council, is 62,121.

Between 1925 and 1975 one new building had been erected in Blessington. Since 1975 new libraries have been built in Wicklow town and Carnew with bigger premises having been acquired for Arklow, Dunlavin and Rathdrum branch libraries. An Chomhairle Leabharlanna supplied a loan of £50,000 for books and the impetus coming from the Council can be clearly seen.

Similar success stories can be quoted from all round the country. Co. Kildare started a library service in 1926 when the County Council adopted the Public Libraries Acts. The two urban areas in the county ceded their library powers, Athy in 1927 and Naas in 1939. Through the foresight of its county librarian J.C. Connolly, Kildare had been able to erect a county library headquarters in Droichead Nua in 1936. In 1957 proposals to improve the service generally were put forward by the county librarian. These were strongly supported by the local press which described the library service, not quite unoriginally perhaps, as the 'Cinderella of our rate-aided activities'. After a long struggle the Library Committee in 1972 submitted to the Library Advisory Council a plan for future development. This included additional accommodation at the headquarters and resulted in an assessment of the short and long term needs of the towns in the area. These included suggestions for purpose-built branches in certain towns, expansion of the bookstock and improved staffing levels.

This plan eventually led to the completion of a new extension to the Droichead Nua headquarters. This was opened in 1978 and was followed in 1982 by the opening of new libraries at Celbridge and Maynooth (see Figure 11.3). In Castledermot a renovated building was acquired and in Ballitore the eighteenth century Quaker meeting house has been converted partly into a library and partly into a Quaker museum. New libraries are planned for Naas, Athy and Kildare and most others are being renovated. In the light of this

# FIGURE 11.3   MAYNOOTH BRANCH LIBRARY OPENED
## 1982

development it is interesting to look back at the year 1935 when the total amount spent on the Naas library was £43 per annum of which £20 was the librarian's salary, £14 went on books and £9 on repairs.

To quote a few more examples of the growth of the library service since the support of An Chomhairle Leabharlanna we can look first at the city of Cork. There the inadequacies of the service became apparent in 1965 with the extension of the city boundaries. But soon a programme of reorganisation and development was adopted. Sites were acquired adjoining the City Library premises and a new City Library was started in 1975 embracing the original building. Known as the Terence McSwiney Library it was opened by Mr Jack Lynch the Taoiseach (leader) on 12 May 1979, thus indicating that interest in library development had changed considerably for the better (see Figure 11.3). It is now the largest public library in the country, containing adult and children's departments, a music library stocking records and cassettes, a newspaper reading room, a general reference library, local history collection, newspaper archive and microfilm library as well as the headquarters for the primary school service with a permanent display of about 10,000 volumes. It also houses the administrative headquarters for the entire service.

Three new branches have opened between 1972 and 1976, and four more are planned. The primary schools library service is relatively new, dating from 1968 and as with other primary school library services the Department of Education makes a contribution of 25p per child, with a matching contribution from the library authority. In fact, as in the case of Cork, many library authorities underwrite primary schools services to a large extent, making contributions far in excess of their original commitments. In 1980-81 the total cost of the scheme in Cork was £28,000 towards which the Department of Education had contributed £6,500. The Library Association of Ireland has submitted a library scheme for post primary schools urging the improvement of the use of existing funds in post primary schools and better funding for the primary schools.

Limerick adopted a library development plan in 1962 with the object of providing more branch libraries, more libraries in primary, secondary and vocational schools, a mobile reference service to outlying areas, and the promotion of a regional library system. The development of the schools library service was far in excess of anything dreamed of previously, aiming to provide children in Co. Limerick with a service comparable to the best anywhere in the world. By 1972 this investment in education through the school libraries had increased children's reading by 350 per cent through enlarged junior book stocks, added advisory service and better expertise. School library schemes for Limerick County had been

**FIGURE 11.4   MR J LYNCH OPENING THE TERENCE MCSWINEY LIBRARY IN CORK IN 1979**

From left: Mr Pearse Wye, T.D., Minister of State Dept of Finance; Mr Sean Bohan, City Libraries; An Taoiseach, Mr. Jack Lynch; Lord Mayor of Cork, Councillor Brian Sloane, Mr. C.J.F. McCarthy, Chairman, Cork City Library Committee.

proposed by the county librarian as early as 1938 at a cost of £500, but had been rejected as being too expensive. A further scheme put forward in 1947 asked for one children's librarian but this had been turned down by the department of local government. Throughout Ireland the professional impetus was there, straining at the leash, but it was too often rejected.

The Limerick proposal for a regional reference library was deferred with a further recommendation that the library of the then proposed National Institute of Higher Education (NIHE) should be unified with that of the region. It was agreed with the Regional Development Organisation for Limerick, Clare and Tipperary (North Riding) that the librarian at the NIHE would be charged with the responsibility for the further promotion of the regional reference library with the Regional Development Organisation subventing the salary of the newly created post of librarian until 1981.

The first Institute was opened in 1970 at Limerick with another proposed Institute at Dublin. The Limerick Institute has adopted Europe as its academic theme and it offers educational programmes to train students for Ireland's role as a member of the European Economic Community. The Institute specialises amongst other things in diploma and degree studies in electronics, engineering, computer engineering, data processing, energy technology and industrial design, all the programmes being designed to reflect technological and managerial careers within the European Community. The Institute also offers a continuing education programme, and a Link-In for Education programme enabling managers and technical specialists to link in to separate modules on the full-time courses. The Mid-West Regional Office of the Institute of Industrial Research and Standards is located on the campus to help make technological information available to local firms and to form links between those firms and the Institute. In addition a Regional Management Centre has been established to meet the training and performance improvement needs of the local industry, commerce and public sectors. The Centre which is located at the Institute provides an integration of the skills of AnCo (the Training Council), the Institute, the Shannon Development Company and other training and consultancy bodies.

The campus library consists of over 100,000 items including audio-visual materials such as slides, films, film loops and microforms. The catalogue is in the process of being converted from card to microfiche. Dewey Decimal Classification is used. Some 1,000 periodicals are currently taken, including Irish, English, European and American newspapers.

In 1973 Patrick Kelly, the librarian of the NIHE, submitted a report to the Regional Development Organisation on the proposed development of the Mid-West Region Information Service. He recommended a network of information centres with the NIHE as the coordinating body. The centres so recommended were at Limerick under the joint control of the Limerick Corporation and Limerick County Council, at Ennis under Clare County Council, at Thurles under the Tipperary Joint Library Committee, and at Shannon under the Shannon Development Company. These proposals were put to the Conference of Mid-West librarians for discussion, and were agreed. With the help of An Chomhairle Leabharlanna the proposals for the development of a Mid-West Regional Library Service was submitted to and approved by the Regional Development Organisation Board in 1977. The Conference of Mid-West librarians joined An Chomhairle Leabharlanna and the librarian of the NIHE to form a library committee of the Regional Development Organisation, which has a consultative, coordinating and advisory role.

The service offered includes the distribution to the participating libraries of the catalogue of the holdings of the NIHE and the Thomond College of Education on a regular basis. A consolidated list of all the periodicals and newspapers in the region has been undertaken, and the large collection of reference material held by the NIHE and the Thomond College of Education is available to enquirers either by letter, telephone or personal visit. The union list of the periodicals in the area does not in any way duplicate the function of the *Union List of Current Periodicals and Serials in Irish Libraries* produced by IADIS as none of the participating libraries with the partial exception of the NIHE are listed.[3]

Thus the NIHE has become a major regional information and documentation source for the area. NIHE has also been chosen by the Documentation Coordinating Committee of the National Science Council as one of the participants in an experimental facsimile transmission network linking the major libraries in the country. It is hoped that other specialist libraries in the region will disseminate their list of holdings on the same basis as soon as possible. The Library Committee is looking at the feasibility of a coordinated computerised cataloguing system for the Mid-West Region.

In Dublin a building programme for a series of new branch libraries and extensions to existing ones was conceived to meet the expanding needs of the city's population. New libraries have been placed in shopping centres such as the one at Roselawn in Blanshardstown, or adjacent to a school as at Coolock, or a college as at Ballyfermot. Other new libraries are those at Deansgrange and

Swords. Services to children include storytelling sessions and leisure activities. A picture lending scheme has been started as well as an information centre for teenagers.

A new headquarters was opened in Fenian Street in 1980, when an automatic ordering system was installed. An automated cataloguing system is planned for 1983. The new central lending library, the ILAC (Irish Life Assurance Co.) Centre in Moore Street, is shortly to open with a reference, commercial and technical service, music library, art collection and language learning facilities.

Many Irish libraries are beginning to take advantage of the new automated information systems. EURONET DIANE (Direct Information Access for Europe) has over thirty subscribers in Ireland, and the EURONET DIANE launch team in Luxembourg is headed by an Irishman, Barry Mahon.

The small public library system at Dun Laoghaire, which has a population of 60,000 and four branches has on-line access to EURONET and SDC through the services of the Institute for Industrial Research and Standards. Dun Laoghaire's agreement with NIHE for the computerisation of its catalogue using BLAISE/LOCAS has been noticed with interest by the rest of the profession.

Problems facing librarians are the same in both parts of Ireland. After the tremendous boost to the profession and the energetic building programme, the economic recession has slowed things down. In addition the break in parity between the Irish punt and the British pound has meant that book budgets in the Republic are smaller. The purchasing power of Irish libraries has been effectively reduced since so many of the books that need to be bought are published in the United Kingdom. To add insult to injury, when Value Added Tax was introduced to the Republic the government saw fit to impose it on books, which has never happened in the United Kingdom. Happily, after very much lobbying, this ignoble tax on learning was taken off in May 1982.

Nevertheless, the future of the library service in all parts of Ireland appears to be brighter than ever before. There is much fertilisation of ideas between librarians in the Republic and in Northern Ireland. The Library Association of Ireland and the Northern Ireland Branch of the Library Association have held joint conferences since 1963, and the existence of the border makes no difference to the profession when it comes to electing the President of the Library Association of Ireland. In its turn, the (British) Library Association has granted an Honorary Vice-Presidency and a Honorary Fellowship to two Irish librarians. A joint periodical is published as *The Irish Library – An Leabharlann*: the journal of the Library Association of Ireland and the Library Association

(Northern Ireland Branch), with an editorial board drawn from both sides of the border. In addition, a joint fiction reserve scheme devised by the two bodies exists for all Ireland. Furthermore, the Irish Central Library, Dublin, serving the whole of Ireland, is now integrated with the British Library Lending Division as one of the regions.

Another joint venture worthy of note is the *Irish Publishing Record* which has appeared since 1967. This includes materials published both in the Republic and in Northern Ireland, including books, pamphlets, new numbers of periodicals, yearbooks, music scores, works on music and also government publications. Since 1969 it has been compiled by the library school at University College Dublin on behalf of IADIS. The Institute of Irish Studies at Queen's University, Belfast helped to publish *Irish Booklore*, which comes out twice a year and is now produced with the aid of a grant from the Arts Council of Northern Ireland.

This book began by referring to the long and honourable history of libraries in Ireland. Despite the various vicissitudes affecting the country over the centuries Irish people, in all Ireland, have always displayed an admirable and inherited love of books, literature and libraries. Now that the era of information technology has arrived, knowledge and the right to knowledge has become the inheritance of a people whose libraries indeed have a long-traced pedigree.


'The past is behind us. We enter the future palpitating with ambitious speculation'.

Dermot Foley in *The Library World* September 1963

# References

**Chapter 1**

1 *The Annals of the Four Masters*, written between 1630 and 1636 by Michael O'Cleary, Peregrine O'Cleary, Peregrine Duignan and Fearfeasa O'Mulconry, in the Franciscan Convent at Bundrowes, Co. Donegal.

**Chapter 2**

1 Mr and Mrs S.C. Hall, *Ireland: its Scenery, Character etc.*, 1843

**Chapter 4**

Mr & Mrs S.C. Hall, *Ireland: its Scenery, Character etc.*, 1843

**Chapter 5**

1 Lord Lieutenant of Ireland for eight months in 1745 and known for his amours.

**Chapter 8**

1 Leslie, T.E. Cliffe, *An Enquiry into the progress and present conditions of Mechanics Institutes, Parts 1 and 2*, Papers read before the Dublin Statistical Society. 1852.

**Chapter 11**

1 Father Brown founded the Central Catholic Library, Dublin in 1922 and was a lecturer at the Library School at University College, Dublin.

2 In 1937 Christina Keogh was appointed as Consulting Librarian and Chief Executive Officer of the Hospital Library Council. In the same year a Government grant of £10,000 had been made out of Hospital Trust Funds for the establishment of a Hospital Library Council. This service was discontinued in 1977.

3 The Irish Association for Documentation was established in 1947 to promote in Ireland the recording, organisation and dissemination of specialist knowledge. In 1967 its title was changed to the Irish Association for Documentation and Information Services (IADIS) with a programme of activities to deal with education and training, the production of a directory of special libraries, and of a Union List of Current Periodicals and Serials.

# Bibliography

**BOOKS**

Adams, Michael. *Censorship: the Irish experience* . Dublin, Scepter Books. 1968.

Adams, W.G.S. *A Report on Library Provision and Policy*. Dunfermline, Carnegie United Kingdom Trust. 1915.

Allen, Robert. *The Presbyterian College, Belfast, 1853-1953*. Belfast, Mullan. 1954.

Anderson, John. *History of the Belfast Library and Society for Promoting Knowledge*. Belfast, McCaw, Stevenson and Orr, Linenhall Works. 1888.

Armagh, Dean of. *A Memoir of the Public Library of Armagh:* a paper read to the 7th Annual Meeting of the Library Association of the United Kingdom, 30 September 1884.

Bassett, G.H. *The Book of Antrim*. Dublin. 1888.

Bieler, Ludwig. *Ireland: harbinger of the Middle Ages*. London, OUP. 1963.

Bonfield, C. and Farrington, A. *The Royal Irish Academy and its Library*. 1964.

Brenan, Revd Martin. *Schools of Kildare and Leighlin, 1775-1835*. Gill and Son. 1935.

Byrne, Kieran. *Mechanics' Institutes in Ireland, 1825-1850*. Proceedings of the Educational Studies Association of Ireland Conference, Dublin 1979. Galway University Press.

Byrne, Kieran. *Mechanics' Institutes in Ireland before 1855*. Thesis presented in partial fulfilment of the regulations governing the award of the degree of Master of Education, Mode B. University College Cork, Faculty of Arts. 1976.

Cameron, Sir C.A. *History of the Royal College of Surgeons in Ireland and Irish Schools of Medicine*. Dublin, Fannin and Co. 1886.

Carnegie United Kingdom Trust. County Library Conference, 4-6 November 1924. Report of the Proceedings. Dunfermline, CUKT. 1925.

*Catalogue of the Library of the Loyal National Repeal Association of Ireland,* to be sold by auction, 15 November 1848.

An Chomhairle Leabharlanna (The Library Council). *The Improvement of Public Library Services, Recommendations, 1st series:*

*County Libraries.* 1955. *2nd series: County Borough, Borough and Urban District Libraries.* 1958.

Corcoran, T. *The Clongowes Record, 1814-1932.* Dublin, Browne and Nolan.

Craig, Maurice. *Irish bookbindings, 1600-1800. London, Cassell. 1954.*

Daunt, W.J. O'Neill. *Ireland and her agitators.* Dublin, John Mullany. 1867.

Downing, P.J. *The Hedge schools of Ireland.* London, Longmans, Green and Co. 1935.

Dublin Mechanics' Institution. Reports from 1839.

Duffy, C.G. *Young Ireland: a fragment of Irish history,* London, Fisher Unwin. 1896.

Foley, Dermot. *Censorship in Ireland: a personal experience.* Speech at University of Michigan, Ann Arbor, Michigan, USA, June 1973.

Gilbert, Sir John. *History of the City of Dublin.* Dublin, Dollard, 1854-59.

Graham, Hugh. *The Early Irish monastic schools.* Dublin, Talbot Press. 1923.

Hall, Mr and Mrs S.C. *Ireland: its scenery, character etc.* 3 v. Jeremiah How. 1843.

Hudson, J.W. *The History of adult education.* London, Longman, Brown, Green and Longman. 1851.

Hyde, Douglas. *A Literary history of Ireland.* London, Benn. 1967 reprint.

Irish Rural Libraries Association. The Organisation of rural libraries in Ireland: memorandum for the use of District Councils and Voluntary Library Associations. Dublin, IRLA, 34 Dawson Chambers, Dawson Street. (ca. 1904).

Jameson, John. *The History of the Royal Belfast Academical Institution, 1810-1960.* Belfast, Mullen. 1959.

Keogh, Christina A. *Report on Public Library Provision in the Irish Free State, 1935.* 1936.

Kildare Place Society (The Society for the Education of the Poor in Ireland). Hints on the formation of lending libraries in Ireland. Dublin. 1824.

Ledwich, Edward. *The Antiquities of Ireland*. Dublin. 2nd ed. 1804.

Leslie, T.E. Cliffe. *An Enquiry into the progress and present condition of Mechanics' Institutions*. Parts 1 and 2. Papers read before the Dublin Statistical Society, 1852. Dublin, Hodges and Smith. 1852.

McCarthy, Muriel. *All graduates and gentlemen – Marsh's Library*. Dublin, O'Brien Press. 1980.

McGregor, J.J. *History, topography and antiquities of the County and City of Limerick*. Dublin. 1827.

Magee, John. *The Linen Hall Library and the Cultural Life of Georgian Belfast*. Library Association of Ireland and Library Association (Northern Ireland Branch). 1982.

Meenan, James and Clarke, Desmond, (eds): *The Royal Dublin Society, 1731-1981*. Dublin, Gill and Macmillan. 1981.

Mitchell, J.M. *The Public Library system of Great Britain and Ireland, 1921-1923*. A report prepared for the Carnegie United Kingdom Trustees. Dunfermline, CUKT. 1924.

Moody, T.W. and Beckett, J.C. *Queen's Belfast, 1845-1949*. 2 v. London, Faber. 1959.

Moore, Kingsmill. *An Unwritten chapter in the History of Education, being the History of the Society for the Education of the Poor in Ireland, generally known as the Kildare Place Society, 1811-1831*. London, Macmillan. 1904.

National University of Ireland. *The National University Handbook, 1908-1932*. Dublin, The Senate of the National University of Ireland. 1932.

Northern Ireland Government. *The Public Library Service in Northern Ireland:* report of the Committee appointed by the Minister of Education and presented to Parliament, April 1966. Belfast, CMD. 494.

Northern Ireland Library Advisory Council. Annual reports, 1980-1981.

O'Connor, Frank. *My father's son*. London, Macmillan. 1968.

O'Neill, M.J. *Lennox Robinson*. Dublin, Twayne. 1964.

O'Sullivan, T.F. *The Young Irelanders*. The Kerryman Ltd. 1944.

Parke, H.W. *The Library of Trinity College*, Dublin, no date.

Robertson, William. *Welfare in trust: a history of the Carnegie United Kingdom Trust, 1913-1963*. Dunfermline, CUKT. 1964.

Robinson, Lennox. *Lady Gregory's Journal, 1916-1930*. London,

Putnam. 1946.

Ryan, John. *Irish Monasticism*. London, Longman. 1931.

Spillane, M.V. *Two centuries of popular education: an historical survey of the educational institutions of Limerick, 1700-1900*. Thesis. NUI Cork. 1973.

Stuart, James. *Historical memoirs of the City of Armagh*. Newry. 1819.

Tallon, Maura. *Church of Ireland Diocesan libraries*. Dublin, The Library Association of Ireland. 1959.

Trinity College, Dublin. *Guide to the Library of Trinity College, Dublin*, no date.

Wall, Thomas. *The Sign of Dr. Hay's Head: being some account of the hazards and fortunes of Catholic printers and publishers in Dublin from the late penal times to the present day*. Dublin, Gill and Son Ltd 1958.

Wilson, R.N.D. *The County Library service in Ireland: a summary for the guidance of local authorities and for the general reader*. Dunfermline, CUKT. 1927.

Younger, Calton. *Arthur Griffith*. Dublin, Gill and Macmillan. 1981.


PERIODICAL ARTICLES

Adams, J.R.R. Library provision for children in County Down prior to 1850. *Irish Booklore*, 4, (1) 19-23, 1978.

Barnard, T. The Purchase of Archbishop Ussher's library in 1657. *Long Room*, 1970, pp 9-14.

Barnes, Margaret. Repeal Reading Rooms. *An Leabharlann*, 23 pp 53-57, June 1965.

Bigger, F.J. Rural libraries in Antrim. *The Irish Book Lover*, 13 (4) November 1921.

Coleman, James. The Cork Library in 1801 and 1820. *Journal of the Cork Historical and Archaeological Society*, 11, (Second series), 1905.

Corkery, Revd S. Maynooth College Library. *An Leabharlann*, 14 (2) pp 51-58, 1956.

Doyle, Daniel. Libraries and public education. *Christus Rex*, 10, pp 115-125, April 1956.

Foley, Dermot. A Minstrel boy and a satchel of books: reminiscences of life as a librarian in County Clare. *Irish University Review*, 4 (Pt 2), pp 204-217, 1974.

Henchy, Patrick. The National Library of Ireland. *An Leabharlann*, **26**, (2), pp 44-49, June 1968.

Kaufman, Paul. Community lending libraries in eighteenth century Ireland and Wales. *Library Quarterly*, **23**, (4) October 1963. (*Also* appears as Chapter XV of Libraries and their users: collected papers in library history, by Paul Kaufman. London, The Library Association, 1969, repr. 1971)

Kirkpatrick, T.P.C. Sir Patrick Dun's Library. *The Bibliographical Society of Ireland*, 1 (Pt. 5), 1920.

Kirkpatrick, T.P.C. The Worth Library, Steeven's Hospital, Dublin. *The Bibliographical Society of Ireland*, 1 (Pt. 3), 1919.

Lawlor, Hugh. Primate Ussher's Library before 1641. *Royal Irish Academy Proceedings*, 3rd series, **6**, pp 216-224, 1900-02.

Library World, **65**, (759), pp 83-117, September 1963. (Special number on Irish libraries and librarianship featuring articles by Dermot Foley, Mairín O'Byrne, Thomas Armitage, Desmond Clarke and Robert Casey)

McCracken, Eileen. The Origins of the Library at Glasnevin Botanic Gardens. *Irish Booklore*, **2**, (1) 1972.

McClintock Dix, E.R. Report on the Waterford Diocesan Cathedral Library. *The Bibliographical Society of Ireland*, 1921, Pt. 1, 5-6.

MacWilliam, Alexander. The Dublin Library Society, 1791-1882. *The Bibliographical Society of Ireland, Publications: Short Papers 2*, (6) pp 120-131, 1925.

Mooney, Revd Canice. The Franciscan Library, Killiney. *Archivum Hibernicum*, **18**, pp 150-156, 1955.

Mooney, Revd Canice. The Franciscan Librarian, Merchant's Quay, Dublin. *An Leabharlann*, **8**, pp 29-37, September 1942.

Mooney, Revd Canice. Irish Franciscan Libraries of the past. *Irish Ecclesiastical Record*, **5**, (60), pp 215-228, September 1942.

Mooney, Revd Canice. The Library of Piers Creagh. *Repertorium Novum*, **1** (pt. 1), pp 117-139, 1953.

Morton, K.G. Mechanics' Institutes and the attempted diffusion of useful knowledge in Ireland, 1825-1879. *Irish Booklore*, **2**, pp 59-75, Spring 1972.

Olden, Anthony. Lennox Robinson's Carnegie 'Librarian'. *An Leabharlann*, **4**, pp 57-67, 1975.

O'Donovan, Revd. J. Village libraries. *The Irish Homestead*, **IV**, (3), Saturday 20 January 1900.

O'Sullivan, William. Ussher as a collector of manuscripts. *Hermathena*, **88**, pp 34-58, 1956.

Petit, S.T. The Royal Cork Institution: a reflection of the cultural life of a city. *Journal of the Cork Historical and Archaeological Society*, **81**, pp 233-4, 1976.

Power, Ellen. Ireland, Libraries in the Republic of. *Encyclopedia of Library and Information Science*, **13**, pp 67-81, 1975.

Quane, Michael. Aspects of education in Ireland, 1695-1795. *Journal of the Cork Historical and Archaeological Society*, **73**, (218), 1968.

Ryan, M.J. Some notes on the libraries and book trade of Dublin. *Book Auction Records*, **4**, (Pt. 4), 1907.

Simms, Most. Rev. G.O., *Bishop of Armagh*. The Founder of Armagh's Public Library: Primate Robinson amongst his books. *Irish Booklore*, **1**, (2), August 1971.

Walker, T. McCallum. Libraries and librarianship in Northern Ireland. *Libri*, **14**, pp 315-329, 1953-4.

Weatherup, D.R.M. The Armagh Public Library, 1771-1971. *Irish Booklore*, **2**, (2) pp 269-299, 1976.

Wheeler, W.G. The Spread of provincial printing in Ireland up to 1850. *Irish Booklore*, **4**, (1) 7-18, 1978.

White, J.D.N. Elias Bouhéreau of La Rochelle: first public librarian of Ireland. *Proceedings of the Royal Irish Academy*, **27**, pp 126-158, 1908-9.

Woodworth, Rev. David. St. Canice's Library. *Old Kilkenny Review*, **22**, (5-10), 1970 and **23**, (15-22), 1971.

# Index

Abbeyleix, 37
Act of Union 1801, 140
Acthicus of Istria, 1
Adams, W.G.S., 185, 187, 189
Adult education, 151-169
Aidan, 9
Aigilbert, 9
Aitchison, C., 159
Alcuin, 7, 9
Aldfrith, King of Northumbria, 9
Alexander, Sir Jerome, 120
An Chomhairle Leabharlanna, *see*
    Chomhairle Leabharlanna
*Anatomical Plates of D'Azyr*, 68
*Annals of Ulster*, 123
Anne, Queen, 120
*Antiphonary of Bangor*, 13
Antrim Co. Lib., 187, 194, 198,
    199, 223, 227
Antrim Library, 128
Apollo Circulating Library, 55
Archer, Eliza, 60
Archer, John, 96, 97
Archer, William, 138
Armagh, 60
Armagh Co. Lib., 81, 198, 201,
    207
Arts Council of Northern Ireland,
    234
Association for Discountenancing
    Vice, etc., 36
Asylum for Aged Printers, 53
Athanaeum News Room Co., 159
Audio-visual services, 208
Automation, 134, 205, 233

Ballymoney, 159
Ballymure, 102
Bangor, 7, 11, 13
Baptist Society, 23
Bardic literature, 1-14
Bardin, Rev. Charles, 27
Bards, 4, 14, 15, 16

Barnard, Dr. J.H., 190
Barrett, Richard, 147
Barry, James, 211
Bates, H.E., 218
Battersby, William J., 52
Beck, Dr., 142
Bede, 9
Beggs, Thomas, 102
Belfast Academy, 126, 127, 128,
    129
Belfast, circulating libraries in, 60
*Belfast Commercial Chronicle*, 61
Belfast Education and Library
    Board, 204-206
Belfast Library and Society for
    Promoting Knowledge, 103,
    131
Belfast Literary Society, 158
Belfast Mechanics' Institute, 158
Belfast Natural History and
    Philosophical Society, 158
*Belfast Newsletter*, 54
Belfast People's Literary Institute,
    159
Belfast People's Reading Room,
    159
Belfast Public Libraries, 177, 198,
    201
Belfast, St. Anne's Cathedral, 80
Belfast Select Reading Club, 159
Belfast Working Classes
    Association, 158
Belfast Working Men's Institute,
    159
Beresford, Hon. Marcus G., Bp.
    of Kilmore, 80
Berkeley, George, 120
Bernard, Saint, 11
Best, Dr. R.I., 138
Bible Societies, 23
Bigger, Francis Joseph, 102, 103,
    183
BLAISE, 137

BLAISE/LOCAS, 233
Blaney, Lord, 76
Blow, James, 20, 54
Bobbio, 11, 12
Bodleian Library, 73, 75, 79
Boggs, William, 61
*Bolg an tSolair,* 105
Bolton, Abp. Theophilus, 78
*Book of Armagh,* 10, 123
*Book of Ballymote,* 4, 71, 95
*Book of Dimma,* 10, 123
*Book of Durrow,* 10, 123
*Book of Kells,* 10,123
*Book of Lecan,* 71, 95
*Book of Leinster,* 123
*Book of Magauran,* 139
*Book of Molling,* 10, 123
*Book of the Dun Cow,* 4, 10
Boole Library, 137
Boru, Brian, 13
Botanic Garden, Glasnevin, 93
Bouhéreau, Elias, 74
Bouhéreau, John, 74
Boyd, M.J., 201
Boyle, Michael, 59
Boyne, Battle of the, 17
Boyton, John William, 67
Bray, 58
Brehon Laws, 1, 2, 3, 6, 9
Brendan, Saint, 5
British and Foreign School
   Society, 27
British Library Lending Division
   (BLLD), 234
British Museum Library, 75
Brock, Stearne, 47
Brooke, Henry, 47
Brown, Fr. Stephen, 217
Brownlee, Isabella, 130
Bruce, Rev. Dr., 127, 128
Bunting, Mr., 105
Burgh, Thomas, 120
Burghley, Lord, 42, 43
Byrne, Felix, 113
Byrne, Patrick, 52
Byron, George Gordon, Lord, 103

Cahirciveen P.L., 190

Caldwell, Sir James, 34
Caldwell, Robert, 61
Campbell, J.J., 201
Campbell, Lord, 215
Campbell, Patrick, 45
Campion, Edward, 15
Carey, P., 107
Carlow, 37
Carnegie, Andrew, 184, 186, 187,
   189
Carnegie United Kingdom Trust
   (CUKT), 186, 189, 190, 191,
   192, 194, 195, 196, 197, 198,
   212, 213
Carpenter, Abp. John, 85
Carr, T.S., 59
Carrick on Suir, 59
Carrickfergus, 61
Carrickfergus YMCA, 159
Carrickmacross, Lough Fea, 88
Carroll, James, 58
Carroll, John, 58
Carson, James, 48
Cary, Matthew, 50, 52
*Case of the Roman Catholics,* 50
Cashel Diocesan Library, 78
Castleisland Library, 189
Castlereagh, Lady, 23
Cathach (Battle Book), 6
Catholic Association, 140
Catholic Relief Act, 123
Catholic Truth Society, 215
Catholic University of Ireland, 132
Caulfield, Dr. Richard, 108
Ceefax, 205
Celtic Literary Society, 180
*Censor, The,* 47
Censorship, 181, 215-219
Censorship Board, 181
Censorship of Publications Act
   1929, 216
Chapmen, 51, 52, 53, 54
Charity schools, 20
Charlemont, Lord, 90, 94, 97
Charles II, King, 63, 70
Charter schools, 20, 21, 22
Cheap Book Society, 26
Chester Beatty Library, 139

Chesterfield, Lord, 100
Chomhairle Leabharlanna, An
  (The Library Council), 203,
  219 *et seq.*
Ciaran of Clonmacnois, Saint, 10
*Cin of Drom Snechta*, 4
Clare Co. Lib., 218
Clarke, Bernard, 47
Clogher Diocesan Library, 76
Clonard, 7
Clonbullogue, 38
Clongowes, 23
Clonmacnois, 7, 11, 13
Clonmel, 59
Clonmel Mechanics' Institute,
  163, 164
Coats, John, 51
Colette, *pseud.*, 218
Colles, G.P.R., 170
Collins, Michael, 18, 93
Columba, Saint, 5, 6, 8, 10
Columbanus, Saint, 11
Company of Stationers, 46
*Computerised List of Serials
  Holdings in Irish Libraries*, 203
Confraternity of the Christian
  Doctrine, 37
Connell, William, 38
Connolly, J.C., 228
Conry, Abp. Florence, 43
Constant, Ellen, 59
Cooldrevna, Battle of, 6
Coombie, Dr., 126
Cooperative Reference Library,
  Dublin, 189
Cooperative societies, 181
Cope, Dr. Henry, 66
Copyright deposit, 120, 121, 126,
  136, 138
Cork, 58
Cork Diocesan Library, 77
*Cork Directory*, 58
*Cork Examiner*, 164
Cork Institution, *see* Royal Cork
  Institution
Cork Mechanics' Institute, 164,
  165

Cork Public Library, 170, 189,
  190, 224, 229, 230
Cork Public Library and Reading
  Room, 59
Cork Scientific and Literary
  Society, 165
Cork Subscription Library, 104,
  108-110
Cork University Library, 77
*Cosmography of the World*, 1
Cotter, Thomas, 45
Cotton, Dr. Henry, 79
Cottrell, Joseph, 114
County Management Act 1940,
  220, 222
Courtney, Mr., 68
Cover, 59
Craddock, T.R.W., 75
Cramsie, James, 159
Crawford, Sharman, 137
Crawley, Ivor, 201
Creagh, Abp. Piers, 83
Crips, Mary, 60
Cromwell, Henry, 69, 120
Cromwell, Oliver, 63, 69
Crooke, John, 46
Crosby, John, 65
Cross, Richard, 50
Crowe, Bp. of Cloyne, 77
Cuala Press, 96
Cumann na Leabharlann (Library
  Association of Ireland), 177,
  178, 179, 180, 211 *et seq.*, 233,
  234
Cumpsty, Andrew, 51
Curran, Rt. Hon. John Philpot, 98
Curry, John, 51
Customs Consolidation Act 1876,
  215
Cuverian Society, 165

Dagobert II, King of France, 9
*Daily Freeman*, 146
*Daily Saunders*, 146
D'Alton, Rev. E.A., 182
D'Alton, J., 141
Daly, Dr. Charles, 109
Daly, John, 95

Dancer, Samuel, 49
Danes, 2, 5, 11, 13
d'Arbois de Juboinville, 137
Dartas, James, 42
Davidson, Samuel, 128
Davies, Thomas, 71
Davis, Thomas, 101, 142, 144, 148
Deeping, Warwick, 216
Derry Diocesan Library, 77
de Valera, Eamon, 93, 122
Dewey Decimal Classification,
    138, 231
Dialog, 205
Diamuid, King, 6
Dick's Coffee House, 45
Dickson, Dr. Stephen, 67
*Dictionary of National Biography*,
    122
Dicuil, 13
Dillon, John, 144, 145
Diocesan libraries, 71 *et seq.*
*Diverting Post*, 45
Dix, E.R. MacClintock, 138, 179
Doagh, 102
Dobbyn, Mr., 79
DOBIS, 137
Dobson, Eliphal, 46, 47
Doheny, Michael, 148
D'Olier Street Club, *see* Dublin
    Library Society
Dominican order, 215
Donegal P.L., 194, 213
Dougatt, Robert, 74, 77
Dowden, Richard, 107, 164, 165
Dowling, J.T., 220
Dowling, Luke, 45
Dowling, Vincent, 49, 55
Down, Connor and Dromore
    Diocesan Library, 80
Down Co. Lib., 198-9, 201
Downes, Bartholomew, 46
Doyle, Dr. James, 34, 52
*Drapier Letters* (Swift), 46
Drew, Rev. Thomas, 80
Drogheda Mechanics' Institute,
    160
Drogheda P.L., 190
Droz, Jean Pierre, 48, 49

Druids, 1, 2, 7
Drum-Ceata, Convention of, 10
Dublin, 61, 62
*Dublin Almanac and General
    Register of Ireland*, 101
Dublin Book Repository, 189
Dublin Christian Citizenship
    Council, 216
Dublin City and County Library
    (formerly Dublin P.L.), 176,
    192, 195, 224, 232, 233
*Dublin Evening Mail*, 55, 56, 99,
    100, 101
*Dublin Intelligence*, 48
*Dublin Journal*, 47, 90
Dublin Library Society, 96, 97,
    98, 99, 100, 101, 104
Dublin Mechanics' Institute
    Library, 153-157
*Dublin News Letter*, 45
Dublin Philosophical Society, 89
Dublin Public Record Office, 78,
    80
Dublin Society for improving
    Husbandry, Manufactures and
    other Useful Arts, *see* Royal
    Dublin Society
*Dublin Weekly Journal*, 48
Duffy, Sir Charles Gavan, 101,
    142, 144, 146, 148, 149
Duffy, James, 150
Du Maurier, Daphne, 218
Dun, Lady, 65, 66
Dun, Sir Patrick, 65, 66, 67, 68
Dun Emer Press, 96
Dun Laoghaire P.L., 233
Dundalk, 58
Dundalk Mechanics' Institute, 160
Dundalk P.L., 175
Dungal of Pavia, 11, 13
Dungannon, 61
Dunlang, 3
Dunne, Rev. Andrew, 125
Dunton, John, 45
Dutton, Hely, 35

East Belfast Talking Newspaper
    for the Blind, 205

Eblana Literary and Debating Society, 179
Edgeworth, Francis, 88
Edgeworth, Richard Lovell, 37
Edgeworthtown, 85
Edkins, Mr., 97
Educational Society, 27
Edwards, Edward, 75
Elizabeth I, Queen, 42, 120
Ennis, 175
ESA/IRS Information Services, 135
Este, Rt. Rev. Charles, 79
EURONET DIANE, 135, 136, 233
European Community (EEC) material, 135, 231
Evans, Alderman Joseph, 115-116
*Evening Mail*, 146
*Evening Packet*, 146
*Evening Post*, 146

Fabrij, Jacques, 48
Fagel, Greffier, 122
Fanin, Mr., 69
Faroe Islands, 13
Faulkner, George, 47
Fearghal, 12
Fenning, W.H., 201
Fermanagh Co. Lib., 198, 199, 201
Fermoy, 174
Fiction reserve scheme, 234
Filid, 2
Fingal, 40
Finlay, Rev. T.A., 190
Finlay, Fr., 190
Finnian of Druim Finn, 5, 6
Fireside Clubs, 179
Fitzgerald-Lennox corresp., 138
Fitzpatrick, Sir Jeremiah, 22
Fivemiletown Branch Library, 208, 209
*Flora Dubliniensis*, 68
Foley, Dermot, 218, 220, 226, 234
Ford Foundation, 121
Forgaill, Dallon, 10
Foster, Abp., 78

*Four Masters*, 3, 9
Four Towns Book Club, 102, 103
Franciscan libraries, 83, 84
Franklin, Benjamin, 52
Frankton, John, 46
Frayne, Pat, 33
*Freeman's Journal*, 47, 147
Fry, Sir Edward, 132

Gaelic League, 179, 181, 197
Gaelic Society, 96
Galland, James, 61
Galt, William, 102
Galway, 59
Galway Mechanics' Institute, 161-2
Gamble, Mrs. Henry, 129
Garnett, John Armstrong, 68
Gately, Canon, 181
Geary, Catherine, 60
Gilbert, Claudius, 122
Gonne, Maud, 188
Gordon, Lionel Smith, 190
Goresbridge, 37
Graham, Robert, 60
Grant, John, 47
Grattan, Henry, 21
Graves, Robert, 218
Gray, Dr. John, 146
Green, John Richard, 135
Greer, Robert, 53
Gregory, Lady, 188, 189
Gregory, Rev. William Tighe, 100
Grierson, George A., 49, 53, 54
Griffith, Arthur, 179, 180
Grimshaw, Robert, 158
Groves, Tenison, 78
Guild of St. Luke, 50
Guinness, Benjamin Lee, 75
Gulbenkian Foundation, 137
Gun, Nat, 48
Guy, Francis, 172-4
Guy's *Directory of Cork*, 110, 136
Gwynn, Stephen, 183

Hall, Rev. George, 131
Hall, Mr. and Mrs. S.C., 18, 19, 34, 124, 125, 144

Halliday, Mrs. Charles, 96
Halliday, William, 96
Hamilton, G.A., 167, 170
Handicapped readers, 206, 207, 208
Hanna, Rev. Samuel, 128
Hardiman, James, 95, 136, 161
Harding, John, 46
Haughton, James, 156, 157
Haughton, May, 201
Havard-Williams, Peter, 199, 201
Hawnt Report, 106, 200-203
Hayes, R.J., 138
Heaney, H.J., 201
Hedge schools, 18, 22, 25, 32, 35, 36, 38
Hemingway, Ernest, 218
Henderson, W.S., 201
Henry IV, King of France, 70, 71
Henry, Rt. Rev. Joseph, 80
Henry, R.M., 133
Heuston, Richard, 59
Heyer, Georgette, 218
Heygate, Sir Frederick, 78
Hibernian Bible Society, 36
*Hibernian Magazine*, 144
Hibernian Society, 21
Higgins, Fr. Brian, 84
Higginson, James, 59
Hill, George, 133
Hill, R., 58
Hincks, Rev. Thomas Dix, 107, 109
*Historical Guide to Dublin* (Wright), 95
*Historical memoirs of the city of Armagh* (Stuart), 82
*Historical memoirs of the Irish Rebellion of 1641*, 50
*History of the County and City of Limerick* (McGregor), 60
Hodges and Smith Collection, 95
Hodgson, John, 60, 61
Hoey, James, 47
Hogan, Fr. Thomas, 83
Hopkins, Ezekiel, Bp. of Derry, 78

Hospital libraries, 206, 207, 208, 212
Howard, John, 22
Hudson, J.W., 143, 151, 166
Hudson, William Elliott, 95
Hume, George, 153
Huntingdon, Henry, 120
Huntingdon, Rev. Dr., 89
Huxley, Aldous, 218
Hyde, Douglas, 10, 136, 149, 178, 180, 183

Iceland, 13
Incorporated Society for the Promotion of Protestant Schools in Ireland, 21, 36
Inglis, Mr., 124
Ingram, John Kells, 122, 179
Institute for Industrial Research and Standards, 135
Institute of Irish Studies (Queen's Univ. Belfast), 234
*Intelligencer, The*, 46
International Federation of Library Associations and Institutions (IFLA), 227
*Iris Oifigiuil* (Official Gazette), 217
Irish Architectural Record Association, 139
Irish Association for Documentation and Information Services (IADIS), 234
*Irish Booklore*, 234
*Irish Catholic Directory*, 52
Irish Central Library, 93, 197, 215, 219, 234
Irish Church Act 1879, 79
Irish Copyright Act 1963, 137
Irish Free State Local Government Act 1925, 195, 211
*Irish Homestead, The*, 182, 183
Irish Mission, 5
Irish Presbyterian Church General Assembly Library, 129
*Irish Publishing Record*, 136, 234
Irish Rural Libraries Association, 183, 184

Irish Society for Promoting
Knowledge of the Native
Language, 24, 27
*Irish Times,* 217
Irish Universities Act 1908, 132
Irish University Education Act
1879, 132
Irish Vigilance'Association, 215
Iveagh, Lord, 121

Jacotin, D., 55
James I, King, 46
James II, King, 45
James, Richard, 49
Jesuits, 17
John Paul II Library, Maynooth,
125
John Rylands Library,
Manchester, 76
Joint fiction reserve scheme, 234
Joly, Dr. Jasper, 91
Joly Collection, 138
Jones, Henry, Bp. of Meath, 123
Jones, Dr. Henry, 70
Jones, Sir Theophilus, 70
Joyce, James, 215
Justell, Christophe, 70

Kaufman, Paul, 54, 55
Kavanagh, Rose, 180
Kelly, Patrick, 232
Kelly, Thomas, 179
Kelso, Ann, 61
Kenmare P.L., 189
Kennedy, James F., 135
Keogh, Christina, 189, 191, 213,
215
Kernohan, J.W., 130
Kildare, 38, 39
Kildare Co. Lib., 228, 230
Kildare Place Society, 24, 25, 26,
27, 28, 29, 30, 31, 32, 33, 35,
130
Kilkenny College, 19
Kilkenny Library Society, 69,
104, 111-119
Kilkenny P.L., 117-118

Kilmore, Elphin and Ardagh
Diocesan Library, 80
King, Richard Ashe, 149
King, Very Rev. R.G.S., 78
King, William, Abp. of Dublin,
65, 77, 78
King's Inn Library, 139, 170
Kingsford, Thomas, 59
Kingsmill, William, 113
Kingston, Felix, 46
Kingstown, 177
Kirwan, Dr. Richard, 96, 97, 98
Knapp, John, 51
Kohl, 85
Koralek, Paul, 122

Lambeth Palace Library, 75
Lamont, Francis, 61
Lane, A., 109
Lanigan, Rev. Dr. John, 90
Laoghaire, King, 2
Lardner, Dr., 108
Larne, 160
Latocnaye, 33
Lawrence, D.H., 216
Lawson, Dr., 72
*Leabhar Breac,* 95
*Leabharlann, An,* 178, 211, 217,
233
Leadbeater, Mary, 55
Leech, Mr., 116
Legal deposit, *see* Copyright
deposit
Le Hunte, Sir Francis, 163
Leighlin, 38, 39
Leinster House, 90, 92, 93
Leinster Literary Society, 179
Leitch, David, 159
Leland, Dr., 90
Leslie, Cliffe, 168, 169
Leslie, Canon J.B., 81
*Liber de Praedestinatione,* 13
LIBIS, 137
Library Advisory Council
(Northern Ireland, 200, 203
Library Association (of the UK),
176, 191

Library Association of Ireland, *see* Cumann na Leabharlann
Library Council of Ireland, *see* Chomhairle Leabharlanna, An
*Library of Ireland*, 148, 149
Library schools, 199-200, 205
*Library World, The*, 234
Limerick, 58, 60
*Limerick Chronicle*, 58
Limerick Institution, 110, 111
Limerick Mechanics' Institute, 165
Limerick P.L., 177, 224-5, 230-232
Linen Hall Library, 60, 61, 104, 105, 106, 107, 126, 127, 201
Lisburn, 159
Lismore, 7
Lismore Castle papers, 138
Lismore Diocesan Library, 79
Listowel P.L., 190
Litton, Dr. Samuel, 90
Llewellyn, Richard, 218
Lloyd, Edward, 123
LOCAS, 136
Local Government Act 1930, 224
Local Government (Officers) Act 1943, 223
Lodge, Rev. William, 81, 82
Lon of Garad, Saint, 8
London Hibernian Society, 23, 25, 27, 36, 151
Londonderry, 61
Londonderry City Library, 198, 201·
Londonderry Co. Lib., 198, 200, 201
Longford-Westmeath Joint Library Committee, 176
Lord, Patrick, 50
Louvain, St. Anthony's College, 125
Lownes, Matthew, 46
Loyal National Repeal Association of Ireland, 141, 145, 147, 148
Lucas, Charles, 47
Lucas, Richard, 58
Luxeuil, 12

Lynch, Jack, 229
Lynch, Patrick, 96
Lyster, T.W., 138, 178, 179, 183, 190

McAdoo, Rt. Rev. H.R., 72
MacAirt, Cormac, 3, 4
McAuliff, John and Thomas, 58
McCagwell, Hugh, 43
McCarthy, Mr., 165
M'Cartney, Louisa, 59
McCormack, John, 135
MacCulloh, Alexander, 47
McCurtin's *Irish Dictionary*, 109
MacDonell, Dr. James, 105
McDonnel, Thomas, 52
McGarel, Charles, 160
McGee, Thomas D'Arcy, 149
McGonigal, A., 201
McGrath, James, 77
McGreevy, Thomas, 190
McGregor's *History of the City and County of Limerick*, 110
Mackay, Rev. James, 127
Macmanus, Seumas, 179
MacMullen, Samuel James, 131
MacNeill, Eoin, 180
MacNevin, Thomas, 148
Macrory Report, 202
MacSwiney, Marquis of Mashanaglass, 95
Madden, Samuel, 34
Magee University College, Londonderry, 134
*Magee's Weekly Packet*, 49
Mahon, Barry, 233
Mahon, N., 109
Mahony, David, 18
Main, Robert, 49
Mallan, Luke, 102
Mallow, 175
Malone, J., 201
Malone, James, 45
Malone, Richard, 45
*Manual of Devout Prayers*, 45
*Manuscript Sources for the History of Irish Civilisation*, 138
Marsh, Abp. Narcissus, 72-76, 83

Marsh's Library, 64, 72-76, 77, 78, 79, 170
Martin, Mr., 161
Martyn, Edward, 179
Matthew, Fr., 108, 141
Maugham, W. Somerset, 218
Maurice, Bp. Edward, 71, 72
Maynooth, 85, 130
Maynooth Act 1795, 124
Mazarin, Cardinal, 69
Mechanics' Institutes, 108, 151-169
Meehan, Fr. C.P., 149
Melanctus, *pseud.*, 98, 99, 101
Melbourne, Lord, 130
*Mercury, The*, 47
Merriman, Brian, 217
Milton, Samuel, 93
Mitchel, John, 148
Mitchell, J.M., 190, 191
Mitchell, L.J., 201
Mitchell, Dr. Patrick, 65
*Model Times*, 205
Moffett, Rev. Canon Benjamin, 76
Moira, Lord, 90
Monasterboice, 7
Monasteries, 8, 11, 12, 13, 16
Monastic literature, 1-14
Moore, Thomas, 96, 103
Morgan, Lady, 97
Morrison, Jack, 121
Mounteagle, Lord, 183
Mountjoy, Lord, 89
Moyne, Lord, 96
Mudie's Lending Library, 83, 93, 105
Mungret, 7
Munn, A.M., 78
Murphy, John, Bp. of Cork, 85
Murray, Dr. Daniel, Abp. of Dublin, 91
Music Circulating Library, 56

*Nation, The*, 116, 140-150
National Central Library, London, 93
National Institute of Higher Education, 231, 232, 233

National Library of Ireland, 91, 92, 93, 138-9, 175
National Literary Society, 180
National University of Ireland, 133
*New Irish Library*, 149
New University of Ulster, Coleraine, 134
Newcastle West P.L., 190
Newman, Cardinal John Henry, 132
Newry, 102
Newtownards, 23
Newspapers, circulation, 54
Normans, 13-14
North Eastern Education and Library Board, 204, 206
Northern Ireland Branch of the Library Association, 199, 212, 232, 234
Northern Ireland Library Advisory Council, 200, 203
*Northern Ireland Local Studies* lists, 206
*Northern Star*, 54, 102, 105

O'Brien, Brien, 60, 111
O'Brien, Dermod, 190
O'Brien, Rev. Paul, 96
O'Brien, Philip, 84, 86, 87
O'Brien, William Smith, 91, 95, 101, 149, 166
Obscene Publications Act 1857, 215
O'Connell, Daniel, 18, 30, 40, 101, 140, 141, 142, 143, 144, 145, 146, 147
O'Connell, John, 143, 146, 147
O'Connor, Arthur, 102
O'Connor, Frank, 192, 217, 218
O'Connor, Rory, 190
O'Currey, Eugene, 170
O'Curry, Eugene, 122
O'Donnell Cathach, 5, 6
O'Donnell, John, 101
O'Donnell, Thomas, 190
O'Donovan, John, 122
O'Donovan, Fr. J., 182, 183, 196

O'Donovan, Michael, *see*
    O'Connor, Frank
O'Faolain, Sean, 218
O'Flanagan, Theophilus, 96
Ogham, 1, 3, 4, 8
O'Grady, Standish, 149
O'Growny, Fr. Eugene, 180
O Heoghusa, Bonaventure, 43
O'Higgin, John 14
O'Keefe, Mr., 69
O'Keefe, Manus, 83
O'Kelly, Sean T., 178
O'Longain, Michael Og, 85
O'Neil, Denis, 38
O'Neill, Charles, 90
Oracle, 205
O'Rahilly, Dr. A., 137
O'Reilly, Edward, 96
Ormond, Duke of, 72
Ormond Archives, 138
Ormonde, Earl of, 16
Orr, James, 102
O'Shaughnessy, Eliza, 60
Ossian, Oscar, 40
Ossory, 8
Ossory Diocesan Library, 71
O'Suilliobhain, Diarmuid, 18
O'Sullivan, Tomás Ruadh, 40, 41
Oswin, King, 9
Otway, Bp. Thomas, 71
Owen, Richard, 77

Pallas, Chief Baron, 135
Palliser, William, Abp. of Cashel,
    122
Palmerston, Lord, 33
Parish libraries, 38, 39
Parish schools, 19
Parks, James, 58
Patrick, Saint, 2, 5, 6, 40
Paulstown, 37
Pearse, Padraig, 178
Peel, Sir Robert, 33, 34, 130
Penal laws, 19, 23
Petrie, George, 95
Petty, Sir William, 89
Phelps, E.A., 79
Philosophical Institutions, 167

Physico-Chirurgical Society, 68
Physico-Historical Society, 90
Pigot and CO's *Directory*, 55, 58,
    60
*Pilot, The*, 142, 146, 147, 162
Plessey book issuing system, 134,
    135, 206
Plunkett, Sir Horace, 189, 191
Pomercy, Abp., 77
Popish schools, 20
Portaferry, 102
Povey, Kenneth, 133
Powell, Humfrey, 42
Power, J., 117
Praegar, Robert Lloyd, 138
Prendergast, 139
Private libraries, 63-88
Protestant Repeal Association, 142
*Psalter of St. Columcille*, 10
Public Bodies Order 1943, 223
Public Hospitals Act 1933, 223
Public libraries, 170-234
Public Libraries Act 1919, 192
Public Libraries (Art Galleries in
    County Boroughs) (Ireland)
    Act 1911, 183
Public Libraries Act (Ireland)
    1855, 170
Public Libraries (Ireland)
    Amendment Act 1877, 176
Public Libraries (Ireland) Act
    1894, 177
Public Libraries (Ireland) Act
    1902, 177, 183
Public Libraries (Ireland) Act
    1920, 184
Public Libraries Act (Northern
    Ireland) 1924, 195, 198, 199
Public Libraries Act 1947, 224,
    226
Public Libraries and Museums Act
    1850, 170
Public Libraries Grant Scheme
    1961, 227
Public Record Office, Dublin, 190
*Public Service Information Bulletin*,
    206
Pue, James, 45

Pue, Richard, 45
Pue, Sarah, 45
*Pue's Occurrences*, 45

Quakers, *see* Society of Friends
Queen's College, Belfast, 128
Queen's University, Belfast, 105, 131, 132, 133
Queen's University, Belfast, Department of Library and Information Studies, 199, 205
Queenstown, 175
Quin, Dr. Henry, 66
Quin, Henry George, 123

Raphoe Diocesan Library, 78
Rathfriland, 24
Rathkeale P.L., 189, 190
Rathkeale R.D.C., 182
Rathmines, 177
Ray, Thomas Matthew, 142, 143, 146, 147
Reeves, Bp. William, 95
Reeves Collection of MSS., 80
Register of Prohibited Publications, 217
Reichenau, 12
Reid, James Seaton, 128, 129
Relhan, Anthony, 66
Religious Tract Society, 24, 31
Repeal Reading Rooms, 140-150
Representative Church Body Library, 80
Resbacus (Rébais), 12
Reynell and Swanzy Collection of MSS., 80
Rhames, Aaron, 45
Robarts, Hon. Francis, 89
Roberts Report, 200
Robertson, John, 93, 94
Robinson, Abp., 201
Robinson, Lennox, 188, 190, 191
Robinson, Richard, Abp. of Armagh, 81, 82, 83
Robinson, Sir William, 73
Rokeby, Lord, 82
Rolleston, T.W., 180

Roman Catholic Education Society, 30
Rooney, William, 179
Royal College of Physicians of Ireland, 64, 65
Royal College of Surgeons, 68
Royal Cork Institution, 107, 108, 109, 164, 165
Royal Dublin Society, 34, 89, 90, 91, 92, 93, 94, 166, 176
Royal Irish Academy, 71, 94-96, 97, 102, 105
Royal Society, London, 89, 105
Russell, George (A.E.), 189
Russell, Thomas, 105
Ryan, Mr., 116

St. Anthony's College, Louvain, 125
St. Brigid's School, Kildare, 6
St. Columba's School, Iona, 6
St. Gall, 11, 12
St. Isidore's College, Rome, 125
St. Patrick's College, Maynooth, 124, 125, 126
St. Patrick's School, Armagh, 6
Sandon, Lord, 92
Saurin, William, 99
School libraries, 30, 177
Science and Art Museum Act 1877, 92
Scott, Sir Walter, 103
Scottus, John, 13
Scribes, 9
Scriptorium, 8, 9
Sebright, Sir John, 123
*Secret History of the Dublin Library Society*, 98
Select Committee on Public Libraries 1849, 167, 170
Sergier, Richard, 46
Sheridan, Thomas, 21, 46
Shirley, Philip Evelyn, 88
Simond, Jacques, 71
Sinn Fein, 187
Skelgy, Co. Tyrone, 33
Skibbereen, 175
Slane, 9

Smiles, Samuel, 150
Society libraries, 89-119
Society of Friends, 24, 163
*Song of the Books*, 40, 41
Sothebys, 72, 88
South Eastern Education and
  Library Board, 204, 206-7
Southern Education and Library
  Board, 204, 207-8
Speer, M., 159
*Spirit of the Nation*, 148, 149
*Standards for Public Libraries*
  (IFLA), 227
Stanmillis College, 134
Stearne, John, Bp. of Clogher, 64,
  74, 76, 122
Steevens, Grissel, 63
Steevens, John, 63
Steevens, Richard, 63
Stephen, Rosamund, 80
Stewart, Alexander, 54
Stillingfleet, Dr. Edward, 73
Stopford, Bp., 77
Stowe Missal, 95
Strange, Fr. Thomas, 71
Stuart, James, 81, 82
Subscription libraries, 89-119
Sullivan, A.M., 148
Sullivan, Sir Edward, 54
Sunday School Society, 24
Swift, Jonathan, 19, 46, 47, 78

Taaffe, Denis, 96
Tara, 3, 6
Taxes, newspaper, 53
Telepen book issuing system, 134
Teletext, 205
Temperance Movement, 141, 142,
  143
Thomas, Mary, 61
Thom's *Irish Almanac and Official
  Directory*, 152, 155
Thomson, Samuel, 102
Thornton, Robert, 49
*Times, The*, 141
Times Book Club, 83
Tims, Mr., 31, 32

Tipperary Joint Library
  Committee, 177, 213
Todd, J. Henthorn, 122
Todd, Mr., 68
*Tomorrow*, 190
Total Abstinence Society, 141,
  160-161
Townshend, Lord, 47
Tralee P.L., 190
Travers, Dr. Robert, 75, 76
Trench, Mrs. M., 55
Trinity College, Dublin, 19, 42,
  64, 65, 67, 69, 70, 71, 72, 73,
  89, 120-123, 130, 132, 170
Tuam Diocesan Library, 80
Tuam, Protestant Abp. of., 161
Tullow, 37
Tyrone Co. Lib., 198, 201, 208
Tyrrel's Library, Dublin, 140
Tyrrell, Sir Timothy, 69, 70

United Nations publications, 138
University College, Cork, 136-138
University College, Dublin, 134-
  35
University College, Dublin,
  Department of Library and
  Information Studies, 212, 234
University College, Galway, 80,
  136
University libraries, 121-138
University of Dublin, 23, 123, 132
Upton, H.A.S., 95
Upton Bequest, 96
Ursgeul, 5
Usher, James, Bp. of Meath, 64
Ussher, James, Abp. of Armagh,
  69, 70, 71, 120, 122
Ussher, John, 42, 43
Ussher, Sir William, 43

Vallence, James, 85
Vallency, General, 94
Value Added Tax, 233
Video, 207, 208
Virgilius (Fearghal), 12
*Voice of the Nation*, 148, 149
*Volunteer Journal*, 52

Wadding, Luke, 71
Wade, Walter, 68
Walsh, Dr. William J., Abp. of
    Dublin, 135
Waterford Diocesan Library, 79
Waterford P.L., 177
Watson, John, 49
Webb, Thomas, 55
*Weekly Freeman*, 146
*Weekly Register*, 140, 146
*Weekly Warder*, 146
Wellesley, Marquis, 99
Wesley, John, 22
Western Education and Library
    Board, 204, 208-210
Westley and Tyrrell, 56, 57
Wexford Mechanics' Institute, 163
Wexford P.L., 194
Whaley, John, 51
White, Gilbert, 42, 47, 54
White, Luke, 51, 52
White, William, 40
Whitehouse, Thomas, 49
Wicklow, 213, 214
Wicklow Co. Lib., 227-228
Wilkinson, James, 189
William III, King, 17, 19, 65
Williams, Bp. Griffith, 71

Williamson, William, 47, 49
Willis, I., 56
Wilson, R.N.D., 195
Wilton Regional Hospital Medical
    Library, 137-8
Windele, John, 95
Wogan, Pat, 50
Wood, Robert, 70
Workers' Educational Association,
    186
*World, The*, 146
Worth, Edward, 63, 64
Worth Library, Dublin, 63, 64
Wren, Sir Christopher, 120
Würzburg, 12
Wynne, Rev. John, 74
Wyse, Sir Thomas, 34, 130

Yeats, Jack B., 186
Yeats, W.B., 180, 189
Youghal, 174
Young, William, 54
Young Ireland League, 176
Young Ireland Movement, 144,
    150, 157, 170

Zimmer, Prof. Heinrich, 135